Contemporary African Political Economy

Series Editor
Eunice N. Sahle, University of North Carolina Chapel Hill,
Chapel Hill, NC, USA

Series Editor Eunice N. Sahle is Associate Professor with a joint appointment in the Department of African, African American and Diaspora Studies and the Curriculum in Global Studies at the University of North Carolina at Chapel Hill, USA.

Advisory Board: Bertha O. Koda, University of Dar es Salaam, Tanzania, Brij Maharaj, University of KwaZulu-Natal, South Africa, Cassandra Veney, United States International University-Africa, Kenya, Fidelis Edge Kanyongolo, Chancellor College, University of Malawi, Law School, Malawi, John Pickles, the University of North Carolina at Chapel Hill, USA, Rita Kiki Edozie, University of Massachusetts, Boston, USA, Willy Mutunga, Office of Former Chief Justice and President of the Supreme Court, Nairobi, Kenya, and Wisdom J. Tettey, University of Toronto, Canada. Contemporary African Political Economy (CAPE) publishes social science research that examines the intersection of political, social, and economic processes in contemporary Africa. The series is distinguished especially by its focus on the spatial, gendered, and cultural dimensions of these processes, as well as its emphasis on promoting empirically situated research. As consultancy-driven work has emerged in the last two decades as the dominant model of knowledge production about African politics and economy, CAPE offers an alternate intellectual space for scholarship that challenges theoretical and empirical orthodoxies and locates political and economic processes within their structural, historical, global, and local contexts. As an interdisciplinary series, CAPE broadens the field of traditional political economy by welcoming contributions from the fields of Anthropology, Development Studies, Geography, Health, Law, Political Science, Sociology and Women's and Gender Studies. The Series Editor and Advisory Board particularly invite submissions focusing on the following thematic areas: urban processes; democracy and citizenship; agrarian structures, food security, and global commodity chains; health, education, and development; environment and climate change; social movements; immigration and African diaspora formations; natural resources, extractive industries, and global economy; media and socio-political processes; development and globalization; and conflict, displacement, and refugees.

More information about this series at
http://www.palgrave.com/gp/series/14915

Shaukat Ansari

Neoliberalism and Resistance in South Africa

Economic and Political Coalitions

Shaukat Ansari
Department of Political Science
University of Toronto
Toronto, ON, Canada

Contemporary African Political Economy
ISBN 978-3-030-69765-5   ISBN 978-3-030-69766-2   (eBook)
https://doi.org/10.1007/978-3-030-69766-2

This Palgrave Macmillan imprint is published by the registered company Springer Nature Switzerland AG
The registered company address is: Gewerbestrasse 11, 6330 Cham, Switzerland

PREFACE

This book began as my Ph.D. project at the University of Toronto. I began the research with the full knowledge that a great deal of scholarship had already been penned on South Africa's democratic, and economic, transition. However, I was particularly interested in two phenomena that had received less attention: Why had the neoliberal growth model, which was officially adopted by the African National Congress (ANC) in 1996, lasted for over twenty years despite its dismal economic performance; and why has the South African population, despite numerous protests and uprisings against privatization and economic stagnation, chosen to re-elect the governing party over successive elections with a sizeable majority? While I was conducting fieldwork in Johannesburg, Pretoria, and Cape Town in 2013, a momentous event occurred that offered a partial answer to the second question: Nelson Mandela, the leader of the liberation movement against apartheid and the former President of the ANC, passed away at the age of ninety-five. Crowds of citizens filled the streets of Johannesburg for days to celebrate the life and achievements of this liberation leader. This provided a clue as to the dynamic driving the ANC's electoral victories: Despite an extremely high and persistent unemployment rate, as well as one of the highest rates of inequality in the world, the legacy of the liberation struggle still resonated with many South African citizens. Thus, the political capital that the ANC had built up during the decades long battle against apartheid provided the party with the insulation needed to implement orthodox economic policies that have benefitted a small coterie of Black South African capitalists, financial actors, and multinational corporations.

Of course, as documented in this book, the above answer is partial: there are many additional complex factors that explain the ANC's popularity, which I discovered during my research. Some of these factors include the Cash-Transfer Programme, the tripartite political alliance that has resulted in labour corporatism, and, thus far at least, the absence of a truly viable alternative political party with mass appeal. Nonetheless, the massive celebrations of Mandela's life and achievements upon his death, and the ongoing popularity of the ANC despite decades of dismal economic accomplishments, did suggest to me that analysing the current neoliberal trajectory, along with its shortcomings, was not enough to impact on-the-ground change. For that, some type of alternative policy framework and social model would need to first be put forward, accepted by the general population, and then pushed onto to the governing party. It would have to be shown that the lofty goals of the anti-apartheid struggle could be better realized through an economic programme divorced from market orthodoxy. Thus, this book is rather different from my dissertation. The latter project focused on unpacking the dynamics and factors driving the reproduction of neoliberal orthodoxy in South Africa over a twenty-year period. As such, it paid little attention to precisely which economic and political variables could potentially usher in a new developmental model predicated on structural transformation and employment generating industrial upgrading. The present book thus fills this gap by offering new chapters highlighting the political factors that historically gave rise to the developmental state, as well as why such a model has so far failed to take root in post-apartheid South Africa.

The urgency of this task was also impressed upon me due to a second significant (though more personal) event that transpired during my fieldwork. While conducting research in Johannesburg, I was mugged by a group of street kids at knifepoint. An elderly man came to my aid after the incident, and we started talking. When I told him that I was in the country to conduct research for my doctoral dissertation on economic policy and inequality in South Africa, he smiled and responded, "Looks like you just got a first-hand taste of your research." It was an astute statement. Economists and political analysts (myself included) too often focus narrowly on the macroeconomic dimensions of public policy, and as a result end up neglecting the impact of such programmes on the micro-interactions between citizens and within local communities. The spatial separation between those who formulate economic policies and those who experience marginalization and structural violence as an unintended consequence of these policies is one reason why economists are able to portray market orthodox programs as "neutral" and "resource efficient."

A large part of my motivation for revising my dissertation and writing this monograph was to flesh out a blueprint that could potentially contribute at some future date to the effort of supplanting the current neoliberal model. In fact, my hope is that this book might serve as an antidote to the conventional mainstream framing of globalization as "There-is-no-alterative" (TINA). While much of the analysis that follows is structural, there is also a clear focus on the importance of political agency and institutional shifts in shaping economic outcomes. Indeed, the distribution and control of resources is always grounded in politics, and the latter is heavily influenced by local as well as domestic forces in addition to global institutions. While my focus is mainly on South Africa, the analysis that follows is also relevant for other developing countries and touches on issues that currently affect much of the population in the advanced capitalist nations as well. Economic and social inequalities have been rising throughout the Global South and the Western World, with growing protest movements calling for progressive policies and a redistribution of wealth away from the top 1%. Endless accumulation and profit-making also pose serious threats to the ecosystem and the global climate. Thus, establishing economic programs and policies that alleviate poverty and inequality, through employment generating inclusive development, should be viewed as a vital necessity in the contemporary period. As the proceeding pages will show, there was nothing inevitable about the implementation of neoliberal orthodoxy in post-apartheid South Africa (even in the context of a unipolar world), and thus there are no insurmountable barriers standing in the way of its replacement with a more egalitarian economic regime. It is my hope that the lessons from this case study travel beyond the South African example.

Toronto, Canada   Shaukat Ansari

CONTENTS

1 Financialization as a New Regime of Accumulation:
   Business, Apartheid, and the Neoliberal Transition   1
   1.1   Introduction   1
   1.2   The Shifting Political Economy of Segregation,
         Autarky, and Liberalization   8
   1.3   Financialization of the Post-apartheid Economy   20

2 Bureaucratic Fragmentation, Cash-Transfers,
   and Financial Markets: Policymaking
   in the Post-apartheid Neoliberal Landscape   41
   2.1   The South African Bureaucracy, Economic
         Development, and Global Financial Markets   43
   2.2   The Fiscal Policy and Income Redistribution: Political
         Consequences of Financial Liberalization   50
   2.3   Financialization and Intergovernmental Conflict:
         Policy Fragmentation and Treasury Dominance   56
   Appendix: A Primer on Bonds and Yields   70

3 Political Resistance to Neoliberalism: Cracks
   in the Post-apartheid Corporatist Arrangement   73
   3.1   The Tripartite Alliance: Origins, Cracks,
         and Implications for Policymaking   75
   3.2   The Marikana Massacre and Labour Unrest   83

3.3   New Political Resistance to the Neoliberal Growth
Model   88
3.4   Zuma's Initial Ascension to Power and the Left-Wing
Political Coalition   92

4   Early Forms of State Resistance to Neoliberalism: The
International Monetary Fund in South Africa   103
4.1   The Policy of the International Financial Institutions
in South Africa During Apartheid   104
4.2   The IMF: Evolution and Involvement in South Africa   109

5   Forging a Developmental State in Post-apartheid
South Africa: A Comparative Analysis of the Structural
and Political Barriers to Industrialization   125
5.1   State-Led Industrialization in the Global South: Policy
Divergence Among the Late-Industrializers   127
5.2   Attempting to Forge a Developmental State
in Post-Apartheid South Africa: Minor Successes Amid
Institutional Failures   141
5.3   The Post-Apartheid Economic Landscape: Monopoly
Capital or Foreign Ownership as a Barrier to State-Led
Inclusive Development and Growth?   146

6   Conclusion: Incentives for 'State Capture'
and Dis-Incentives for Industrialization   159
6.1   Incentive Structures Driving State-Capacity   160
6.2   Zuma, State Capture, and Economic Transformation   168

Index   177

LIST OF FIGURES

Fig. 1.1   The unemployment rate and trade protection
           in post-apartheid South Africa (*Note* The gaps represent
           the years for which data was missing. *Source* SARB
           for the unemployment rate, The World Bank for South
           Africa's average weighted tariff)   2

Fig. 1.2   South Africa's current account and government
           deficit/surplus as a ratio of GDP, 1995–2019 (*Source*
           South African Reserve Bank)   4

Fig. 1.3   South African merchandise and manufacturing exports
           (*Note* The gaps in the series represent years for which
           data is missing. *Source* SARB for total merchandise
           exports; World Bank database for manufacturing and high
           technology exports)   19

Fig. 1.4   Dividend income and exports in post-apartheid South
           Africa (*Source* SARB, author's calculations)   24

Fig. 1.5   Manufacturing, mining, and total private investment
           in post-apartheid South Africa (*Source* SARB, author's
           calculations)   26

Fig. 2.1   Reserve accumulation in South Africa, 1995–2018 (*Source*
           South African Reserve Bank, author's calculations)   48

Fig. 2.2   South Africa's ten-year-government bond yield, 1970–2018
           (*Source* South African Reserve Bank)   50

Financialization as a New Regime of Accumulation: Business, Apartheid, and the Neoliberal Transition

1.1 Introduction

South Africa's transition away from apartheid and racial segregation has been the subject of numerous scholarly tracts and popular celebrations. As of this writing in October 2019, liberal democracy in the country has endured over a 25-year period. Despite this political victory, majoritarian democratic governance has not succeeded in effectively addressing or alleviating the economic and social injustices created by decades of white minority rule. In 2017, for example, the *New York Times* ran a story in which the author asserted that in contemporary South Africa "Apartheid has essentially persisted in economic form," as evidenced by the fact that thousands of black families continue to reside in segregated townships that were the product of apartheid. Additionally, millions of citizens lack the capital required to start businesses and less than half of the working age population have been able to secure official employment.[1] The *New York Times* article was highlighting a persistent problem in the post-apartheid landscape, one which has generated political unrest and the rise of radical opposition parties such as the Economic Freedom Fighters (EFF). Unemployment in South Africa has also stubbornly hovered above 20% since the shift to liberal democracy, and in July of 2019 the official rate reached a record level of 29%, the highest documented figure since 2008.[2] The high official unemployment rate in the country has in

© The Author(s), under exclusive license to Springer Nature Switzerland AG 2021
S. Ansari, *Neoliberalism and Resistance in South Africa*, Contemporary African Political Economy, https://doi.org/10.1007/978-3-030-69766-2_1

turn been driven by a number of state measures (see Fig. 1.1) predicated on economic liberalization and neoliberal orthodoxy, which the African National Congress (ANC) has adhered to despite the economy's poor performance in terms of growth. This cluster of policies, it will be shown, has served as a driver of both poverty and economic inequality in the country.[3]

The pattern of social and economic destitution for large swaths of the South African population has thus persisted since the governing party of national liberation, the African National Congress (ANC), ascended to power in 1994 after the first democratic general elections held in the country since the termination of apartheid. The ANC led the political struggle against segregation and subsequently ran their electoral campaign on an economic platform predicated on wealth redistribution through state expenditure and the nationalization of key strategic sectors.[4] However, in 1996, two years after the party's electoral victory and in the midst of a financial panic precipitated by the depreciation of the rand, the Finance Ministry released the Growth, Employment, and

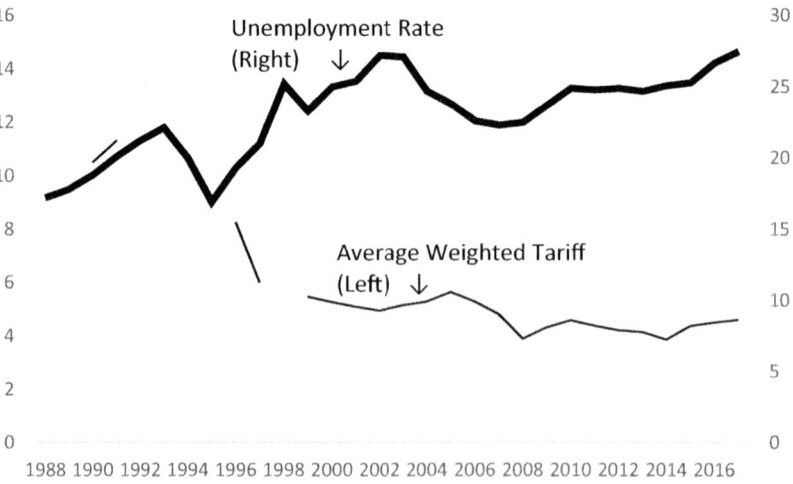

Fig. 1.1 The unemployment rate and trade protection in post-apartheid South Africa (*Note* The gaps represent the years for which data was missing. *Source* SARB for the unemployment rate, The World Bank for South Africa's average weighted tariff)

Redistribution package (GEAR), which committed the new government to a market orthodox programme that was tied to fiscal restraint, trade and financial liberalization, and inflation targeting. Although the rationale behind GEAR was to generate employment growth via private sector investment and exports by creating a hospitable economic environment for foreign and domestic capital, the programme largely failed to deliver the policy objectives outlined by state technocrats. For instance, despite optimistic predictions about employment prospects based on the country's integration with the global economy, from 1996 to 1998 nearly 300,000 jobs were lost as a result of liberalization, and the projected targets for private sector investment fell massively short.[5] Moreover, despite some progress in the realm of poverty reduction and housing, the World Bank continues to classify South Africa as a "dual economy with one of the highest inequality rates in the world."[6] With respect to economic progress, a 2019 piece in the *Financial Times* noted that "Africa's most industrialised economy has suffered a sustained period of sluggish growth and its economy has failed to expand by more than 2% a year since 2013."[7]

Figure 1.1 depicts South Africa's official unemployment rate alongside the average weighted trade tariff on imported goods from 1988 to 2017. The two series follow divergent trajectories; as the tariff structure was dismantled and barriers lowered beginning in the mid-1990s, the country's unemployment rate has steadily trended upwards, and the correlation coefficient of 0.73% suggests a rather strong association between sluggish employment growth on the one hand and the systematic removal of protection for the country's labour intensive industrial base. Figure 1.2 shows South Africa's current account and fiscal expenditure trajectory since the transition. Note that the trade balance and the state budget have consistently been operating in a deficit since the adoption of market orthodoxy, again suggesting that liberalization measures have thus far failed to generate sustained economic growth and competitive advantages. Yet, despite economic stagnation, rising unemployment, and deepening social inequality the ANC has, as noted earlier, persisted with their adherence to neoliberal orthodoxy along crucial macroeconomic policy domains. Moreover, government policy failures related to the unemployment rate and social inequality have not translated into significant electoral losses. In fact, since the democratic transition the ANC has won successive national elections despite renewed labour strikes and serious allegations of corruption and state capture that were levelled against

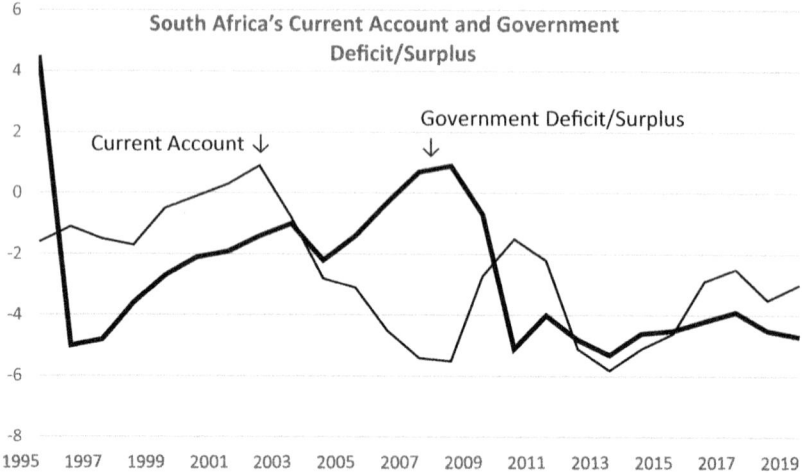

Fig. 1.2 South Africa's current account and government deficit/surplus as a ratio of GDP, 1995–2019 (*Source* South African Reserve Bank)

the Zuma administration by opposition parties and former members of parliament.[8]

Persistent adherence to market orthodoxy by the governing party of national liberation, specifically in the context of political unrest and severe economic inequality, raises some crucial questions. Why has the ANC continued with the implementation of a macroeconomic programme that has failed to meet very clearly outlined social and economic targets over a 25-year period? What political and economic factors are responsible for shaping and constraining South Africa's narrow policy trajectory throughout the post-apartheid period? Perhaps most importantly, why have large sections of the South African population, who have not reaped the material benefits of over two decades of neoliberal orthodoxy, chosen to successively re-elect the governing party that has reneged on numerous post-liberation promises pertaining to economic justice and structural transformation?

The purpose of this book is to provide answers to these questions. The central argument advanced in the chapters that follow is that the neoliberal macroeconomic programme in South Africa has been underwritten by a loose coalition of political and economic actors consisting of bureaucrats in the Treasury and Reserve Bank, ANC political elites, the

Congress of South African Trade Unions (COSATU), global investors and rating agencies, multinational corporations operating in the country, and even citizens benefitting from the ANC's redistributive Cash-Transfer Programme. The alliances that have coalesced around this orthodox growth path can be further disaggregated into their economic and political components. For instance, as will be emphasized in Chapter 2 in the context of a critical examination of public policymaking within the post-apartheid bureaucracy, South Africa's financial integration into the international capital markets after decades of isolation created a space for global finance to shape and constrain domestic policymaking in the country. The post-transition deregulation of the capital account has enabled policymakers to borrow on global financial markets to fund social expenditures and domestic programmes at reduced interest rates. It has also allowed the multinational corporations operating within the country to borrow capital and raise equity on the international capital markets to fund operations outside the borders of South Africa.

However, in the context of persistent fiscal and current account deficits throughout the post-apartheid period, domestic political elites and technocrats within the Treasury must carefully craft policies in accordance with the interests of global asset managers and investors in order to access global finance. In other words, the influx of foreign portfolio capital has permitted the governing party to finance certain non-productive expenditures, such as the cash-transfers to impoverished households as well as civil service salaries, at a lower cost of borrowing. Yet, in the absence of sufficient economic growth, this type of state facilitated redistribution and unproductive expenditure has provided credit rating agencies and international investors with a de-facto veto over "high risk" heterodox economic programmes that could potentially facilitate industrial diversification and generate employment growth. Under these conditions, certain aspects of market orthodoxy related to financial liberalization and anti-inflationary monetary policies are championed by portfolio investors and transnational corporate actors who profit from financial activities. Moreover, these programmes are upheld by orthodox policymakers in the Finance Ministry and Reserve Bank. As Chapter 2 will further document, financial integration and neoliberal orthodoxy have generated significant policy conflicts and debates between orthodox bureaucrats in the Treasury and Central Bank and their more heterodox counterparts in the Department of Trade and Industry (DTI) and the Economic Development Department (EDD).

The persistence of neoliberal orthodoxy is also upheld by a political tripartite alliance consisting of the ANC, COSATU, and the South African Communist Party (SACP). The democratic transition cemented a corporatist arrangement between the governing party and the main trade unions in the country. This agreement incorporated the representatives of organized labour into the state apparatus, thereby sealing off a potentially important radical source of opposition to neoliberal policies while delivering the votes of organized labour to the ANC. In addition to the support enabled by their alliance with the major trade unions, ANC elites can utilize the cash-transfer programme as a tool to generate political support while also capitalizing on the party's legacy in the struggle for liberation against apartheid. Of course, this is not to suggest that orthodox policies have not been met with any resistance from civil society actors. As will be documented in detail in Chapter 3, the neoliberal programme has faced intense opposition in recent years from break-away unions, radical political parties, and segments of organized labourers and impoverished citizens who are not adequately represented by the unions. While this source of protest may indeed prove to be formidable in the future in terms of carving out a new macroeconomic growth path, thus far the official post-apartheid democratic political alliance has remained stable.

In the course of formulating and building these arguments, the book draws on interviews with South African policymakers and contextualizes the implications of this qualitative data by grounding the findings within some noteworthy theoretical frameworks informed by the critical political economy literature on neoliberalism. Specifically, Chapter 2 will employ Thomas Pepinsky's study on economic coalitions in the context of capital mobility and differing investment strategies. Although his argument focuses largely on authoritarian governments and regime durability, Pepinsky's framework highlights how macroeconomic policy-making might differ based on whether the dominant economic actors in the society are owners of mobile or fixed assets. This distinction is important because mobile owners of capital are outward oriented and will prefer policies anchored in financial and trade liberalization. Part of the discussion in the second chapter will also be situated within the theoretical analysis offered by Wolfgang Streeck in his timely and pioneering study, *Buying Time: The Delayed Crisis of Democratic Capitalism*. Streeck's central argument—that under contemporary capitalist relations the primary locus of class conflict now revolves around global investors and nation-state citizens—is particularly relevant to the examination of South Africa's integration into international financial markets and its impact on policymaking. Chapter 2 also utilizes Layna Mosley's important study, *Global Capital and National Governments*, as a framework for exploring the manner in which international asset managers are able to exert influence on the policies enacted by emerging market governments. In addition to building on these critical approaches to political economy, portions of the book draw heavily on the literature dealing with developmental states, especially Chapter 5. This latter chapter offers a comparison between South Africa, India, South Korea, and several other emerging market economies in order to identify the factors behind the divergent growth paths and industrial trajectories in specific developing countries, while also analysing the Zuma era narrative of "White Monopoly Capitalism." Chapter 4, which examines the influence of the multilateral organizations on economic policymaking in South Africa, utilizing the heterodox literature on debt conditionality and policy networks. The conclusion offers a critical analysis of the political and economic incentives that have historically driven industrialization in the developing world, and then employs this framework to unpack the factors that incentivized the phenomena of "state capture" under the Jacob Zuma presidency.

The remainder of this chapter will examine the political and economic variables responsible for South Africa's democratic transition, as well as the evolution of the economic indicators most often tied to neoliberalism. In doing so, it will draw on the Post-Keynesian and Marxian scholarship on the political economy of apartheid, industrial policy, and the turn to market orthodoxy. Portions of the chapter will also delve into the literature on financialization in order to highlight the new investment strategies adopted by the domestic business community and the consequences of this post-apartheid corporate shift. These structural factors will be situated within the broader policy conflicts and developmental debates that crystallized within the ANC's research teams and upper party ranks in the period prior to, and immediately following, the democratic transition. The objective of this section is not to offer a comprehensive and exhaustive review of the political and economic forces that combined to facilitate the ANC's initial shift away from a Keynesian platform of redistribution to the neoliberal programme. This has already been done quite effectively elsewhere.[9] However, it is important to note that the social and economic coalitions underpinning policymaking in South Africa have not remained static. Thus, in order to understand the dynamics behind these shifting alliances and interests, it is necessary to trace and unpack the precise manner in which domestic and global conditions have shaped the preferences of socioeconomic classes and political elites from the era of segregation to the contemporary period. Special attention will be paid to the shift in the investment and profit-making strategies of the business community, with special reference to the large conglomerate corporations that expanded during apartheid. As noted, these structural forces will be linked institutional shifts that occurred within post-apartheid South Africa, including the centralization of economic policymaking within the Treasury, and their link to the persistence of neoliberal orthodoxy.

1.2   The Shifting Political Economy of Segregation, Autarky, and Liberalization

The popular narrative surrounding South Africa's break with apartheid, and the subsequent democratic transition, is generally well known at this point. Nelson Mandela, the leader of the banned African National Congress, in alliance with students, labour unions, and regular South African citizens, fought a valiant battle against racial injustice and segregation. The brutalities of the apartheid system, exposed through the efforts of journalists and human rights activists, led to global outrage and the imposition of economic sanctions against the National Party (NP), all of which eventually compelled state officials to enter into negotiations with the leaders of the ANC and capitulate to popular demands for a liberal democratic election. While this official recounting of the struggle for democracy and racial justice in South Africa certainly captures a crucial component responsible for the democratic transition, what is less well known outside of academic circles is the role played by the business community in integrating the country back into the liberal international order and facilitating apartheid's demise. Yet the influence of big business was not only an integral component in the transition to democracy, it has also shaped South Africa's economic trajectory before and after the disintegration of racial segregation.

South Africa's modern history, including the historical origins of racially infused capitalist social property relations, is inextricably tied to the emergence and eventual economic dominance of the mining industry. The discovery of gold and diamonds in the nineteenth century prompted the British colonial mercantile elite to initiate the production and distribution of minerals in a fashion that would maximize profitability given the economic costs and global conditions confronting investors in the industry. Since the price of gold was fixed internationally, and because mining required a large outlay of fixed capital to begin production, the British mining companies pioneered the system of racial segregation establishing a hierarchical labour market in order to push down wage costs and raise profit margins—a task that became especially important in the context of the inflationary outbreak associated with the First World War.[10] From the end of the nineteenth century until the close of the First World War the British colonial elites, who were interested in promoting the interests of the mining sector, generally prioritized the preservation of a dual labour market predicated on race. The demand for cheap African labour to work in the mines soon led to political tension with the Dutch farmers and the Afrikaner Kruger government in the surrounding regions. The subsequent conflict over the control of cheap exploitable labour power eventually culminated in the Boer War, with the British victory establishing the dominance of mining capital and the implementation of economic policies largely reflecting the free trade ideology of Metropolitan Britain.[11]

Nonetheless, a nascent manufacturing class had also begun to develop and organize into a cohesive group across the Cape during the late nineteenth and early twentieth centuries. This manufacturing community, made up of Boers and other European immigrants who were largely English-speaking, had a vested interest in lobbying for state programmes that would promote industrial expansion centred on protectionism and other interventionist policies.[12] Yet, it must be noted that this budding socioeconomic class sought to obtain state concessions in the context of an inclusive South African nationalism that was mindful of the importance of the entire business community. Manufacturing associations understood that the future prosperity of the industry would be dependent on the continuing expansion of other sectors, most specifically, the mining industry.[13] In fact, for a variety of political and economic reasons, the mining sector and South African manufacturing developed and evolved through a symbiotic relationship with one another that was complex, entailing both conflict and cooperation between the industries.

For instance, the Chamber of Mines, the official business association of the mining industry that was formed in 1897, established a fund in 1916 to provide financing for the expansion of manufacturing companies in order to deal with the problem of unemployment and to service

the mining sector. This led to the creation of the Industrial Development Company (IDC) as well as the Industries Advisory Board (IAB); the
former was initially entirely funded and staffed by gold mining magnates
in 1917. The IAB was formed on the recommendation of the IDC and
was charged with advising the Department of Mines and Industries on
"industrial matters," and was also largely comprised of private business
officials from the mining companies.[14] Moreover, the establishment of
South Africa's State-Owned-Enterprise (SOE) sector was also facilitated
through close collaboration with the mining industry. Mining magnates
wanted to ensure that the SOE's would not employ their market power to
charge high markups to private industry and therefore lobbied for close
collaboration with the government on such matters. As a result, the 1922
Electricity Act, which created the state-owned energy giant Eskom, was
approved by a committee chaired by the Minister of Mines before it was
passed in Parliament.[15]

The dependence of South Africa's manufacturing sector on mining
for its expansion is also evident in terms of sales. From 1925 to 1985
the share of manufacturing in GDP nearly doubled, rising from 36.4 to
64.3%, with the vast majority of this growth centred around the production of industrial consumables for the mining companies.[16] Additionally,
both industries were vertically integrated in a crucial fashion. The mining
sector provided the manufacturing companies with vital inputs. Iscor, the
state-owned steel producer created in 1928 to further stimulate industrial
production, received and processed raw materials such as iron ore and coal
from the domestic mining companies. Furthermore, many sub-sectors
identified with the manufacturing industry, such as non-ferrous metals,
plastics, basic chemicals, and fertilizers, were intricately connected to the
large mining companies.[17] This type of interpenetration between the
industries has led Fine and Rustomjee to characterize the South African
economy in accordance with a "Minerals-Energy-Complex" (MEC) as
a general system of accumulation, one which has shaped the country's
political and socioeconomic evolution from the nineteenth century to
the present.[18] Indeed, segregation, apartheid, and industrialization have
served the interests of the MEC in one fashion or another. In fact, even
the SOEs, once established, employed cheap African labour from the
reserves to reduce costs.[19] Segregation allowed for below subsistence
wages to be paid since the land reserves served to subsidize the costs
of reproduction.

The large mining houses in South Africa, including Anglo-American, DeBeers, and Goldfields and Harmony, were instrumental during this period in the creation of the domestic capital and money markets, and often acted as investment banks in addition to mining companies.[20] Moreover, the state played a crucial role in the cultivation of a long-term domestic financial market through the establishment of the National Finance Corporation (NFC) in 1949. The NFC channelled its deposits into mining company debt and Treasury Bills. In addition, by directing funds from Anglo-American's diamond ventures into the mining operations in the Gold Fields of the Orange Free State, the institution helped to erode the distinction between Afrikaner and English Capital.[21] The South African economy underwent a further series of crucial structural changes from the late 1960s to the early 1990s. The National Party's ongoing commitment to apartheid provoked protests, boycotts, as well as social and political unrest that at times compelled the government to respond with ruthless state violence. In the aftermath of the 1960 Sharpeville massacre, which involved the killing of dozens of unarmed protestors by the South African police, the NP imposed a stringent set of capital controls on non-residents in order to stem financial outflows. The regulations, known as the "blocked-rand-system," stipulated that while non-residents could continue to liquidate their South African equities and bonds, they could not repatriate the funds unless the blocked-rand were used to purchase additional domestic securities that would be subsequently sold on foreign exchanges, such as the London Stock Exchange, with a matching buyer of the assets. This measure served to prevent additional capital outflows from South Africa through legal means, thereby insulating the rand from downward selling pressure and preserving the country's foreign exchange reserves.[22]

Between 1984 and 1989 over 300 multinational firms disinvested from South Africa as a result of sanctions, political unrest, and economic disturbances marked by the debt crisis. This disinvestment enabled the domestic conglomerates to acquire the subsidiary shares of the blue-chip firms, which in turn generated heightened levels of domestic-conglomerate economic concentration.[23] Diversification by South Africa's core mining firms through their acquisition of non-core businesses eventually led to the emergence of six giant conglomerates that dominated the Johannesburg Stock Exchange (JSE), which together represented 80% of market capitalization by 1992.[24] As a result of this development, by the late 1980s South Africa's economy was effectively controlled by six wealthy families.[25] The post-1948 period was thus marked by a coalitional class alliance consisting of white organized labour and conglomerate groupings with investments in mining, finance, and industry, operating in the context of state protection and racialized capitalism.[26]

This type of economic system, however, was not without its own contradictions and social instabilities. First, although high levels of economic concentration and cross-ownership patterns between the various conglomerates raised the business community's market power, this trend also increased the type of inefficiencies and distortions which tend to manifest as economic stagnation.[27] However, as will be discussed in Chapter 5, the existence of oligopoly on its own was not primarily responsible for stagnationist tendencies; rather, it was the absence of a comprehensive industrial programme targeting the capital goods sector. Industrial policy in South Africa was always constrained by the existence of a mining sector dominated by foreign capital. The South African Party, under Botha and General Smuts, initially pursued a very weak programme of protection that did not substantively disrupt the colonial ideology and practice of free trade, despite numerous protests from the manufacturing associations. The tariff structure, up until 1924/5, was designed solely to generate revenue and not to protect infant industries.[28] While this policy underwent a modification with the election of the Pact government, state industrial programmes continued to unfold, and were thus shaped, according to the economic interests of the Minerals-Energy-Complex. As a result, the limited ISI policies that were adopted by the National Party did not substitute for advanced capital goods, a policy gap which eventually served to raise the country's import bill. Moreover, advanced sectors were under the control of transnational corporations, and exports remained concentrated among natural resources and minerals.[29] Over time, this trend generated a balance of payments and debt crisis by the 1980s.[30] The political uncertainty and social instabilities associated with apartheid and international boycotts also served to discourage long-term investment in fixed capital assets. Expansion thus took the form of mergers and acquisitions in contrast to capacity expansion. Moreover, in this context, the conglomerate firms began to channel funds into financial assets, further eroding employment stability and industrial growth.[31] This latter development was a precursor to the shift to financialization as an integrated business model, a point which will be discussed more thoroughly later in this chapter.

In addition to the economic contradictions generated by apartheid and racially exclusive state-led development, the social and political coalitions underpinning the system were also subjected to destabilizing forces beginning in the 1970s. As the economic historian Sampie Terreblanche has noted, racial segregation was essentially a growth model endorsed and facilitated by the Chamber of Mines in collaboration with the state. The model was predicated on an "alliance of gold and maize," thus incorporating a loose coalition between mining capital, Afrikaner farmers, and organized white workers.[32] As noted, this system, even in the later years of apartheid when industrialization and economic diversification were prioritized by the government, fundamentally revolved around an economic model dominated by the MEC through a series of backward and forward linkages. Racial segregation underwrote the mining companies' profitability, and economic autarky and state intervention were viewed as tolerable even in the midst of certain developmental contradictions—so long as the international environment was conducive for mining profits.[33] In the 1970s, following President Nixon's decision to delink the dollar from gold, stagflation facilitated a steady rise in gold prices as global investors sought to hedge their risks. However, in 1979 there was a reversal of this trend as the US Federal Reserve began an unprecedented hike in domestic interest rates through a contraction of the money supply. The subsequent "Volker Shock" ushered in a period of deflation and signalled the beginning of the debt crisis in the Third World. The fall in gold prices and earnings in the 1980s, in conjunction with the social crisis of legitimacy surrounding the apartheid system, signalled to business the need for a new investment and growth model predicated on outward expansion beyond South Africa, which in turn necessitated a certain degree of internal political stability.[34] The business community became receptive to a transition to political democracy based on the liberal precepts of equality and internationalism.

As negotiations between the National Party and the ANC began in the late 1980s, big business increased its efforts to steer the direction of economic policymaking in a future post-apartheid government. To this end, the South Africa Foundation (SAF) and the Anglo-American Corporation sponsored several economic planning scenarios aimed at government officials in order to highlight the potential dangers of the ANC's initial growth through redistribution platform. Two of the most influential economic seminars were the "Professional Economist's Panel" and the *Mont Fleur* planning scenario. The former was sponsored by Nedcor/Old Mutual, was published in the *Weekly Mail*, and specifically stated that "Neither individual [economic] proposals nor the package as a whole should result in any additional taxation or any increase in government expenditure overall."[35] The *Mont Fleur* scenario, which was designed to illustrate the destructive potential of any type of populist redistributive programme, was sponsored by the Institute for Social Development and included the participation of top ANC officials such as Trevor Manuel, as well as business executives from companies such as Shell. The scenario was packaged as a video and offered the core message that in attempting to meet the unrealistic expectations of the working class, populism would quickly crash and maim the economy.[36] Jeremy Cronin, former Deputy General Secretary of the SACP, summarized the cumulative effect of the business community's lobbying efforts on policymaking: "The think tanks, the safari junkets? I'm sure these had an impact."[37]

In addition to this type of overt lobbying, Terreblanche has noted that a set of informal discussions were held between ANC leaders and members of the South African corporate elite behind closed doors in the early 1990s. This exchange played a crucial role in consolidating the market-oriented nature of the economic policies implemented in the mid-1990s, and culminated in an "elite compromise" on economic policymaking in 1993. The pre-election "Statement on Economic Policies" contained a commitment to a "redistribution through growth" strategy, which entailed a clause for fiscal balance as well as a commitment to reduce deficit spending over the long-term and a pledge not to raise taxes.[38] The "elite compromise" meant that macroeconomic policymaking in post-apartheid South Africa had already been injected with a strict dose of market orthodoxy even before GEAR was officially unveiled by technocrats in the Finance Ministry in 1996.[39]

Alan Hirsch, who was one of the authors of the GEAR document and who served as a senior official in the Department of Trade and Industry and the Office of the Presidency following the democratic transition, has stressed that the effort by big business to subvert the ANC's electoral platform of redistribution and progressive taxation was quite significant. Hirsch noted that by taking the initiative to facilitate peace talks between the National Party and the ANC, the corporate sector hoped to preserve certain elements of South Africa's economic structure, such as the market power possessed by the large firms, while removing obstacles to further expansion. Thus, exchange and capital account liberalization were promoted while progressive corporate taxation was discouraged. The primary driver behind the campaign by big business to terminate racial segregation and influence post-apartheid economic policy was the desire to internationalize investment operations.[40] However, it is important to note that the business community was able to succeed with their project largely because there were different and opposing economic strands of thought within the party. A 2002 discussion paper released by COSATU, entitled "Theory of the Transition," identified two separate socioeconomic perspectives within the liberation movement, one which advocated for an interventionist state, and a second position which pushed for a far more cautious approach in light of the globalization of capital and the disintegration of the Soviet Union. The corporate sector was able to exploit this divide quite effectively to secure the eventual post-transition "elite compromise."[41]

The most recent and comprehensive account of the policy debates surrounding the post-apartheid economic transition is to be found in Vishnu Padayachee and Robert Van Niekerk's study, *Shadow of Liberation*.[42] The authors argue, based on interviews, archival research, and first-hand experience, that the ANC leadership abandoned their earlier strategy of Keynesian redistribution for several reasons. Firstly, they note that by the late 1970s a group of policymakers schooled in market orthodoxy had already begun, under the support and encouragement of PW Botha (who had earlier removed many of the statist apartheid hardliners from the bureaucracy), to implement several reforms in the areas of exchange controls, trade, and labour market policies. This move was in line with the new trend towards economic liberalization. The rationale driving this decision was economic as well as political in nature. For instance, Hentz has argued that the privatization of SOEs under apartheid, while cloaked in economic language, was fundamentally a political calculation. More specifically, privatization of the industrial SOEs was implemented in order to facilitate a reliable "exit strategy" for investors in the event that the ANC succeeded in establishing a truly redistributive economic democracy.[43] In this context, once such measures were introduced the momentum driving liberalization would prove difficult to disrupt. As a result, when formal negotiations were launched between the ANC and the NP, the latter simply maintained their current macroeconomic policy stance, supported by their well-staffed research and government departments, while ANC leaders were limited in their ability to adequately challenge these orthodox proposals.[44] One important factor responsible for the ANC's impotency in this area was that the liberation movement had prioritized the struggle against political domination, which manifested itself in the form of segregation and apartheid. As a result, economic policies in a post-apartheid South Africa received less attention from the party, thereby rendering the leadership far more susceptible to external influence from business and the apartheid government in the economic domain.[45] Indeed, it is telling that during the informal discussions between representatives of the apartheid government and the ANC leadership, economic issues were largely absent from the talks.[46]

This relative neglect of the macroeconomic policy agenda on the part of the ANC would also account for the party's rejection of viable alternative economic programmes, specifically those predicated on an interventionist industrial programme and Keynesian redistribution. For example, in June of 1990 the Canadian government, working through the International Development Research Center (IDRC), helped facilitate the establishment of the Macroeconomic Research Group (MERG). The unit was composed of international and domestic researchers who were tasked with formulating economic policy proposals in order to compensate for the weakness of the ANC's Department of Economic Planning (DEP).[47] Vella Pillay, a London trained economist and a member of the South African Communist Party (SACP), was appointed as the director of the research team. Despite producing some well-supported and comprehensive policy measures to alleviate apartheid era inequality and promote industrial diversification, the DEP and ANC leaders rejected the Group's proposals in December of 1993. Padayachee and Van Niekerk have put forward a number of possible reasons for this rejection, including tension between the international and domestic researchers, the lack of any substantive involvement in the process by the SACP and COSATU, and the drift towards more orthodox economic positions within the DEP during this period—such as their acceptance of Reserve Bank independence.[48]

Once MERG was rejected by the ANC, it was a short leap to the Growth, Employment, and Redistribution (GEAR) programme adopted by the party in 1996. The abandonment of a heterodox policy package enabled the proponents of neoliberal orthodoxy within the business community, academia, the media, and the party to push for further economic liberalization based on the notion that "there is no alternative."[49] The consolidation of this worldview meant that perfectly reasonable proposals for state intervention to alleviate the inequalities of apartheid were jettisoned. For example, when Mboweni, then Deputy Head of the DEP, proposed a reconstruction levy (essentially a wealth tax) in order to generate a special fund for developmental purposes, the suggestion was vetoed by the ANC leadership as a result of opposition from the media.[50] Indeed, Segatti and Pons-Vignon have argued that the rejection of MERG by the ANC leadership marked the beginning of a trend in which macroeconomic policymaking would be insulated from democratic scrutiny, and internal party processes emanating from within government departments, specifically the Treasury, would take precedence over broader policy initiatives based on academic research and outside consultation.[51] Overall, in the context of this ideologically driven campaign to discredit heterodox economic policies—as well as the National Party's earlier shift to liberalization—the adoption of market orthodoxy must be understood as the culmination of a concerted effort on the part of certain actors to defeat the alternative option of wealth redistribution and state-led industrial diversification. However, the key point is that internal fracture and conflict within the ANC, as well as the triumph of conservative officials over left-wing forces with respect to the key economic policy debates, created the space for external actors to exert their interests and shape the economic programme that was eventually adopted.

Overall, the lobbying efforts by the press, private industry, and apartheid officials allowed big business to reap dividends on the economic front. As noted, average trade tariff rates were reduced as part of the GEAR package to liberalize trade, and capital controls on non-residents were removed in 1995. In the years following the transition, businesses expanded their operations and increased the level of investment throughout Africa. By the year 2000, South Africa had emerged as the largest source of FDI for the rest of the continent. In 2001, investment throughout the continent had increased by 300% since the democratic transition.[52] Throughout this period, South African transnational corporations established control over 80% of the regional economy, which enabled the country to reap the benefits of a 9:1 trade balance with other economies in the region.[53] South African firms accumulated substantial interests in Tanzania's national electricity company, Cameroon's national railroad, and shopping centres throughout the continent.[54] By 2005, all but 8 of the largest 100 corporations listed on the JSE had operations in other African countries. Yet, after subtracting for infrastructure, the composition of this investment has been largely extractive, comprising mainly of Mining, Telecommunications, and Oil & Gas.[55]

This outward investment has benefitted multiple companies within the MEC. Such firms include AngloGold Ltd, Sasol Ltd, Stanbic Africa, ABSA, and Naspers Ltd, as well as telecommunications firms such as MTN Group Ltd.[56] It is noteworthy that the expansion by South African capital throughout the Southern Africa region has bred resentment among the local populations. A great source of this resentment arises from the trade surplus the country enjoys with the rest of the continent, as well as the fact that South African transnational corporations have aggressively acquired local counterparts through vertical integration. As a result, "very few inputs are sourced locally, and there is very little knowledge and skills transfer, let alone training and hiring locals at management levels."[57] Indeed, much of the trade surplus South Africa enjoys with the continent has its roots in this type of vertical integration. For example, South African retailers opened shopping malls and entertainment franchises in the city of Lusaka, and then imported devalued inventories of goods from South Africa.[58] Also of importance is that this process of regional expansion through trade and vertical integration has provided an outlet for South African produced goods that are not competitive on international export markets.[59]

Outward investment by South Africa's corporate sector was accompanied by a fundamental restructuring of these firm's operations and holdings. In the aftermath of economic liberalization, economic concentration on equity markets began a marked decline from the previous levels of the 1980s. For instance, by 2004, the equity owned by the top six conglomerates on the JSE dropped to 38.5%.[60] This unbundling of conglomerate holdings was facilitated through heightened merger and acquisition activity following exchange and capital account liberalization, which enabled firms to divest their holdings of diverse operations in order to focus on core competencies. A 2000 budget review by the National Treasury highlighted the link between corporate restructuring following the adoption of market orthodoxy and the global orientation of South African firms and capital inflows. It was noted that the removal of capital controls and the overseas listing of large domestic corporations have allowed them to reorganize into "focused international groupings," and that foreign investors have taken advantage of this unbundling by purchasing shares previously held by South African companies.[61] While corporate restructuring in line with core competencies facilitated the post-apartheid outward accumulation strategy and increased the appeal of such companies to global investors, the sectoral balance within South Africa has only shifted slightly. Indeed, while the number of firms engaged in finance and services has increased significantly since 1994, six of the top twenty companies are still predominantly involved in mining operations, despite the fact that a crucial rationale of economic liberalization was that dismantling regulations would facilitate FDI inflows and promote industrial diversification.[62]

Figure 1.3 depicts South Africa's trade trajectory for merchandise, manufacturing, and high technology exports. As the graph illustrates, manufacturing exports have followed an upward trend since 1981 and stood at 50% of total merchandise exports in 2014. However, the percentage of strategic, high technology goods that make up this proportion is low, reaching a high of 8.7% of all merchandise exports in 1998 and then declining to 5.9% in 2014. Much of the surge in the manufacturing share of South African exports is attributable to the DTI's Automotive

Fig. 1.3 South African merchandise and manufacturing exports (*Note* The gaps in the series represent years for which data is missing. *Source* SARB for total merchandise exports; World Bank database for manufacturing and high technology exports)

Investment Scheme (AIS), which incentivized the production of automobile component parts by offering a tax-free cash grant of 25% of the investment in productive assets.[63] However, if agro-based and mineral-based manufactures are excluded from the manufacturing category, then resource-intensive products still account for 60% of all of South Africa's exports.[64] The post-transition period has not altered the fundamental dynamic of the South African economy, which still largely revolves around its Minerals-Energy core. Rather, post-transition the MEC has been fused with a financialized component driven by increased capital mobility, shareholder value, corporate unbundling, and outward expansion.

1.3   FINANCIALIZATION
OF THE POST-APARTHEID ECONOMY

The ascendance of financial activities can be understood primarily as a new accumulation strategy which originated in the advanced industrial economies in response to the decline in manufacturing profitability in the United States in the early 1970s.[65] As a new pathway for private profit-making, financialization has also shaped the South African business community's approach to investment throughout the post-apartheid period. The term can refer to a vast array of practices, including the internationalization of financial assets, the dominance of financial actors and institutions over the non-financial economy, the subordination of firm managers to shareholders, and the re-emergence of the rentier—a financial actor who siphons funds from the productive sphere through either speculative activity or usurious interest rates.[66] Gretta Krippner, in her study on the financialization of the US economy, has defined the phenomena as a "pattern of accumulation in which profits accrue primarily through financial channels rather than through trade or commodity production."[67] Such channels would include interest payments, stock dividends, and capital gains. Krippner's definition of financialization is useful because it does not rigidly separate the domestic economy into a financial and productive sphere, but rather recognizes that even traditionally "productive" enterprises will devote their resources towards financial activities given a certain socioeconomic environment. As a result, private investment could potentially be geared in favour of speculative endeavours that have unintended and negative consequences for the economy. For example, financial sector activities tend to employ far fewer individuals per unit of investment than more traditional industries such as manufacturing,[68] and financial speculation tends to generate instability and eventually the outbreak of crises.[69]

The global trend of a shift to increasingly financialized operations has had significant consequences for post-apartheid South Africa in terms of domestic growth, productive investment, and the unemployment rate. During the apartheid years, trade protection enabled the economy to generate current account surpluses from the mid-1980s to the democratic transition. However, with the implementation of rapid trade liberalization in the 1990s, foreign portfolio capital inflows became an important source of finance to fund the persistent trade deficit.[70] In 2000, the Reserve Bank, under the governorship of Tito Mboweni, instituted a monetary regime anchored to inflation targeting (IT), which necessitates high short-term interest rates within a 3–6% band. Although the official rationale of such a regime, as outlined initially in the GEAR document, was that a low and stable inflation rate would create an economic environment conducive to foreign investment and employment growth, this argument has been called into question by economists who have pointed out that high interest rates raise the cost of capital and discourage borrowing and productive domestic investment, thus contributing to South Africa's persistently high unemployment.[71] Moreover, attempting to suppress inflation through high short-term interest rates will fail if inflationary tendencies are triggered primarily through import shocks caused by currency depreciation, a common phenomenon in a primary commodity exporting country such as South Africa.[72]

In fact, the IT regime largely complements the liberalized capital account; in order to mitigate periodic and rapid capital outflows, high short-term interest rates are required to attract foreign funds to buttress the rand and avoid the depletion of foreign exchange reserves during currency crises.[73] This type of policy package is reflective of a general trend within emerging market economies that reflects their subordinated position within the global financial architecture. Their subordinate position is anchored to the lower "liquidity premia" that global investors attach to the currencies of developing countries in comparison to those in industrialized states. This subordinated status compels developing country governments to offer higher short-term interest rates in order to increase demand for assets that fall lower on the currency hierarchy.[74] The prevailing monetary regime in South Africa is thus in actuality tied to this larger process of financialization—it compensates for the capital flight that has occurred since the removal of capital controls and deregulation, buttresses the currency against speculative pressures by drawing in capital, and also supports profit generation among global and domestic financial actors.[75]

This shift to financialization has also generated a series of economic incentives and distortions within the post-liberalization South African economy in a fashion that has important implications for income distribution and corporate decision-making. To begin with, the country's integration into the global financial markets has created "New Forms of External Vulnerability" that directly and indirectly impact policy and the profit-making strategies adopted by domestic and international financial actors.[76] One important aspect of financialization is the proliferation and rapid turn-over of equity assets, debt instruments, and financial and currency derivatives by private investment funds and institutions whose primary motivation is not long-term investment based on capital formation and development, but simply the quest for short-term profit generation through the materialization of capital gains.[77] This type of investment horizon and profit regime has generated volatile price movements and encouraged speculative behaviour which, during certain periods, has caused a rapid appreciation and subsequent depreciation of the South African currency in a fashion that has no connection to the country's economic fundamentals.[78]

Indeed, domestic price gyrations and capital flows in this environment are driven by conditions of global liquidity that are often dependent on the Central Bank policies of developed economies.[79] This aspect of financial integration has had significant consequences for economic stability. In fact, in 2011 the Treasury raised the issue of volatile capital inflows and their destabilizing impact on the rand during economic booms.[80] The potential fall-out from this trend is encapsulated in theoretical models such as the "Dutch Disease"; as the currency appreciates, manufacturing and agricultural exports become less competitive, strengthening the mining and natural resource sector and further constraining industrial investment and diversification. Rapid currency depreciation then leads to costlier imports and, as noted, triggers inflationary outbreaks that further discourage investment and savings.

Additionally, the post-apartheid economy's integration into the global financial architecture has fundamentally impacted the operations of the corporate sector in both the financial and non-financial industries. The restructuring of the large South African multinational companies in the aftermath of the democratic transition was to a large extent motivated by a desire to attract foreign financial inflows and higher rates of investment. This, in turn, necessitated a renewed focus on certain core profit-making activities. In a financialized and globalized economy transnational corporations must meet certain metrics set by international investors, such as dividend payments and asset prices, in order to compete for steady inflows of portfolio capital.[81] At the same time, the benchmarks associated with financialization have served to exacerbate inequality and stifle productive investment and employment generation through capacity expansion. For example, during the commodities boom, which lasted from 2000–08, three of the largest platinum producers distributed nearly half of their entire value-added profits to their shareholders as dividend payments, a management decision that came at the expense of potential future wage increases in the industry.[82]

Speculative and short-term financial activity has, in fact, structured the investment decisions of the large mining houses throughout the period of the global commodities boom and beyond. One manifestation of this form of financialized activity among non-financial corporations (NFCs) is that a growing number of mining companies in the basic materials industry are "over-capitalized." Put differently, their cash/liabilities ratio exceeds 45% in the context of stagnating productive investment, a development which suggests that this liquidity is primarily utilized for the purpose of short-term capital gains in the equity markets.[83] Furthermore, an increasing quantity of the cash reserves of NFCs are also held in accounts with the large South African commercial banks where they can capitalize on rising depositor interest rates. In an economic environment marked by a high unemployment rate and a productive "investment strike" by the corporate sector, the circulation of these funds throughout the economy may further fuel speculative activity. To highlight one example of this trend, in the 1990s South African NFCs issued equity shares which were largely purchased by international portfolio investors. The proceeds of these sales were placed in the South African commercial banks, which have leveraged these reserves to issue mortgage credit to households and underwrite debt fuelled consumption, thereby contributing to price inflation in the real estate markets.[84] In this sense, the shift away from productive investment in industries such as manufacturing has increased financial fragility in the South African economy.

Figure 1.4 depicts three series: the ratio of dividends to exports, the ratio of dividends paid to dividends received for all private non-financial

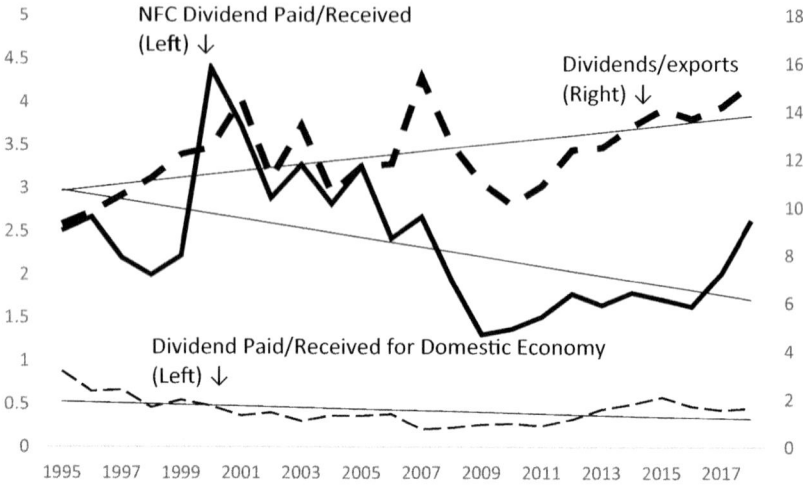

Fig. 1.4   Dividend income and exports in post-apartheid South Africa (*Source* SARB, author's calculations)

corporations (NFCs), and the ratio of dividend income paid/received for the whole domestic economy. The ratio of dividends paid/received for both the entire economy and non-financial companies has, while fluctuating, followed a downward trajectory. However, this may simply reflect the extent to which the South African economy has financialized, since the income received by NFCs in the form of dividends and interest has outstripped their payments to investors since 1995. This latter metric is one indicator of a general pattern of accumulation that is based on financial, as opposed to productive, channels.[85] The ratio of dividends paid to exports, on the other hand, has trended upwards since the democratic transition. This is a significant development, since the upward trajectory of this ratio is one signal of a net outflow of foreign exchange. The payment of dividend income to foreign investors is largely responsible, along with trade liberalization, for the persistent current account deficit that the post-transition South African economy has experienced.[86]

As noted, this deficit has been funded by international portfolio capital inflows. In this context, the adherence to capital account liberalization by policymakers is to a certain extent a response to the problems associated with an appreciating exchange rate caused by foreign bond and equity purchases. Instead of imposing regulations on inflows which could jeopardize foreign financing of the twin deficits, Treasury officials have chosen to allow non-residents to repatriate capital without restrictions in order to partially alleviate the effects of an overvalued exchange rate.[87] However, this has also meant that capital that could have potentially been invested in productive endeavours within the country has been siphoned off by foreign investors in the form of dividend and interest payments.

The argument here is not that the financialization of the post-apartheid South African economy is the causal factor driving low investment rates in productive industries. It has been shown for several industrialized economies, for example, that financialization is driven not through the utilization or depletion of corporations' internal reserves, but rather by massive borrowing on the capital markets.[88] In fact, as of 2017, the South African NFCs were sitting on R719-billion in cash reserves held in domestic financial institutions, hence the term "investment strike."[89] The decision by corporations to not invest in productive endeavours could be explained by a variety of factors, one of which is the general decline in the rate of return on manufactured and tradable industries, at the sectoral and aggregate level, caused by the saturation of global export markets.[90] It has also long been recognized that oligopolistic market power can serve as an impediment to private productive investment, since in this type of economic environment companies have an incentive to restrict output in order to maintain high price-markups.[91]

The latter factor remains especially relevant for the post-apartheid economy. Despite the shedding of non-core activities by the South African conglomerates in the aftermath of liberalization, the economy remains highly oligopolistic at the sectoral level. A 2013 report issued by the Reserve Bank, for example, attributed the country's stagnant growth rates and unemployment problem to persistent oligopoly, noting that "the high levels of market concentration shown in mark-up studies represent a serious underlying constraint to South Africa's potential for achieving sustained higher growth."[92] Under such conditions, large corporations could be compelled to either invest in countries with less mature industries and higher rates of return or, barring more interventionist measures by the state, simply invest in liquid financial assets. As a senior official in the Reserve Bank stated, "even if you were to lock down the capital migrating abroad, it would simply sit in the bank and earn interest."[93] The issue of monopoly capital, and the extent to which it might serve as a barrier to productive investment and employment generation in South Africa, will be examined in greater detail in Chapter 5.

Figure 1.5 depicts the trajectory for private investment in fixed assets as a ratio to GDP, as well as the series for manufacturing and mining investment as a ratio of total investment, calculated in 2010 chained currency. Total investment, which includes investment in the finance sector, has trended upwards since the democratic transition. Manufacturing investment, however, has followed a downward trajectory since 1995, illustrating that the industry has not benefitted from deregulation and economic liberalization. Investment in the mining industry has followed a flat trend line during the same period. Note the uptick in investment that began around the time of the global commodities boom in 2003 and continued to peak until 2010 before beginning a slow descent. This heightened investment activity in additional capacity represents a peculiar feature of the mining industry's integration with financialized circuits: the appreciation of primary commodity prices necessitates increased M&A activity and the expansion of fixed assets as a means of capitalizing on rising profits in a manner that satisfies shareholders.[94] However, once the boom ended and commodity prices started falling,

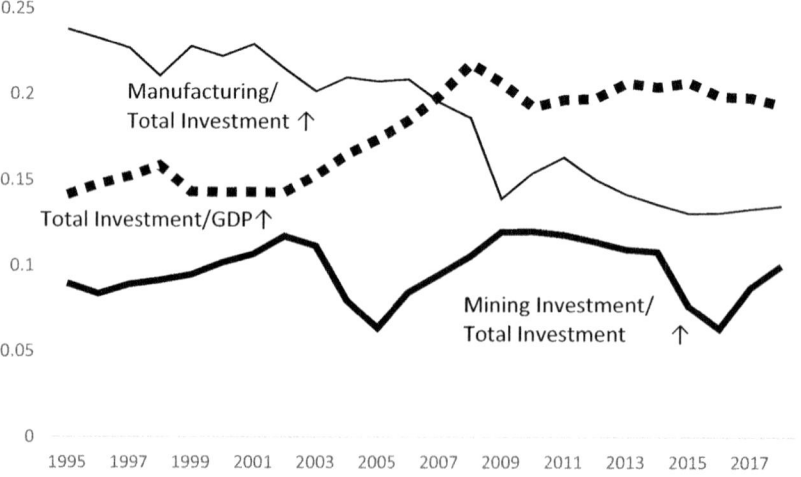

Fig. 1.5 Manufacturing, mining, and total private investment in post-apartheid South Africa (*Source* SARB, author's calculations)

investment in fixed mining assets—as shown in the chart—levelled out and then began to decline in 2011.

The low rates of productive investment and employment growth can be partially attributed to the absence of Keynesian style interventionist policies by the state since the democratic transition. The rationale for economic liberalization was based on the "myth of neutrality," the idea that the market could be entrusted to adequately allocate resources across sectors and among economic actors.[95] According to this school of thought, state expenditure will serve to crowd out private investment by competing for scarce capital. However, it has now long been recognized that state expenditure, specifically spending on capital goods and public infrastructure, often has the effect of crowding in investment by raising the profit forecast of firms and reducing risk and uncertainty.[96] Fiscal austerity, in combination with high levels of economic concentration and oligopoly, could explain why corporations retain liquid assets while abstaining from large productive investments in new capacity outside of global primary commodity booms for the mining industry.

The financialization of the post-apartheid economy resulting from liberalization has political and economic implications that go beyond the risks associated with rising macroeconomic fragility and financial crises. It has also influenced the perpetuation of neoliberal orthodoxy through several distinct policy channels. Firstly, integration into the global capital markets has rendered the government susceptible to the same type of judgments by international financial actors and credit rating agencies as private firms. The ANC must exercise fiscal restraint in order to borrow from international private creditors and fund the budget deficit, which serves to discipline the state and reproduce elements of economic liberalization by deepening market relations. As a former Chief of Fiscal Policy at the Treasury put it: "Expansionary fiscal policy is a privilege, one that is bestowed upon us by the financial markets—you can only borrow as much as foreign lenders are prepared to lend you at a given price."[97] The initial deregulation of the capital account has, in this sense, facilitated the structural power of financial markets over state policy in a fashion that has served to lock in specific aspects of market orthodoxy, such as ongoing fiscal austerity.

Secondly, the structural power of the business community has also served to reinforce the existing economic trajectory throughout the post-apartheid period. One important and unique aspect of private industry in South Africa is that it is large in relation to the state, especially when compared to other countries on the continent where state-owned-enterprises tend to monopolize production in the natural resource sector. The sheer size of the business community thus renders the state sensitive to the perceived investment climate in the country, and any deterioration of "business confidence" represents the potential threat that firms will simply opt to disinvest in response to perceived hostile economic programs.[98] This form of structural power serves to discipline the state and circumscribe interventionist policies, such as, for example, progressive forms of corporate taxation. Attempts to impose higher tax rates on corporations, in the absence of capital controls on outflows, could result in even lower rates of domestic investment and capital flight. In addition, the integration of South African multinational firms into global supply chains and the number of corporate subsidiaries operating on the continent and across the globe would make higher tax rates difficult to enforce. The South African corporate tax rate, for both resident and non-resident companies, is currently 28%, and policymakers in the Treasury are fully aware of the possibility that higher statutory corporate taxes would trigger tax evasion through transfer pricing between subsidiaries or other forms of capital flight.[99]

The prerequisite socioeconomic conditions of the corporate sector's new investment regime are therefore prioritized in policymaking circles, specifically in the Finance Ministry, which tends to generally adopt a conservative stance when it comes to regulating the capital markets. A former senior official in the Treasury, for example, stated that a liberalized capital account was a necessity in the current period because of the reality that under economic globalization firms "require fluidity" in order to enhance their "linkages with global value chains." Moreover, it was asserted that multinational companies in South Africa want the ability to access funds and shift their resources out of the country if necessary.[100] As noted, this type of policy stance recognizes that the corporate sector has adopted a post-apartheid strategy of outward investment. This internationalization of South Africa's corporate base is also partially linked to the large quantities of foreign capital inflows noted earlier, despite stagnating domestic production in many industries. As the Wall Street Journal noted, global investors and asset managers continue to invest in South African corporations even in the midst of slow growth due to the simple fact that a great deal of the corporate profits generated by such companies are linked to operations outside of South Africa.[101] Policymakers are aware of the potential blowback that could come from regulating the capital account in a context of foreign capital inflows that are predicated on this type of outward profit-making strategy.

Lastly, the corporate sector in South Africa has relentlessly promoted the perpetuation of neoliberalism and financial liberalization through direct lobbying efforts, mostly through their business associations. This type of lobbying often takes the form of opposition to any state policies that are viewed as violating the tenets of market orthodoxy. For example, the Chamber of Mines was staunchly opposed to the Mineral and Petroleum Resources Development Act, a bill which sought to impose a royalty tax of 5% from mining firms' gross sales. The Chamber lobbied vigorously against the idea, releasing a memorandum in 2000 to the Director General at the Department of Minerals and Energy. The Chamber argued in this 225-page memo that several of the proposed elements within the Minerals Resources Act violated the economic principles outlined in the ANC's 1996 GEAR document. For instance, the memorandum took issue with the proposal to impose an export duty on diamonds as a method of promoting beneficiation, stating that such a policy would not produce "international competitiveness or align itself with market trends." Moreover, the memo asserted that if the government did in fact insist on an interventionist policy then such a strategy should aim to boost the "competitiveness of the South African diamond cutting industry" through "training, increased labor flexibility, and broadening diamond skills and enhancing market capabilities." Most tellingly, the memo stated that the "economic thinking" behind the interventionist policies outlined in the MPRDA was "autarkic and simply not aligned to government policy to liberalize all regulated sectors of the South African economy."[102] Although the bill was passed through Parliament in 2002, the Chamber's lobbying efforts succeeded in eliminating the proposed export levy increase on diamonds and other natural resources, and in 2005 the export duty that had been put in place on diamonds in 1985 was further reduced.[103]

Also active in the area of domestic macroeconomic policymaking is the Business Leadership South Africa (BLSA), formerly known as the South Africa Foundation. The BLSA represents the largest multinational firms and investors operating or domiciled in South Africa, and many of these businesses are among the multinational companies that have significant investments in other countries on the continent. In 2004, the BLSA surveyed executives and managers at twenty-five of the largest corporations listed on the JSE and asked them what type of economic policies might compel them to increase their investment in fixed capital assets. The main factors highlighted by members had to do with labour market flexibility, tax relief for investment, wage restraint, crime reduction, lower interest rates, and the continued reduction of trade tariffs and exchange controls.[104] Additional position papers released by the association advocated against the utilization of tariff protection by the DTI to stimulate investment, arguing that persistent trade liberalization and exchange rate manipulation should be emphasized to promote exports.[105] The overall position of the BLSA is thus similar to the Chamber of Mines; namely, that the deepening of market orthodoxy should be relied upon by policymakers as a mechanism to guide economic growth and solve unemployment and economic inequality.

The above analysis shows that economic liberalization has emerged from, while also structuring, the South African business community's new investment regime. Despite the unbundling of non-core activities to meet the metrics of shareholder value and financialized redistribution, the corporate sector generally remains, as noted, highly oligopolistic in terms of the prevailing market structure. However, the crucial difference is that under racial segregation domestic capital, which revolved largely around the MEC and mining operations, was for the most part tied to a specific geographic locale as a result of heavy state regulation and its dependence on coerced black labour. In contrast, domestic capital is now highly mobile and significantly depends on outward investment to compete for transnational investment flows. In the post-transition socioeconomic environment mining and minerals remain central to the South African economy; however, as has been illustrated, the removal of state protectionist measures and the rapid inflows and outflows of capital have lowered productive and long-term investment levels while significantly raising the unemployment rate.

Finally, it must be noted that a key demographic underwriting the reproduction of the apartheid regime has now been replaced by a new strata of privileged income earners as a pillar of support for the ANC. Under segregation, the white working and middle classes emerged as a crucial electoral base championing the persistence of their formal racial privilege. In the aftermath of the democratic transition, the ANC began implementing the "Black Economic Empowerment" (BEE) programme, a policy platform designed to alleviate the historical legacies of racial disparity by propping up a socioeconomic category of black entrepreneurs integrated into the capitalist class through state intervention. The programme was in fact initiated by Sanlam, a financial conglomerate, and Anglo-American during the negotiations between ANC officials and the business community.[106] It mandated that funds be made available, and a specific quantity of equity shares of pre-existing enterprises be transferred, to a certain number of politically connected black investors.[107] Kgalema Motlanthe, who served as President of South Africa for a brief period in 2008 after Mbeki resigned, has stated that the BEE was an innovation of the mining industry designed to co-opt South Africa's black nationalist class of leaders: "They [mining companies] basically went out in search of blacks who were 'connected' and therefore could guarantee some sort of protection" against the possibility of radical redistribution. As a result, they cultivated "a small pool of people that they could rope into the first BEE deals."[108]

This incorporation of Black South African capital into mining and other industries is similar to the incorporation of Afrikaner capital into the MEC that took place in the aftermath of the First World War,[109] although an important difference is that the latter involved investment in the real economy and the formation of new manufacturing—though primarily mining—industries. The BEE has entailed very little new investment in pre-existing enterprises; rather, it has facilitated the transfer of shares to well placed black entrepreneurs. As such, while the programme has helped to facilitate a certain degree of state capacity by enabling bureaucratic intervention into the investment schemes of large landed mining corporations such as Anglo-American,[110] the primary political accomplishment of the initiative has been the shoring up of a crucial political base driving the ANC's electoral victories and the reproduction of the post-transition neoliberal project. As a senior official in the South African Communist Party stated, "the BEE basically entails inserting a Black bourgeoisie into the pre-existing capitalistic structures without altering the current system of economic distribution."[111] Moreover, the programme applies mainly to the mining companies which lack the option of exit due to the landed nature of their operations. In fact, the requirements mandating equity transfers to Black investors do not apply to fully foreign owned companies,[112] which highlight some of the limitations of the model's alleged transformative element. The programme's primary purpose has thus not been to substantially redistribute income, as promised in the ANC's initial electoral platform, but rather to ensure a modicum of social stability by empowering a new coalition partner with a vested interest in financialized neoliberal orthodoxy. To this end, the governing party has been willing to employ coercion when necessary—for example, by threatening to withhold mining licenses to Anglo-American in 2005 unless the company met the requirements stipulated by BEE at a faster pace, which was accomplished by 2009.[113]

It is clear that the implementation of the neoliberal growth model was largely promoted by, and thus can be at least partially attributed to, the South African business community. The large conglomerate firms were actively seeking a new investment and profit-making strategy in light of the economic stagnation and isolation that emerged during the latter years of the apartheid regime. Outward investment, along with deregulation and financialization, offered a solution to this competitive disadvantage. While economic liberalization did lead to an influx of foreign portfolio capital inflows and, during commodity booms, an upsurge in private investment, the minerals-energy sector, with a new financialized component, continues to dominate the post-transition South African economy. A consequence of this continuity, as has been shown, is that unemployment and economic inequality remain high. Although the current growth model has clearly benefitted business, the persistence of market orthodoxy cannot simply be explained by a functional analysis which posits that the corporate sector has profited from neoliberalism. An important question that must be addressed is why domestic policymakers have not altered the current economic trajectory by implementing heterodox protectionist measures to lower unemployment and regulate the capital account. An answer to this question must examine the politics structuring the South African state bureaucracy, as well as the policy constraints and incentives generated by the country's integration into the global financial markets. This will be the topic of the next chapter.

NOTES

1. Peter S. Goodman, "End of Apartheid in South Africa? Not in Economic Terms," *The New York Times*, October 24, 2017. https://www.nytimes.com/2017/10/24/business/south-africa-economy-apartheid.html?action=click&pgtype=Homepage&region=CColumn&module=MostEmailed&version=Full&src=me&WT.nav=MostEmailed&_r=0.
2. Ed Stoddard, "Desperate Times as SA Unemployment Rate Hits 11-Year High," *Business Maverick*, October 30, 2019. https://www.dailymaverick.co.za/article/2019-10-30-desperate-times-as-sa-unemployment-rate-hits-11-year-high/.

3. Geeta Kingdon and John Knight, "Unemployment in South Africa, 1995–2003: Causes, Problems, and Policies," *Journal of African Economies* 16, 5 (2007), p. 814.
4. African National Congress (ANC), "The Reconstruction and Development Programme (RDP): A Policy Framework" (Pretoria, 1994).
5. Fantu Cheru, "Overcoming Apartheid's Legacy: The Ascendancy of Neoliberalism in South Africa's Anti-poverty Strategy," *Third World Quarterly* 22, 4 (2001), pp. 508–509.
6. World Bank Group, "An Incomplete Transition: Overcoming the Legacy of Exclusion in South Africa" (World Bank, Washington, DC, 2018), p. iii.
7. Joseph Cotterill, "South Africa's Economic Growth Stutters," *Financial Times*, March 5, 2019. https://www.ft.com/content/1688aa70-3f53-11e9-b896-fe36ec32aece.
8. Kgothatso B. Shai, "South African State Capture: A Symbiotic Affair Between Business and the State Going Bad," *Insight on Africa* 9, 1 (2017), pp. 62–75.
9. See, for example, Patrick Bond, *Elite Transition: From Apartheid to Neoliberalism in South Africa* (Pluto Press, London, 2000); Adam Habib and Vishnu Padayachee, "Economic Policy and Power Relations in South Africa's Transition to Democracy," *World Development* 28, 2 (2000), pp. 245–263; Thomas A. Koelble, "Economic Policy in the Post-colony: South Africa Between Keynesian Remedies and Neoliberal Pain," *New Political Economy* 9, 1 (2004), pp. 57–58; Hein Marias, *South Africa, Limits to Change: The Political Economy of Transition* (Zed Books, London, 1998).
10. Frederick A. Johnstone, *Class, Race, and Gold: A Study of Class Relations and Racial Discrimination in South Africa* (Routledge and K Paul, London, 1976), Chapter 1.
11. Michael Burawoy, "The Capitalist State in South Africa: Marxist and Sociological Perspectives on Race and Class," *Political Power and Social Theory* 2 (1981), pp. 300–301.
12. Stefan Schirmer, "Manufacturers and the Formulation of Industrial Policy in 1920s South Africa," *African Historical Review* 41, 2 (2009), pp. 4–5.
13. Ibid., 6–7.
14. Nancy L. Clark, *Manufacturing Apartheid: State Corporations in South Africa* (Yale University Press, New Haven, 1994), p. 36.
15. Ibid., p. 54; see also Nancy L. Clark, "South African State Corporations: 'The Death Knell of Economic Colonialism?'," *Journal of Southern African Studies* 14, 1 (1987), p. 103.

16. Aregbeshola R. Adewale, "Does Import Substitution Industrialization Strategy Hurt Growth? New Evidence from Brazil and South Africa," *African and Asian Studies* 11, 3 (2012), p. 299.
17. Ben Fine, Sam Ashman, and Susan Newman, "Systems of Accumulation and the Evolving MEC," in B. Fine, J. Saraswati, and D. Tavasci (eds.), *Beyond the Developmental State: Industrial Policy into the Twenty-First Century* (Pluto Press, London, 2013), pp. 8–9.
18. Ben Fine and Zavareh Rustomjee, *The Political Economy of South Africa: From Minerals-Energy-Complex to Industrialization* (Hurst and Company, London, 1996).
19. Nancy Clark, "South African State Corporations," p. 101.
20. Daniel Antin, "The South African Mining Sector: An Industry at a Crossroads" (Hanns Seidel Foundation: Economy Report South Africa, Johannesburg, 2013), p. 4.
21. Sam Ashman and Ben Fine, "Neoliberalism, Varieties of Capitalism, and the Shifting Contours of South Africa's Financial System," *Transformation: Critical Perspectives on Southern Africa* 81, 82 (2013), p. 160.
22. Eric Schaling, "Capital Controls, Two-Tiered Exchange Rate Systems and Exchange Rate Policy: The South African Experience," *South African Journal of Economics* 77, 4 (2009), p. 507.
23. Dan O'Meara, *Forty Lost Years: The Apartheid State and the Politics of the National Party, 1948–1994* (Ravan Press, Randburg, 1996), p. 358.
24. David King et al., "Institutional Forces and Divestment Performance of South African Conglomerates: Case Study Evidence," *South African Journal of Economic and Management Sciences* 18, 3 (2015), p. 340.
25. Gertrude Makhaya and Simon Roberts, "Expectations and Outcomes: Considering Corporate Power in South Africa Under Democracy," *Review of African Political Economy* 40, 138 (2013), p. 557.
26. Rebecca Davies, "Afrikaner Capital Elites, Neoliberalism and Economic Transformation in Post-apartheid South Africa," *African Studies* 71, 3 (2012), p. 395.
27. Antoinette Handley, "Business, Government, and Economic Policy-making in the New South Africa, 1990–2000," *Journal of Modern African Studies* 43, 2 (2005), p. 214.
28. On South Africa's early industrial policy, see William G. Martin, "The Making of an Industrial South Africa: Trade and Tariffs in the Interwar Period," *The International Journal of African Historical Studies* 23, 1 (1990), pp. 59–85.
29. William G. Martin, *South Africa and the World Economy: Remaking Race, State, and Region* (University of Rochester Press, New York, 2013), pp. 138–142.

30. Robert M. Price, *The Apartheid State in Crisis: Political Transformation in South Africa, 1975–1990* (Oxford University Press, Oxford, 1991), p. 274.
31. Ben Fine et al., "Systems of Accumulation and the Evolving MEC," p. 9.
32. Sampie Terreblanche, *A History of Inequality in South Africa* (University of KwaZulu-Natal Press, Scottsville, 2002), p. 69.
33. Jonathan Nitzan and Shimshon Bichler, "Going Global: Differential Accumulation and the Great U-Turn in South Africa and Israel," *Review of Radical Political Economics* 33, 1 (2001), p. 43.
34. Ibid., p. 23.
35. Patrick Bond, *Elite Transition*, p. 56.
36. Ibid., p. 56.
37. Cited in Antoinette Handley, "Business, Government, and Economic Policymaking," p. 217.
38. Sampie Terreblanche, *A History of Inequality*, pp. 96–97.
39. Ibid., p. 98.
40. Personal Interview, Alan Hirsch (Cape Town, January 10, 2017).
41. Neil Coleman, "Theory of the Transition" (COSATU, 2002).
42. Vishnu Padayachee and Robert Van Niekerk, *Shadow of Liberation: Contestation and Compromise in the Economic and Social Policy of African National Congress, 1943–1996* (NYU Press, New York, 2019). The following paragraphs draw heavily from Chapter 4 of this study.
43. James J. Hentz, "The Two Faces Privatization: Political and Economic Logics in Transitional South Africa," *The Journal of Modern African Studies* 38, 2 (2000), pp. 203–223.
44. Ibid., pp. 75–76.
45. Sagie Narsiah, "Neoliberalism and Privatization in South Africa," *GeoJournal* 57 (2002), p. 5.
46. Vishnu Padayachee and Robert Van Niekerk, *Shadow of Liberation*, pp. 84–85.
47. Ibid., p. 88.
48. Ibid., pp. 94–95.
49. Ibid., p. 103.
50. Ibid., p. 112.
51. Aurelia Segatti and Nicolas Pons-Vignon, "Stuck in Stabilisation? South Africa's Post-apartheid Macroeconomic Policy Between Ideological Conversion and Technocratic Capture," *Review of African Political Economy* 40, 138 (2013), pp. 545–547.
52. Adekeye Adebajo, "South Africa in Africa: Messiah or Mercantilist?" *South African Journal of International Affairs* 14, 1 (2007), p. 40.
53. Ibid., p. 30.
54. Ibid., p. 40.

55. Padraig Carmody, "Another BRIC in the Wall? South Africa's Developmental Impact and Contradictory Rise in Africa and Beyond," *The European Journal of Development Research* 24, 2 (2012), p. 225.
56. Garth Le Pere and Chris Alden, "South Africa in Africa: Bound to Lead?" *Politikon* 36, 1 (2009), p. 156.
57. Ibid., p. 160.
58. Richard Saunders, Darlene Miller, and Olajide Oloyede, "South African Corporations and Post-apartheid Expansion in Africa—Creating a New Regional Space," *African Sociological Review* 12, 1 (2008), p. 2.
59. Ian Taylor, "South African Imperialism in a Region Lacking Regionalism," *Third World Quarterly* 32, 7 (2011), p. 1238.
60. Neo Chabane, Simon Roberts, and Andrea Goldstein, "The Changing Face and Strategies of Big Business in South Africa: More than a Decade of Political Democracy," *Industrial and Corporate Change* 15, 3 (2006), p. 553.
61. Budget Review, "Economic Policy and Outlook" (Department of Finance, Pretoria, 2000).
62. Neo Chabane et al., "The Changing Face and Strategies of Big Business," p. 557.
63. "A Guide to the DTI Investment Schemes" (Department of Trade and Industry, Pretoria, 2014), p. 5.
64. Phil Alves and Lawrence Edwards, "South Africa's Export Performance: Determinants of Export Supply," *South African Journal of Economics* 74, 3 (2006), p. 478.
65. See, for example, Hans Despain, "Sweezyian Financial Instability Hypothesis—Monopoly Capital, Inflation, Financialization, Inequality and Endless Stagnation," *International Critical Thought* 5, 1 (2015), p. 73; Bill Lucarelli, "Financialization and Global Imbalances: Prelude to Crisis," *Review of Radical Political Economics* 44, 4 (2012), p. 429.
66. For a survey, see Natascha van der Zwan, "Making Sense of Financialization," *Socio-Economic Review* 12, 1 (2014), pp. 99–129.
67. Greta Krippner, "The Financialization of the American Economy," *Socio-Economic Review* 3, 2 (2005), p. 174.
68. Ibid., pp. 177–179.
69. Sara Hsu, "The Increasing Virulence of Man-Made Crises: Financial Crises and Global Instability," *Journal of Economic Issues* 46, 2 (2012), pp. 491–498.
70. Personal Interview, Senior Reserve Bank Official (SARB, Pretoria, October 4, 2013).
71. Martin Grandes and Nicolas Pinaud, "Which Policies Can Reduce the Cost of Capital in Southern Africa?" (Policy Brief 25, OECD Development Center, 2004).

72. Guangling Liu, "Will the SARB Always Succeed in Fighting Inflation with Contractionary Policy?" *South African Journal of Economics* 81, 3 (2013), pp. 330–345.

73. Shaukat Ansari, "The Neoliberal Incentive Structure and the Absence of the Developmental State in Post-apartheid South Africa," *African Affairs* 116, 463 (2016), p. 221.

74. Annina Kaltenbrunner and Pablo G. Bortz, "The International Dimension of Financialization in Developing and Emerging Economies," *Development and Change* 49, 2 (2017), p. 382.

75. Gilad Isaacs and Annina Kaltenbrunner, "Financialization and Liberalization: South Africa's New Forms of External Vulnerability," *Competition & Change* 22, 4 (2018), pp. 437–463.

76. Ibid.

77. Annina Keltenbrunner and Pablo G. Bortz, "The International Dimension of Financialization."

78. Thomas A. Koelble and Edward LiPuma, "Currency Devaluations and Consolidating Democracy: The Example of the South African Rand," *Economy and Society* 38, 2 (2009), pp. 203–229.

79. "Emerging Markets: Don't Panic," *The Economist*, February 1, 2014, pp. 8–9.

80. Peter Wonacott and Rebecca Blumenstein, "South Africa Seeks Currency Fix," *The Wall Street Journal*, April 14, 2011. https://www.wsj.com/articles/SB10001424052748703730104576260482927796392%20.

81. Andrew Bowman, "Financialization and the Extractive Industries: The Case of South African Platinum Mining," *Competition and Change* 22, 4 (2018), p. 390.

82. Gilad Isaacs and Andrew Bowman, "The 2014 Platinum Strike: Narratives and Numbers," *Review of African Political Economy* 42, 146 (2015), p. 648.

83 Ewa Karwowski, "The Finance-Mining Nexus in South Africa: How Mining Companies Use the South African Equity Markets to Speculate," *Journal of South African Studies* 41, 1 (2015), pp. 9–28.

84. Ewa Karwowski, "Corporate Financialization in South Africa: From Investment Strike to Housing Bubble," *Competition & Change* 22, 4 (2018), pp. 413–436.

85. Greta Krippner, "The Financialization of the American Economy," pp. 181–182.

86. See Ian Strauss, "Understanding South Africa's Current Account Deficit: The Role of Foreign Direct Investment Income," *Transnational Corporations* 23, 2 (2017).

87. Brittany A. Baumann and Kevin P. Gallagher, "Post-crisis Capital Account Regulation in South Korea and South Africa" (Working Paper Series, Number 320, 2013), p. 2.

88. Andrew Kliman and Shannon D. Williams, "Why Financialization Hasn't Depressed US Productive Investment," *Cambridge Journal of Economics* 39 (2015), pp. 67–92.
89. Lynley Donnelley, "No 'Investment Strike—Kganyago," *Mail & Guardian*, May 5, 2017. https://mg.co.za/article/2017-05-05-00-no-investment-strike-kganyago.
90. Robert Brenner, "The World Economy at the Turn of the Millennium Toward Boom or Crisis?" *Review of International Political Economy* 8, 1 (2001), pp. 6–44.
91. Cedric Durand and Maxime Gueuder, "The Profit-Investment Nexus in an Era of Financialization, Globalization, and Monopolisation: A Profit-Centred Perspective," *Review of Political Economy* 30, 2 (2018), pp. 143–146.
92. "Achieving Higher Growth and Employment: Policy Options for South Africa" (SARB, Pretoria, 2013), p. 11.
93. Personal Interview, Senior Reserve Bank Official (Pretoria, December 9, 2016).
94. J.A. Reyes de los, "Mining Shareholder Value: Institutional Shareholders, Transnational Corporations, and the Geography of Gold Mining," *Geoforum* 84 (2017), pp. 251–264.
95. Gilad Isaacs, "The Myth of Neutrality and the Rhetoric of Stability: Macroeconomic Policy in Democratic South Africa" (Working Paper, MWG, 2014), pp. 11–13.
96. Arthur H. Goldsmith, "Rethinking the Relation Between Government Spending and Economic Growth: A Composition Approach to Fiscal Policy Instruction for Principles Students," *Journal of Economic Education* 39, 2 (2008), pp. 153–173.
97. Personal Interview, Former Chief of Fiscal Policy (Department of Finance, Pretoria, October 8, 2013).
98. Antoinette Handley, "Business, Government, and Economic Policy-making," p. 235.
99. Personal Interview, Former Director of Debt Issuance and Management (Department of Finance, Pretoria, December 13, 2016).
100. Personal Interview, Former Senior Treasury Official (Department of Finance, Pretoria, October 3, 2013).
101. Alexandra Wexler, "Stocks Soar as South African Economy Stumbles," *The Wall Street Journal*, July 13, 2015. https://www.wsj.com/articles/stocks-soar-as-south-african-economy-stumbles-1436814200.
102. "Memorandum to the Director-General of Minerals and Energy on the Draft Minerals Development Bill" (Chamber of Mines, Johannesburg, 2000), pp. 32–33.
103. "Explanatory Memorandum for the Diamond Export Bill" (Department of Finance, Pretoria, October 11, 2006), pp. 1–2.

104. "Business in Change" (Business Leadership South Africa, Johannesburg, Occasional Paper No. 2, 2004).
105. "Déjà vu? The Department of Trade and Industry's National Industrial Policy Framework" (Johannesburg, Occasional Paper No, 2, 2007), p. 8.
106. Leonard Gentle, "What About the Workers? The Demise of COSATU and the Emergence of a New Movement," *Review of African Political Economy* 42, 146 (2015), p. 670.
107. Roger Tangri and Roger Southall, "The Politics of Black Economic Empowerment in South Africa," *Journal of Southern African Studies* 34, 3 (2008), p. 700.
108. Neil Coleman, "Do We Have to Choose Between a Predatory Elite and White Monopoly Capital," *Daily Maverick*, April 21, 2017. https://www.dailymaverick.co.za/opinionista/2017-04-21-do-we-have-to-cho ose-between-a-predatory-elite-and-white-monopoly-capital-part-one/.
109. Stefano Ponte, Simon Roberts, and Lance Van Sittert, "'Black Economic Empowerment,' Business, and the State in South Africa," *Development and Change* 38, 5 (2007), p. 938.
110. Okechukwu C. Iheduru, "Why 'Anglo Licks the ANC's Boots': Globalization and State-Capital Relations in South Africa," *African Affairs* 107, 428 (2008), pp. 333–360.
111. Personal Interview, National Spokesperson, South African Communist Party (Johannesburg, December 28, 2016).
112. Bill Freund, "South Africa: The End of Apartheid and the Emergence of the 'BEE' Elite," *Review of African Political Economy* 34, 114 (2007), p. 669.
113. Okechukwu C. Iheduru, "Why 'Anglo Licks the ANC's Boots'," pp. 353–354.

CHAPTER 2

Bureaucratic Fragmentation, Cash-Transfers, and Financial Markets: Policymaking in the Post-apartheid Neoliberal Landscape

Chapter 1 examined the South African business community's investment and profit-making strategies as they evolved over the decades, as well as the mechanisms linking their shifting socioeconomic preferences to the demise of apartheid and the adoption of a neoliberal economic programme. This chapter will critically evaluate the structure of South African policymaking in the context of financial liberalization throughout the post-apartheid period. It will also flesh out the nature of the bureaucratic conflict between the various government departments. The primary purpose of this investigation is to provide an answer to the puzzle surrounding the persistence of the neoliberal growth model over a twenty-five-year period, especially in the context of stagnant growth and rampant social inequality. Why has the ANC thus far refused to substantively deviate from the 1996 market orthodox policy package, despite the fact that unemployment is structurally high and a rising proportion of the population is dissatisfied with the current economic and developmental trajectory?

Aside from the influence exerted by the business community through their lobbying efforts and structural power, as discussed in the previous chapter, the policy constraints and incentives created by South Africa's integration into the global financial markets are an important component driving the reproduction of the neoliberal growth model throughout

© The Author(s), under exclusive license to Springer Nature Switzerland AG 2021
S. Ansari, *Neoliberalism and Resistance in South Africa*, Contemporary African Political Economy, https://doi.org/10.1007/978-3-030-69766-2_2

41

the post-apartheid period. It will be argued that the international capital markets have enabled the ANC to turnover the public debt, and hence fund redistributive social service programmes, despite stagnating economic growth and high unemployment. Moreover, while integration into the global capital markets has permitted the ANC to fund persistent fiscal deficits and maintain current spending, it has also placed the Treasury at the centre of economic policymaking, and has led to the consolidation of an "investor class"—to borrow a term used by the author Wolfgang Streeck. It is important to note, however, that the argument in this chapter is not that the global financial markets are able to dictate the direction of policymaking against the interests of policymakers in departments like the Treasury and Reserve Bank. As noted in the introduction, in the aftermath of the ANC's rejection of MERG, the party leadership largely internalized and accepted many of the neoliberal prescriptions that have been in place throughout the post-apartheid period. My own interviews with senior bureaucrats have revealed that key policymakers in specific government departments sincerely believe that global capital inflows are a crucial component of economic development and thus important for the country's advancement within the global value chain hierarchy. The focus here will be on highlighting the relevant *incentives* as well as constraints on policymaking that have been generated through South Africa's integration with the international capital markets. Senior policymakers in the Finance Ministry and other bureaucratic centres do not, in other words, view themselves as passive victims or spectators of global capital according to this argument. Yet, it is also the case that structural changes in the economy since the transition have bolstered this policy stance. Throughout much of the apartheid period, especially in the aftermath of international sanctions, state managers had to increasingly run current account surpluses to meet expenditure needs. However, with the advent of trade liberalization and other orthodox measures, the trade balance went into a deficit, and global finance has come to occupy a prominent role in filling this gap.[1] Indeed, it will be shown that very specific policy decisions have been required to facilitate and maintain specific types of capital inflows throughout the post-apartheid period. The chapter will first outline the features of the South African bureaucracy, as well as the underlying factors responsible for the absence of a more coordinated heterodox approach to economic development among key government departments. The next section will examine the impact of the international capital markets on policymaking and how global investors have managed to exert informal control over the trajectory of economic policy through their alliance with senior officials in the Finance Department and Reserve Bank.

2.1 THE SOUTH AFRICAN BUREAUCRACY, ECONOMIC DEVELOPMENT, AND GLOBAL FINANCIAL MARKETS

It has now been recognized by numerous heterodox scholars that the structure of a country's bureaucracy has important implications for economic policymaking and state-led industrial diversification. For example, in his pioneering work on state capacity, Peter Evans put forward the argument that diversified economic development in late-industrializing countries was, contrary to the myth of conventional and neoclassical economics, tied to the interventionist policies of strong states. The ability of some states to intervene with the aim of stimulating diversified economic growth was, however, largely shaped by the level of bureaucratic competence and linkages with important socioeconomic classes—a set of relationships denoting "embedded autonomy."[2] In the context of a highly efficient and meritocratic bureaucracy, state capacity is determined by the extent to which technocratic experts are able to adequately regulate market forces and channel financial resources into strategic industries by employing a variety of allocative tools and innovative policy measures.[3] Moreover, this concept of state capacity runs along a spectrum, with certain cases of late industrializers such as Japan, and in the twentieth century other East Asian countries such as South Korea, falling near the ideal end of the spectrum in terms of bureaucratic expertise and relative state autonomy from business classes.[4]

It should be noted that bureaucratic capability and technocratic expertise need not encompass every government department for effective interventionist policies to be implemented. It could be sufficient to simply have certain pockets of bureaucratic capacity and highly skilled technocratic experts within specific government departments to accomplish even a modicum of state-led industrialization, so long as the goals of political officials either align with the interests of certain propertied interests or if the business class is relatively weak in comparison with the state. This latter point is quite important. In South Korea, for example, it was not merely a highly evolved level of state capacity and bureaucratic expertise that permitted diversified industrial development in the 1960s and 1970s to take place. A series of events, including comprehensive land reform and the Korean War, ensured that state industrial policy was not subverted by other powerful societal actors. In contrast to other developing countries, such as Mexico and Indonesia, the South Korean bureaucracy was dealing with a weak propertied class that it could politically subordinate. This factor enabled the state, in cooperation with the middle classes, to construct institutions such as the Economic Planning Board to effectively direct industrial policy while also ensuring an adequate degree of social protection and reducing poverty.[5] However, even in countries where the propertied and dominant socioeconomic classes have not been weakened or fully subordinated to the political class, state-led industrial development or economic growth may still be possible when there is an alignment of economic and political interests among bureaucrats and sectors of the business community. For instance, in Mozambique in the 1990s, one section of the ruling economic elite forged an alliance with foreign companies. As a result, with the support of a cluster of bureaucrats in the relevant government department, this economic/political alliance was able to rapidly increase production and exports of sugar. This economic activity then secured a steady stream of financial rents for the actors involved.[6]

The importance of technocratic expertise and state-society relations in the effective formulation of industrial policies is clear. However, the actual structure of the bureaucracy also plays a highly significant role in terms of facilitating state coordination among the relevant government departments. Indeed, in the absence of this type of internal coherence and coordination it becomes extremely difficult to implement the relevant economic programmes in an efficient manner, especially in the context of potential challenges and opposition from political and socioeconomic classes. In fact, one crucial hallmark of successful developmental states is the presence of a strong and highly centralized economic planning ministry with the authority to actively intervene in other government departments. Japan's Ministry of Trade and Industry (MITI), South Korea's Economic Planning Board, and Malaysia's Economic Planning Unit all serve as successful examples of centralized state units marked by capacity, skilled and disciplined bureaucrats, and the overall political resolve to overcome opposition to intervention and the implementation of national development goals.[7]

South Africa's post-apartheid bureaucracy occupies a rather ambiguous space along this continuum of state capacity and technocratic expertise. On the one hand, it is not hard to identify the earlier referenced "pockets of efficiency" located within the bureaucratic structures of the country's government departments. For example, centres such as the National Treasury, the Reserve Bank, and the South African Revenue Service possess the hallmarks of Weberian meritocracy marked by highly skilled and educated technocrats.[8] Yet, it is also the case that large sections of the bureaucracy and government departments are plagued by a shortage of skilled personnel, a focus on affirmative action to rectify the ills of apartheid at the expense of an emphasis on qualifications, and weak institutional design.[9] Despite this general level of bureaucratic corruption, however, there exists sufficient expertise within the relevant departments for the implementation of a sound national industrialization programme should the political establishment decide to embark on such a path. The central issue with the post-apartheid bureaucracy is the fragmented nature of policymaking which, in the absence of the type of concentrated bureaucratic resolve and centralized planning characteristic of other developmental states, can trigger constant debates over policy issues between government departments.

Thus, in the early years of the democratic transition, the absence of a strategic ministry that could have been tasked with formulating broad macroeconomic programmes to bolster inclusive development and industrialization frustrated early attempts at redistribution. Leading up to their electoral victory, the ANC created the Reconstruction and Development Program (RDP) Ministry in order to facilitate the implementation of certain redistribute policies, which were an important component of the government's initial "growth through redistribution" platform. Given the rejection of the MERG, however, the motivation behind the ANC's adoption of the RDP is unclear. According to Padayachee and Van Niekerk, by 1992 the party leadership had committed to certain aspects of macroeconomic orthodoxy, and certain officials, such as Joe Slovo, would no longer support the term "privatization." Additionally, Reserve Bank independence seems to have been largely accepted at this point in the ANC's evolution.[10] Moreover, the RDP was crafted without the input of many academic and economic specialists, and was released primarily as a manifesto prior to the elections. One reason for this development is that by this point the party and grass-roots leadership had little faith in outside technocrats and academics. Thus, it has been suggested that the document was largely a symbolic act designed to generate electoral support for the ANC.[11]

Nonetheless, during this period the RDP department was created and served as the central hub through which the macroeconomic programmes outlined in the document were to be rolled out and implemented. However, progress on these policies was extremely limited due to the fact that the RDP Ministry was denied adequate funding and, from the very beginning, clashed with the Treasury's mandate.[12] In fact, a 2002 paper by the Congress of South African Trade Unions (COSATU) argued that the RDP department was largely dismantled because there was no centralized planning unit charged with the authority of integrating the RDP proposals into all the government departments. As a result, the broad redistributive programme associated with the ANC's electoral campaign fell victim to the maneuverings of the Finance Ministry.[13] Additionally, as was discussed in the previous chapter, the informal agreement reached between the business community and the ANC prior to the actual democratic transition had already doomed many of the progressive populist policies outlined in the RDP document.

In 1996, with the closure of the RDP department and the unveiling of the Growth, Employment, and Redistribution Programme (GEAR) as the ANC's new macroeconomic growth strategy, the Finance Ministry took the reigns of economic policymaking and promoted fiscal discipline as the mechanism that would draw in foreign investment and stimulate industrialization. The rationale for GEAR was discussed in the previous chapter. It was also shown that the business community played an instrumental role in terms of influencing the governing party's decision to adopt an economic programme predicated on liberalization. It needs to be stressed, however, that post-apartheid South Africa's integration into the global financial markets added an additional layer of external influence over the trajectory of economic policymaking. This point was highlighted by Alec Erwin, who served as the Minister of the Department of Trade and Industry, the Minister of Public Enterprises, as well as the Deputy Finance Minister. In reference to the ANC's abandonment of redistributive populist policies in the early years of the transition, Erwin highlighted a trip to London to raise funds where, he stated, "We recognized the strength of the international capital markets."[14] Indeed, the country's integration into the global financial markets has continued to structure the post-apartheid policy landscape. Specifically, financial liberalization has generated a series of constraints and incentives that have shaped how officials in the National Treasury and Reserve Bank have consistently reacted to the possibility of alternative policy proposals predicated on inclusive development. The economic constraints on state autonomy through financial market integration, specifically in emerging market economies, have been fleshed out in a number of important studies. One of the most comprehensive examinations of the impact of capital market integration on state autonomy and policy formulation is Layna Mosley's monograph, *Global Capital and National Governments*. Mosley investigated the influence international bond investors wield over government policy through a statistical and qualitative analysis. In her interviews with institutional investors and asset managers in London and New York, the author asked what criteria international bond traders and investors evaluate when deciding which currencies and national assets to select for their portfolio. She found that in the case of developed and OECD nations investors examine a small number of macro-variables, such as the current account and rate of inflation, while for emerging market economies micro-variables, such as the distribution of state spending, as well as broader political issues, were also highly relevant in investment allocation decisions.[15]

Mosley tested her hypothesis through a multiple regression analysis in order to measure the importance of each individual macro-economic variable as a determination of the yield on ten-year government securities, which is often the instrument that influences long-term interest rates. The regression model illustrated that in the case of developed nations bond investors are most concerned with the rate of inflation, although it was also shown that a one percentage increase in the US long-term interest rate would lead to a 0.40% increase in international long-term rates.[16] However, in the case of emerging market economies, the market actors interviewed by Mosley emphasized the importance of politics in influencing investment decisions.[17] The implication of this difference between the two categories, according to Mosley, is that international bond traders and investors are able to constrain government policies in emerging markets by virtue of their practice of evaluating politics as one of the main criteria guiding their investment decisions. This emphasis placed on micro-policies and political matters by bond investors when examining the business climate in emerging markets stems from their overall understanding of the credit-worthiness of specific governments. As Mosley's analysis shows, the government budget deficit in developed democracies is not a significant factor in terms of influencing the long-term yield

on government securities. States which possess a high degree of financial credibility in international bond markets are able to navigate certain
neoliberal constraints and engage in deficit spending at levels that often
surpasses 70% of their GDP.

Theoretically, deterioration in one of the fundamental macro-economic
variables should lead to a higher long-term interest rate because the
risk associated with the instrument has now increased which, all else
being equal, will motivate investors to demand a higher yield on the
security. As was noted in the introductory chapter, the elimination of
capital controls in 1995 removed any remaining barriers to foreign capital
inflows. Figure 2.1 depicts the trajectory of South Africa's ten-year bond
yield since 1970 (readers unfamiliar with the mechanics of bonds and
interest rates may want to consult the Appendix). Starting at 7.75% in
the latter year, the yield began trending upwards in 1980 and remained
high throughout the decade as a result of the debt crisis, isolation, and
economic stagnation. After spiking in 1992, the series has followed a
downward trajectory since the transition to democracy, indicating that
investors have responded favourably to the Treasury's policy of fiscal
restraint. The brief uptick of the yield in 2017 represents the influence of
international asset managers over macroeconomic indicators. According
to the 2019 Treasury Budget Review, non-residents were still the largest

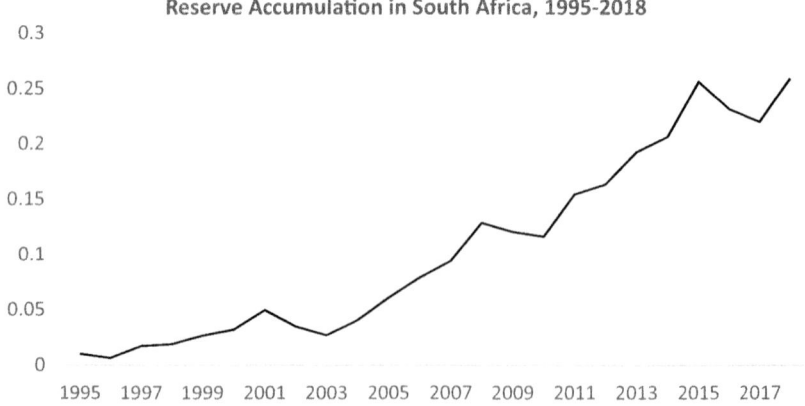

Fig. 2.1   Reserve accumulation in South Africa, 1995–2018 (*Source* South
African Reserve Bank, author's calculations)

category of investors in domestic South African government bonds in 2018, holding 37.7% of the state debt, only slightly down from 41.4% in 2017.[18] This outflow of foreign capital was attributed to the anticipated downgrading of the country's public debt to junk status by Moody's.[19] In this context, and in line with Mosley's general analysis on the influence of foreign asset managers over developing country governments, global portfolio investors in South Africa's public debt have served as a disciplining force and constraint against potentially heterodox policies of industrial diversification and economic redistribution.

One strategy that South Africa, as well as other emerging market economies, have adopted to counteract sudden capital outflows by foreign investors has been reserve accumulation. This entails purchasing foreign debt instruments, usually US Treasury Securities, in order to placate foreign investors by signalling the availability of insurance in case of defaults. A senior policymaker at the Reserve Bank stated that reserve accumulation was initially adopted by South Africa after the East Asian crisis because the "lesson taught was that you do not want to be in a position where your national balance sheet is weak and you have these big contingent liabilities reflected in the current account deficit and foreign capital funding that, if it dries up, could result in a recession."[20] This development, in conjunction with the general shift to economic liberalization in the aftermath of the transition, was also partially designed to offset the influence of the International Financial Institutions (IFIs) in the event of an economic downturn and balance of payments crisis. In other words, reserve accumulation was partially a strategy designed to safeguard the country's autonomy from foreign interference.[21] Figure 2.2 depicts the evolution of the country's foreign exchange reserves, comprised of gold and hard foreign currencies, as a ratio to GDP expressed in 2010 constant dollars from 1995 to 2018. As clearly indicated by the series, South Africa has been accumulating foreign exchange reserves at an increasing pace since the democratic transition, and the figure breached 25% of national income by 2018.

The drawback to this strategy, however, is that the practice entails a significant opportunity cost, diverting resources away from potential development programmes and necessitating a reduction of capital spending in other vital areas.[22] Moreover, in an emerging market country such as South Africa, rapid currency depreciations require the accumulation of foreign exchange reserves as a buffer, which again involves an opportunity cost in the form of reduced productive state expenditure on

Fig. 2.2 South Africa's ten-year-government bond yield, 1970–2018 (*Source* South African Reserve Bank)

infrastructural upgrades or the loss of vital imports.[23] In this sense, while reserve accumulation in response to global capital market integration may have enhanced South Africa's state autonomy in relation to international organizations such as the International Monetary Fund (IMF), economic liberalization has also reduced policy autonomy by subjecting state officials to the disciplinary tools of private financial investors and global asset managers. In addition to these constraints, integration into the international financial markets has generated a number of economic incentives to which policymakers respond, often with significant political implications. The next section will examine such incentives, and their policy consequences, in detail.

2.2   THE FISCAL POLICY AND INCOME REDISTRIBUTION: POLITICAL CONSEQUENCES OF FINANCIAL LIBERALIZATION

It was noted in the previous chapter that the South African economy, in the post-apartheid period, has persistently generated fiscal and trade deficits (Fig. 1.2). This has posed a challenge to bureaucrats and political elites, who must take into account the concerns of public debt investors when formulating redistributive programmes. An implicit inference to be drawn from this tension is that in the context of persistent state deficits, there exists a potential conflict between the interests of voters/citizens and the preferences of international bond investors. This tension can be fleshed out through an examination of the ANC's Cash-Transfer Programme (CTP), which distributes funds to 17 million impoverished South African households in the rural areas and the townships. This social assistance programme has been credited with alleviating both poverty and, to certain degree, mitigating the impact of economic inequality in the country. For example, it has been estimated that, when starting with a poverty line of 2,532 R per person a year in 2000 prices, the distribution of social grants has generated a decrease in poverty by 13 percentage points in 2005.[24] Moreover, some research has suggested that in the absence of the Cash-Transfer Programme South Africa's Gini coefficient would be significantly higher.[25]

As a result of these (albeit limited) redistributive successes, the CTP has been instrumental in the ANC's electoral victories. A survey conducted by the Centre for Social Development at the University of Johannes-burg revealed that 49% of respondents from two poor urban regions and one rural area were under the impression that social grants were tied to the party in power, and not a constitutional right tied to the state.[26] In the 2014 national election, the ANC secured more than 60% of the vote, despite some inroads made by the main opposition parties. A survey of 3,782 voters from sixteen impoverished townships around Gauteng Province found that while good governance and the legacy of national liberation figured prominently as the factors influencing voter's decision to select the ANC (31 and 27% respectively), the provision of material and social welfare benefits came in third at 16%.[27] The distribution of social grants is especially important in shoring up support for the ANC in the rural areas of the county, where many of the recipients depend on the payments as their sole source of income.[28] However, given the persistent trade and fiscal (twin) deficits in the post-apartheid period, the governing party must factor in the impact that heterodox economic policies could have on the country's economic and political risk profile based on the evaluations of credit-rating agencies and bond investors.

In the previous chapter, it was noted that South Africa's GDP has been declining over the last several years, and that at the current trajectory the unemployment rate would remain high well into the future. Thus, given the current reality of economic stagnation, the CTP, a remnant of the RDP platform, is not only a crucial component in alleviating poverty, but it also represents a peculiar form of social welfare expenditure, one which is predicated not so much on income and wealth transfers through progressive taxation, but rather on borrowing from the international financial markets. In other words, the CTP represents a form of redistribution without adequate economic growth or a substantive alleviation of economic inequality. Therefore, in the absence of a steady and sufficient stream of government revenues to close the fiscal deficit, social welfare payments are dependent on the marketability of government bonds, and this in turn necessitates the implementation of economic measures that placate investors, such as fiscal discipline and monetary policies designed to repress inflation. In other words, social grants demand limited austerity.

Moreover, the Treasury must primarily factor in the economic and political interests of *international* investors in the public debt. Despite the fact that the South African Pension Funds control billions of rand which could potentially be invested in state debt instruments, fund managers prefer to invest primarily in private equity shares, and only shift their capital into public debt when the yield on the ten-year government bond reaches 10–11%—the type of spike which generally follows on the heels of a sell-off by global investors.[29] Data released by the Treasury in 2019 revealed that from 2011 to 2018 foreign investors held a larger share of government bonds in comparison with the South African pension funds for every year except one, specifically, 2011, when the ownership share of the latter reached 33% of the public debt in comparison with 29.1% held by non-residents.[30]

The global capital markets and international asset managers have therefore filled the gap in the demand for state debt securities and, as noted in Chapter 1, have generally been more than willing to exploit the higher interest rate differential between developed and developing countries through carry trade practices. Treasury officials are fully cognizant of the fiscal benefit of financial liberalization, particularly as it pertains to the debt market and the impact of the entry of global investors on bond prices and domestic interest rates. As one former senior official in the Finance Ministry stated:

Since 2008 we have had increased participation from foreigners in the domestic bond market, which has changed the dynamic somewhat. Traditionally the SA institutional investors have preferred higher yield, but with the international investors their preference for yield is much lower.[31]

Moreover, a senior bureaucrat in the Reserve Bank reaffirmed the country's reliance on foreign capital inflows to fund a variety of activities and noted that policymakers would have little incentive to threaten this source of capital. In fact, the official asserted that if foreign investors were discouraged from purchasing government bonds then the debt would have to be funded by domestic capital, which would entail a shift of resources out of the private economy, an event that could potentially disrupt economic growth.[32] The centrality of the global financial markets as a source of capital was also emphasized by a former Director of Debt Issuance and Management at the Treasury, who made the following point regarding the imposition of capital controls:

> To be honest, we would not generally consider employing capital controls, because we need foreign capital to at least partially fund our fiscal and current account deficits. So we would not impose regulations on capital inflows, and imposing them on outflows would also have a negative effect by sending a signal to future investors that they could not repatriate their funds.[33]

The country's integration into global financial circuits thus entails adherence to a specific policy trajectory, the implications of which were outlined by Business Leadership South Africa (BLSA) in a policy document: "The reliance of foreign rather than domestic savings creates certain constraints...continued foreign investment in our bonds requires low and stable inflation as well as fiscal deficits."[34] In other words, the states' reliance on the global capital markets has served, alongside the lobbying efforts of the business community, to lock-in the current neoliberal growth path.

The influence that portfolio capital investors wield over post-apartheid South Africa's policy trajectory can put into perspective by drawing on the theoretical framework employed by Thomas Pepinsky in his study of capital controls and authoritarian regime durability. Pepinsky posited that governments may choose to maintain an open capital account if officials have cemented alliances with investors with mobile and liquid assets. The argument is premised on the notion that coalitional alliances between the relevant state officials and private economic actors offer a particularly fruitful framework for understanding why certain regimes might implement different economic policies in response to the same type of events. "Coalitions," the author writes, "are the political link that mediate how economic interests translate into adjustment policies."[35] Thus, if regimes depend on economic and political support from coalitional alliances composed of labour and fixed capital, then state officials will be more likely to adopt heterodox economic programmes, such as capital account restrictions and an expansionary monetary policy. In contrast, state dependence on an alliance made up largely of mobile capital will translate into orthodox economic policies predicated on an open capital account and a restrictive monetary regime.[36] The author buttresses his argument through a comparative analysis of the divergent economic policies adopted by the Malaysian and Indonesian regimes during the 1998 East Asian financial crisis. The former regime rejected IMF advice and adopted a pegged exchange rate and capital controls, while the latter maintained an open capital account and vacillated between tight and loose monetary policies. The outcome was regime survival in Malaysia and democratic transition in Indonesia, a variation in policy outcomes which the author argues can be accounted for by the different type of economic actors supporting the regimes in the two countries.[37]

It should also be noted that Pepinsky draws an important distinction between "mobile" and "liquid" capital. Whereas all capital is potentially liquid, not all capital is mobile. The distinction is to be found in the end goal or overarching purpose of the different economic activities, which is not necessarily determined by sector or industry classification. For example, while property developers would be classified as fixed capital owners, property speculators would be categorized as mobile capital. Moreover, while owners of fixed capital assets, such as plant and machinery, are potentially liquid if their ownership takes the form of control in the majority shares of a publicly traded company, their preferences for long-term growth and profitability distinguish them from short-term portfolio capital owners and speculators.[38] A crucial component of Pepinsky's argument is that the economic conditions prevailing during the period of regime formation shape the coalitional alliance that emerges to underwrite the regime's foundational support. As a result, the economic adjustment policies implemented by policymakers, especially during periods of financial crisis, are determined by the preferences arising from the specific actors making up such coalitions. Thus, the author asserts that when mobile capital owners, both domestic and foreign, dominate the alliance, then "orthodox" economic solutions to crises will be pursued, such as austerity, an open capital account, and a restrictive monetary policy.[39] This preference stems from the fact that owners of mobile capital are outward oriented and generally seek to divest their holdings and migrate to a different location in response to a crisis or better profit opportunities. In contrast, owners of fixed capital, and labour organizations, prefer expansionary fiscal and loose monetary policies, which require capital account restrictions in order to prevent capital flight and cost-push inflation.[40]

Although Pepinsky's framework was employed in the course of an investigation of authoritarian regimes, his method and theoretical framework can be applied to the period after the democratic transition in South Africa as well. The transition to democracy occurred in a macroeconomic environment in which trade and fiscal policy were predicated on the country's integration into the global financial markets. In this context, owners of "mobile assets" emerged as the primary constituents driving the new policy trajectory. It was noted in Chapter 1 that the post-apartheid economy has become increasingly financialized, to the point where even Non-Financial Corporations (NFCs) have started to purchase and trade assets for short-term capital gain as opposed to long-term productive investment. Capital account liberalization, however, has also contributed to the global marketability and liquidity of South Africa's public debt—global institutional investors are not only investing in government bonds, but also generally demand capital mobility as a precondition for investment. As a result, technocrats within the Reserve Bank and Treasury must craft policies that not only ensure macroeconomic stability, such as the inflation targeting (IT) regime, but also those that guarantee capital mobility and liquidity.

This is precisely where Pepinsky's model can be operationalized in the South African context. The post-apartheid economy has been structured around the interests of mobile asset investors to an extent where even in industries with a high amount of fixed capital, such as the mining sector, investment decisions are mediated by the international financial markets. Thus, Treasury officials strive to ensure that investors are able to operate in an environment of mobility and liquidity, which explains why, even when in the midst of a currency crisis, the Finance Ministry has opted to allow capital outflows to accelerate as a method of facilitating downward pressure on the rand, as opposed to imposing temporary restrictions on currency convertibility and capital repatriation.[41] However, this policy regime has not gone completely unchallenged by other government departments, as we will now explore.

2.3   FINANCIALIZATION AND INTERGOVERNMENTAL CONFLICT: POLICY FRAGMENTATION AND TREASURY DOMINANCE

The absence of an overarching centralized economic planning ministry has, on several occasions, generated policy conflict between the Treasury, Reserve Bank, and other bureaucratic centres, such as the Department of Trade and Industry, the Economic Development Department, and the Ministry of Public Enterprises. In the event of a disagreement regarding a fundamental policy proposal, the President mediates between the ministers of the various government departments in an effort to reach a compromise. This is what happened from 2005 to 2008, for example, when a disagreement took place between the Department of Public Enterprises and the Treasury over how to utilize the primary surplus that had built up over these years. The Finance Ministry fought to have the surplus diverted to buttress the country's foreign exchange position, as opposed to employing the funds to capitalize the country's public corporations.[42]

Additional policy conflicts have, on several occasions since the transition, emerged between Treasury and Reserve Bank officials and bureaucrats from the Department of Trade and Industry on issues related to the exchange rate, capital controls, and inflation targeting. The appreciating exchange rate, and solutions on how to deal with its impact on export competitiveness, has been a point of contention between technocrats from these ministries since the onset of the worldwide commodities boom. The event prompted the DTI to lobby the Treasury to implement policies that could potentially depreciate the rand. The Finance Ministry initially responded by instructing the Reserve Bank to purchase foreign currencies on the FX markets. Since the long-term viability of such a strategy is limited, the Treasury also held several meetings between 2004 and 2006 to contemplate the efficacy of capital controls on inflows. In the end, the policy prescription was rejected by the ministry for two reasons: first, officials concluded that such measures had not succeeded in producing the desired result in other emerging market economies, such as Brazil. Secondly, officials within the department argued that prior to 2001 it had been extremely difficult to attract inward flows of capital into the country, and that measures that could potentially minimize access to funds and discourage capital flows should be avoided.[43]

The Treasury's reluctance to deviate from economic orthodoxy was in fact evident in the early period after the democratic transition. From 1995 to 2000, for instance, the DTI lobbied to introduce export taxes on primary commodities such as coal and iron ore in order to encourage value added production and alter the composition of GDP in South Africa. The Finance Ministry, which must sign-off on any new taxes, vetoed the proposal on the grounds that such an unorthodox policy would trigger a negative reaction from financial actors and discourage investment in the primary commodities sector.[44] The Treasury also opposed any industrial cluster initiatives, which would have provided funding to specific, strategic sectors, on the grounds that the government could not be perceived as selecting favourites, and that if one industry was provided with state resources then other sectors would have to be subsidized as well.[45] Since 2000, officials within the DTI have also periodically protested against the IT regime. The argument against a stringent inflation targeting policy proffered by such bureaucrats was that high short-term interest rates were discouraging domestic borrowing and hence investment and economic growth. In response, technocrats in the Treasury have argued that in the absence of a tight monetary programme to anchor inflationary expectations, then international investors would begin to attach a higher risk premium to the country, which would in turn raise long-term interest rates.[46] In other words, a looser monetary policy would raise the ten-year government bond yield.

These intergovernmental tensions were highlighted in a 2013 conference organized by the Economic Development Department (EDD) on financialization and state regulation, which included presentations from officials in the Treasury, the DTI, the EDD, and policymakers from other emerging market economies. Officials from the National Treasury were generally very supportive of financial integration, and financialization more broadly, while officials from the DTI were far more pessimistic and advocated for some form of controls. For example, Kuben Naidoo from the Treasury argued that growth in South Africa would have proceeded at a far slower pace had it not been for liberalized capital flows, and that government management should focus on the "consequences" of financial liberalization as opposed to regulating the process itself.[47] In contrast, policymakers from the DTI and the EDD drew attention to the negative consequences of increased financial integration and offered recommendations for some form of government regulation. For instance, Dr. Neva Makgetla of the EDD gave a presentation on the concept of financialization and linked it to increasing financial flows and the general shift to shareholder value and a turn to financial instruments and activities as the dominant channel for profit-making activities. Makgetla also pointed out that in the last decade the financial sector in South Africa had only increased its employment by 1% per annum, which is a much slower rate than the rest of the private economy.[48] The presentation by Makgetla ended with a call for financial regulation in the form of capital controls, which could potentially direct investment into productive sectors and prevent asset bubbles from forming. This position was supported by Stephen Hanival, Chief Economist for the DTI, who argued that South Africa has generally not felt the benefits of financial globalization, and that portfolio inflows are for the most part destabilizing, rendering the performance of manufacturing exports quite unpredictable because of the possibility of sudden surges and reversals.[49]

In order to deal with these ongoing conflicts and problems of horizontal coordination between government departments, the Jacob Zuma administration established the National Planning Commission in 2010 with Trevor Manuel, the former Finance Minister who headed the Treasury when the GEAR programme was introduced, as its first Chairperson. This decision followed the 2007 Polokwane Leadership Conference, where the ANC proposed to set up a specialized National Planning Body, to be located in the Office of the Presidency, tasked with the development of medium as well as long-term economic planning.[50] The 2007 Leadership Conference is where delegates voted out Mbeki as the ANC president and replaced him with Zuma. The coalition that was largely responsible for this decision consisted of the party's rank and file membership represented primarily by COSATU and the SACP. These organizations had grown increasingly dissatisfied with Mbeki's style of governance, particularly his tendency to centralize power and nullify the influence of party activists over the direction of policymaking.[51] Mbeki's drive to centralize authority over policymaking marked the deepening of a pattern that began under President Mandela, who facilitated the concentration of political power within core ministries, especially the Treasury.[52] However, Mbeki further increased the level of difficulty for the South African parliament to "perform legislative and oversight functions," and further cemented the position of the presidency as the final arbiter of policy disputes between the government ministries.[53] Thus, the coalition that ousted Mbeki and replaced him with Zuma did so with the aim of injecting democratic accountability and populist input into the policymaking process.

Yet, despite Zuma's ascension to power and the establishment of a National Planning Commission, his course of conduct during his tenure simply succeeded in shifting the locus of policy conflict to a series of showdowns between the Treasury and the Presidency. This conflict was rooted in disagreements over populist policies, specifically fiscal expansion, and allegations of state capture and corruption. More specifically, the tension between the Presidency and the Finance Ministry began after a decision by the Zuma administration to enter into an agreement with Russia to construct a number of nuclear power plants in South Africa. The nuclear plants would have been supplied with uranium from a mine in the Northwest, Oakbay Resources and Energy, owned by the Gupta Family, which also has a subsidiary, Shiva Uranium, on which Zuma's son held a chairmanship.[54] The Russian deal would have provided the SOE Eskom with much needed electricity, while also further enriching the Gupta and Zuma Families, but it was blocked by Finance Ministers Nene and Gordhan as too expensive.[55] As a result of this disagreement, Zuma initially replaced Nene with David van Rooyen, a less experienced Finance Minister. Although the president succumbed to the pressure exerted by the international financial markets and reversed this decision, in late March of 2017 he again removed Gordhan from his post during a cabinet reshuffle, setting off another negative reaction on the currency markets followed by a sharp decline in the rand's value.[56]

The reappointment of Pravin Gordhan to the post of Finance Minister, while calming the financial markets, did not put an end to the internal factional battles within the ANC or the conflict between Zuma and the Treasury. In the aftermath of the disappointing 2016 municipal elections, which registered historic losses for the ANC, aggregate electoral support fell below 60% for the first time since the democratic transition,[57] Zuma came under increasing pressure to implement heterodox policies and increase fiscal expenditure. However, this policy stance conflicted with the Treasury's commitment to cut the budget deficit and restore investor confidence in South Africa's financial instruments.[58] In this context of fresh political turmoil, it was reported that "ANC lawmakers loyal to Mr. Zuma have argued that technocratic policies advocated by Mr. Gordhan are dislocating the party from its base."[59] Alan Hirsch, the former head of economic policy with the office of the Presidency and a former senior official with the DTI, stated that Zuma's removal of Nene, and his replacement by an unknown but loyal official, was based on Nene's refusal to "allocate national resources carelessly," and that "his successor was chosen because he [was] not expected to be so careful." Moreover, it was expected that the removal of Nene would "weaken the currency, raise the cost of borrowing," and undermine the country's fiscal credibility.[60]

However, the reappointment of Gordhan to the post of Finance Minister was short lived, as he was subsequently removed again in another cabinet reshuffle by Zuma in March of 2017. Zuma announced that the reshuffle and the removal of Gordhan would usher in "radical socio-economic transformation."[61] Nonetheless, the move was also criticized by leading officials within the ANC, including Mbeki, as well as trade unions and civil society groups, while the SACP warned against the possibility of "state looting."[62] The reshuffle was also condemned by Deputy President Cyril Ramaphosa, who called the firing "totally unacceptable," a statement reflecting the general reaction of many top ANC officials, though in the end Ramaphosa decided not to resign as a protest against the move.[63] Although a precise justification was not provided by Zuma for the firing, it was reported that the tension between the President and the Finance Minister had escalated because the two officials differed on the issue of state expenditure, and Zuma publicly stated after the reshuffle that he had directed his new cabinet to "work tirelessly" in order to "ensure that the promise of a better life for the poor and the working class becomes a reality."[64] It was further reported that the bond and foreign exchange markets were reacting negatively to news of the firing, as Gordhan was viewed by investors as a source of stability in light of his long-standing priorities of controlling inflation and imposing fiscal discipline, two goals which, as noted, clashed with Zuma's populist thrust.[65]

Chapter 6 will delve into this issue more deeply and partially locate Zuma's actions within the phenomenon of state capture and the institution of Black Economic Empowerment. However, it must also be noted that this conflict between Zuma and the Treasury, as well as the general fiscal crisis confronting the South African state, was rooted in the contradictions built into the country's neoliberal growth model and the ruling party's commitment to limited redistributive policies. As was noted in Chapter 1, the central axis of South Africa's economy remains the Minerals-Energy-Complex, a cluster of industries organized around mining operations and the export of primary commodities. As such, the country's post-transition developmental trajectory was largely predicated on the global commodities boom. Once this global demand began to dry up in 2008, state revenues began to stagnate, which placed strain on the Zuma administration's patronage circles and service delivery to impoverished and unemployed citizens—the very networks that have enabled political elites to maintain their hold on power over the last twenty-five years.[66] Indeed, employment in the provincial and national governments rose by 27% from 2005 to 2012, while the cash-transfers to the unemployed and low-income households increased from 12.6 to 14.2% from 2008 to 2012, leading to the projection that together public sector remuneration and social grants would draw in the entirety of government revenue by 2026.[67]

The Treasury has aimed to find a solution to this problem through various channels. For instance, Nhlanhla Nene, Zuma's Finance Minister in 2014, attempted to deal with the fiscal crisis by introducing a budget statement that called for cutbacks in government expenditure, an increase in tax revenue, and the capping of compensation for public servants.[68] However, in light of the ANC's precarious political position with respect to its electoral platform and promises of redistributive social justice, strict austerity has its limits and cannot be implemented in a fashion that threatens social service delivery. This was clearly illustrated in the 2015 budget, which, unveiled by the then Finance Minister Pravin Gordhan, sought to strike a delicate balancing act between the interests of the citizenry and bondholders. It was by no means a conventional austerity budget. For example, Michael Sachs, the former Chief of Fiscal Policy, pointed out that the budget did not retrench any programmes aside from freezing public sector staff levels, and noted that the number of South Africans who receive social grants had increased to 16.5 million, up from 7.9 million in 2004. The budget also increased expenditure on social services by 9.4% over a three-year period. It is important to note that Sachs also drew attention to the fact that interest payments on the debt would increase at a faster rate than capital expenditure, and that for every rand collected in taxes 12 cents would be transferred to bond holders, 40% of whom are non-residents.[69] The 2018 budget also increased spending in real terms, again allocating additional revenue to public servants and income transfers to impoverished households.

In light of the chronic problem of economic stagnation and unemployment in the post-apartheid period, one question that needs to be posed is how exactly the governing party has managed to gradually increase spending via borrowing over the years while avoiding sharp-cuts in social expenditure or the implementation of a progressive tax programme? This chapter has suggested that the country's post-transition integration into the international financial markets has allowed the ANC to turn over the state debt on a regular basis to continue funding social service programmes, as well as other expenses, by placating the interests of *global*, as distinct from domestically domiciled, bond investors. This willingness on the part of international asset managers to continue purchasing South African state debt despite economic stagnation, a persistently high unemployment rate, and consistent deficit spending, is largely predicated on the country's economic base, which is dominated by transnational and multinational corporations. As was noted in Chapter 1, international investors have continued to channel funds into South Africa's equity and bond markets in the midst of extremely sluggish economic growth due to the fact that a large portion of the profits of South African companies are generated outside of the country. Additionally, and as also previously illustrated, the domestic operations of these firms are centred around mining and extraction for export on the global markets. The stability of these sectors and activities as generators of foreign exchange, and thus their ability to serve as a tax base for the country despite high unemployment, has meant that foreign investors are willing to underwrite the public debt without imposing strict austerity and cutbacks so long as the government strives to maintain a stable macroeconomic environment anchored to high short-term interest rates/low inflation, financial and trade liberalization, and reasonable fiscal restraint.

The upshot of this policy package is that it has enabled the governing party to implement modest income transfers to poor households in the context of twin deficits and sub-optimal economic growth without facing the imposition of a strict austerity programme by investors. The trade-off, however, has materialized in the form of Treasury and Reserve Bank dominance over economic policymaking, as well as the prioritization of mobile asset investors, even during currency crises. It has also meant that heterodox interventionist policies, such as capital and exchange controls, export taxes, and an expansionary monetary policy, have been avoided by the Finance Ministry as anathema to international asset investors, who demand anti-inflationary macroeconomic measures, and an appreciating exchange rate, in exchange for lower long-term interest rates. Moreover, fiscal expansion has been primarily driven by current expenses as opposed to productive capital expenditure on infrastructure,[70] thereby failing to capitalize on the "crowding-in" effect deficit spending could potentially have had on private investment levels. Thus, paradoxically, by utilizing the international financial markets to implement programmes predicated on poverty alleviation and income transfers, the ANC and the Finance Ministry must adhere to a neoliberal growth path by avoiding interventionist policies that could facilitate industrial diversification, lower unemployment, and reduce economic inequality and poverty over the long-run.

The analysis offered here points to a fundamental flaw in the argument put forward by James Ferguson in *Give a Man a Fish*, a comprehensive study on the politics of redistribution and social justice in sub-Saharan Africa. With the best of intentions, Ferguson points out that critics of neoliberalism have failed to take note of the fact that in several Southern African countries, particularly South Africa, market orthodox programmes have been implemented in conjunction with an *expansion*, as opposed to retrenchment, of a new type of welfare state.[71] The author further notes that the cash-transfers to impoverished households are unique in the sense that, in contrast to state income transfers in many Latin American countries, the social grants in South Africa are generally not linked to conditionality.[72] Ferguson frames these novel cash-transfer programmes as a new form of governance, a potential rupture from a global capitalist system that treats marginalized segments of the population as largely superfluous and no longer necessary to the reproduction of the labour force.[73] This regime, it is argued, represents a new, and potentially radical, form of economic distribution that no longer links citizenship to productivity and labour force participation. As a result, CTPs signal a disconnect with the classic European welfare states and the starting point for a substantive redefinition of citizen rights.[74]

Interestingly, portions of Ferguson's thesis are echoed by policy-makers within the South African bureaucracy. For example, as one senior economist in the Reserve Bank put it, "What we have is not neoliberalism; we have the inflation targeting (IT) regime, we have capital account liberalization, but then we have a lot of state spending."[75] Indeed, the implementation of South Africa's cash-transfer programme is susceptible to framing in such a manner that the country's orthodox growth path is obscured, which may partially explain the ANC's successive electoral victories. However, this type of argument simply serves to conceal the economic factors responsible for persistent unemployment and the absence of a truly viable and effective developmental state during the post-apartheid period; specifically, financialization and the dominance of internationally oriented and mobile capital over the economy. In fact, the present reality of South African society is better captured by Wolfgang Streeck's broad study on state debt and investor power: *Buying Time: The Delayed Crisis of Democratic Capitalism*.

Streeck sets out to analyse the evolution of international class dynamics in the context of global capitalism since the 1970s. The author argues that conventional class categories, such as wage-earner and capital, are rather outdated in the era of neoliberalism and financial globalization. More relevant are categories such as investors vs creditors, a dynamic which can define the relationship between individuals and nation-states. Streeck argues that under neoliberal restructuring there has been a general transition from what he calls the "tax state" to the "debt state." The shift to financialization and the revolt of the business community against postwar regulations and the capital/labour compact led to declining tax progressivity and state revenues on a global scale, which was not matched by a proportionate decrease in state expenditure, leading to a fiscal crisis of public finances and with it rising levels of public indebtedness.[76]

The author further posits that the ascendance of finance and the consolidation of the debt state have empowered a class of asset owners/investors who, in the context of declining rates of taxation, now lend the state money and receive interest payments in return.[77] The investor class, who Streeck refers to as the *Marktvolk* (people of the market), compete with the general citizenry, or the *Staatsvolk*, in order to influence and shape government policy in the direction of their own interests.[78] Streeck argues that though the state is largely dependent on the *Marktvol* in order to meet its fiscal obligations it must, nonetheless, balance between the competing interests of the creditor class and national citizens. Although the author confined his analysis to the United States and the OECD countries, Streeck's concept of the *Marktvol* can be extended to analyse economic policy formulation in emerging market countries as well, though with slightly different implications. For instance, developing and middle-income countries, as evidenced by the case of post-apartheid South Africa, face significant constraints that are imposed by creditors over policymaking despite much lower debt/GDP ratios. Streeck's analysis thus highlights the coercive class mechanisms underpinning the economic and coalitional alliances outlined by Pepinsky. However, the author also notes that the democratic debt state must "manoeuver" carefully between its two stakeholders, the *Marktvol* and the *Staatsvolk*, without allowing either constituent to fully monopolize government policymaking in one direction.[79]

This consolidation of the "debt state," and the decline of progressive taxation in general, illustrates a fundamental problem with Ferguson's framing of social welfare programmes in the Global South as inherently radical or transcendental of neoliberal orthodoxy. While the author is certainly correct in arguing that South Africa's cash-transfer programme has alleviated some of the poverty and inequality in the country, and that in the absence of such social grants the situation in the post-apartheid environment would indeed be far worse, integration into the global financial markets is precisely what has largely made such state expenditure and limited redistribution possible in the context of twin deficits. As this chapter has illustrated, capital account liberalization, and the shift to neoliberal orthodoxy in general, has centred the Treasury, the Reserve Bank, and the Office of the President at the forefront of policymaking. Policymakers within specific bureaucratic centres, especially the Finance Ministry, must carefully evaluate the interests of global investors when formulating economic programmes designed to facilitate industrial diversification and lower unemployment.

This dominance of international portfolio investors, especially in instruments such as government debt, adds an additional layer to the economic and political dynamics driving neoliberal orthodoxy in the post-transition period. Integration into the global capital markets thus offers an important component of the explanation as to why state bureaucrats and political officials have continued to pursue policies that have largely failed to solve the country's developmental and employment problems. Economic programmes and policy solutions to stagnation are therefore enmeshed in the same logic of financialization that was outlined in the introduction, and the process has enveloped and drawn in political elites and key bureaucratic centres into the coalition promoting the perpetuation of the neoliberal growth model. However, as subsequent chapters will show, this economic paradigm has not gone unchallenged by societal and, at times, political actors.

NOTES

1. Personal Interview, Senior Policymaker, Reserve Bank (Pretoria, October 3, 2013); see also Shaukat Ansari, "The Neoliberal Incentive Structure

and the Absence of the Developmental State in Post-apartheid South Africa," *African Affairs* 116, 463 (2017), pp. 226–227.

2. Peter Evans, *Embedded Autonomy: States and Industrial Transformation* (Princeton University Press, Princeton, NJ, 2005).

3. Alice Amsden, "Like the Rest: South East Asia's 'Late' Industrialization," *Journal of International Development* 7, 5 (1995), pp. 791–798.

4. Chalmers Johnson, "The Developmental State: Odyssey of a Concept," in Meredith Woo-Cumings (ed.), *The Developmental State* (Cornell University Press, Ithaca, NY, 1999), p. 38.

5. J.A. Teichman, *The Politics of Inclusive Development: Policy, State Capacity, and Coalition Building* (Palgrave Macmillan, New York, NY, 2016), pp. 145–146.

6. Lindsay Whitfield and Lars Buur, "The Politics of Industrial Policy: Ruling Elites and Their Alliances," *Third Word Quarterly* 35, 1 (2014), p. 131.

7. Abdulrazak Karriem and Mark Hoskins, "From the RDP to the NDP: A Critical Appraisal of the Developmental State, Land Reform, and Rural Development in South Africa," *Politikon* 43, 3 (2016), p. 339.

8. Ibid., p. 338.

9. Karl von Holdt, "Nationalism, Bureaucracy, and the Developmental State: The South African Case," *South African Review of Sociology* 41, 1 (2010), pp. 4–6.

10. Vishnu Padayachee and Robert Van Niekerk, *Shadow of Liberation: Contestation and Compromise in the Economic and Social Policy of the African National Congress, 1943–1996* (NYU Press, New York), pp. 110–111.

11. Ibid., p. 114.

12. Sagie Narsiah, "Neoliberalism and Privatization in South Africa," *GeoJournal* 57, 1 (2002), p. 31.

13. "Theory of the Transition" (COSATU Paper for the ANC Bilateral, February, 2002), p. 9.

14. Personal Interview, Former Senior Official, DTI (Cape Town, January 9, 2017).

15. Layna Mosley, *Global Capital and National Governments* (Cambridge University Press, Cambridge, 2003).

16. Ibid., p. 83.

17. Ibid., p. 129.

18. Government of South Africa "2019 Budget Review" (National Treasury, Pretoria, 2019), p. 82.

19. Colleen Goko, "Investors Ditch South African Bonds as Moody's Junk Threat Looms," *Bloomberg*, October 1, 2019. https://www.bloomberg.com/news/articles/2019-10-01/investors-ditch-south-african-bonds-as-moody-s-junk-threat-looms.

20. Personal Interview, Senior Official, Reserve Bank (Pretoria, October 3, 2013).

21. Ibid.
22. Dani Rodrick, "The Social Cost of Foreign Exchange Reserves," *International Economic Journal* 30, 3 (2006), pp. 253–266.
23. Thomas A. Koelble and Edward LiPuma, "Currency Devaluations and Consolidating Democracy: The Example of the South African Rand," *Economy and Society* 38, 2 (2009), pp. 223–224.
24. Paula Armstrong and Cobus Burger, "Poverty, Inequality, and the Role of Social Grants: An Analysis Using Decomposition Techniques" (Stellenbosch Economic Working Papers, 2009), p. 12.
25. Bhorat and Cassim, cited in A. Karriem and Mark Hoskins, "From the RDP to the NDP: A Critical Appraisal of the Developmental State, Land Reform, and Rural Development in South Africa," *Politikon* 43, 3 (2016), p. 332.
26. Linda Ensor, "Poor Believe Grants Tied to Party, Not State," *Business Day*, May 23, 2014. https://www.businesslive.co.za/bd/national/2014-05-23-poor-believe-grants-tied-to-party-not-state/.
27. Marcel Paret, "Contested ANC Hegemony in the Urban Townships: Evidence from the 2014 South African Election," *African Affairs* 115, 460 (2016), p. 438.
28. Chris Webb, "Profiting from Poverty in South Africa" (Review of African Political Economy, Blog Entry, 2016).
29. Personal Interview, Senior Official, National Treasury (Pretoria, December 7, 2016).
30. "2019 Budget Review" (National Treasury), p. 82.
31. Personal Interview, Former Senior Official, National Treasury (Pretoria, October 3, 2013).
32. Personal Interview, Senior Official, Reserve Bank (Pretoria, December 15, 2016).
33. Personal Interview, Former Senior Official, National Treasury (Pretoria, December 13, 2016).
34. "Five Million Jobs: A Job for Every South African, Practical Proposals" (BLSA, 2009), pp. 3–4.
35. Thomas Pepinsky, *Economic Crises and the Breakdown of Authoritarian Regimes: Indonesia and Malaysia in Comparative Perspective* (Cambridge University Press, Cambridge, 2009), p. 7.
36. Ibid., pp. 14–15.
37. Ibid.
38. Ibid., p. 25.
39. Ibid., pp. 26–27.
40. Ibid., p. 29.
41. Mariam Isa, "South Africa's Currency Dilemma," *The Wall Street Journal*, March 4, 2011. https://www.wsj.com/articles/SB10001424052748703409904576174403336128310.

42. Personal Interview, Former Senior Official, Public Enterprises (Cape Town, January 9, 2017).
43. Personal Interview, Senior Official, Reserve Bank Official (Pretoria, December 15, 2016).
44. Personal Interview, Alan Hirsch (Cape Town, January 10, 2017).
45. Ibid.
46. Personal Interview, Senior Official, National Treasury (Pretoria, December 7, 2016).
47. "Financialization Conference Report" (Pretoria, Economic Development Department, November 26, 2013).
48. Ibid.
49. Ibid.
50. Andre Kraak, "Horizontal Coordination, Government Performance, and National Planning: The Possibilities and Limits of the South African State," *Politikon* 38, 3 (2011), pp. 343–365.
51. Shane Mac Giollabhui, "The Fall of an African President: How and Why Did the ANC Unseat Thabo Mbeki?" *African Affairs* 116, 464 (2017), pp. 394–395.
52. Ibid., p. 397.
53. Ibid.
54. Allister Sparks, "Is This Why the Guptas Zipped-Out of South Africa?" *Times Live*, April 14, 2016. https://www.timeslive.co.za/ideas/2016-04-14-is-this-why-the-guptas-zipped-out-of-south-africa/.
55. Ibid.
56. Nicholas Megaw, "Rand, Banks, and Bonds Hit as Zuma Fires Gordhan," *Financial Times*, March 31, 2017. https://www.ft.com/content/46e ff1ba-15dd-11e7-b0c1-37e417ee6c76?mhq5j=e1.
57. Christopher Vandome, "South Africa Left in Limbo by Landmark Election Results," *Newsweek*, August 9, 2016. https://www.newsweek.com/south-africa-left-limbo-landmark-election-results-488670.
58. Justina Crabtree, "Rand Slides Amid Fresh Political Uncertainty in South Africa," *CNBC*, August 26, 2016. https://www.cnbc.com/2016/08/26/rand-slides-amid-fresh-political-uncertainty-in-south-africa.html.
59. Joe Parkinson, "South Africa's Rand Slides Amid Renewed Cabinet Tensions," *The Wall Street Journal*, August 24, 2016. https://www.wsj.com/articles/south-africas-finance-minister-pravin-gordhan-could-face-charges-1472040772.
60. Personal Interview, Alan Hirsch (Cape Town, January 10, 2017).
61. Gabriele Steinhauser and Joe Parkinson, "South Africa's Government in Turmoil After Zuma Ousts Finance Chief," *The Wall Street Journal*, March 31, 2017. https://www.wsj.com/articles/south-africa-dismisses-finance-minister-prompting-jitters-over-economy-1490943187.
62. Ibid.

63. "South Africa Leaders Divided After President Zuma Sacks Gordhan," *BBC News*, March 31, 2017. https://www.bbc.com/news/world-africa-39451040.
64. Ibid.
65. Nicholas Megaw, "Rand, Banks, and Bonds Hit as Zuma Fires Gordhan," *Financial Times*, March 31, 2017. https://www.ft.com/content/46e ff1ba-15dd-11e7-b0c1-37e417ee6c76?mhq5j=e1.
66. Roger Southall, "The Coming Crisis of Zuma's ANC: The Party State Confronts Fiscal Crisis," *Review of African Political Economy* 43, 147 (2016), pp. 73–88.
67. Ibid., p. 75.
68. Ibid., p. 74.
69. Michael Sachs, "Budgeting in the Real World," *Daily Maverick*, March 17, 2015. https://www.dailymaverick.co.za/author/michaelsachs/.
70. Lerato Mothibi and Precious Mncayi, "Investigating the Key Drivers of Government Debt in South Africa: A Post-apartheid Analysis," *International Journal of Business and Government Studies* 11, 1 (2019), p. 17.
71. James Ferguson, *Give a Man a Fish: Reflections on the New Politics of Distribution* (Duke University Press, Durham, NC, 2015), p. 3.
72. Ibid., p. 6.
73. Ibid., p. 12.
74. Ibid., pp. 17–18.
75. Personal Interview, Midlevel Official, Reserve Bank (Pretoria, October 3, 2013).
76. Wolfgang Streeck, *Buying Time: The Delayed Crisis of Democratic Capitalism* (Verso, New York, 2014), pp. 47, 66.
77. Ibid., p. 78.
78. Ibid., pp. 80–81.
79. Ibid., p. 83.
80. Private firms can also issue shares (equity) in order to raise funds. There are multiple reasons why a firm might issue debt as opposed to ownership shares, but this is not relevant to the present study.
81. Robert E. Hall and John B. Taylor, *Macro-Economics: Theory, Performance, and Policy* (New York: W. W. Norton, 1986), p. 299. Bonds and interest rates are inversely correlated because when the latter falls, the fixed coupon payments on earlier issued bonds are now above the prevailing market yields, and so investors must pay a higher price for the older assets.
82. Ibid., 308.
83. Ibid, 35. This equality exists purely as the result of the accounting procedure employed.

84. See, for example, Gretta Krippner, *Capitalizing on Crisis: The Political Origins of the Rise of Finance* (Harvard University Press, Cambridge, 2009), pp. 92–95.
85. See Shaukat Ansari, "The Neoliberal Incentive Structure and the Absence of the Developmental State in Post-apartheid South Africa," *African Affairs* 116, 463 (2017), pp. 217–218.

APPENDIX: A PRIMER ON BONDS AND YIELDS

A bond is a fixed income asset. When governments or private firms need to raise funds in order to finance their operations, one way of doing so is to borrow on the capital markets.[80] A bond is therefore a form of debt; it represents a liability to the borrower and an asset to the lender. In exchange for providing cash to the borrower, the lender receives a fixed revenue stream, referred to as the "coupon interest rate," on an annual or semi-annual basis, along with the principal once the bond reaches maturity. For example, if the borrower needs $1000, then the lender would supply this capital on the date of issuance, and if he/she receives $50 a year in interest until maturity, then the coupon rate is 5%.

It is important to note that while the bond's coupon rate is a fixed dollar amount (e.g. $50 annually), the yield fluctuates based on the bond's price on the secondary markets. For instance, if the price of the asset rises to $1500, the investor continues to receive $50 annually, as agreed upon when the bond was initially issued, but the yield has now declined to 3.3% (50/1500). As a result, bond prices and interest rates are inversely correlated.[81] The order in which this correlation occurs is irrelevant—if bond prices spike, interest rates will decline, and vice versa. Monetary authorities may also employ open market operations and bond sales as part of a sterilization policy to reduce inflation. For example, if the Reserve Bank targets the value of the rand on the foreign exchange markets in order to depreciate the currency, authorities might then attempt to mop up the excess liquidity circulating in the economy by selling government bonds to the private sector.

The inverse relationship between bond prices and interest rates explains some aspects of South Africa's neoliberal policies. When a country's monetary authorities want to affect the prevailing short-term interest rates, one common method they employ involves altering the economy's monetary base. If the Central Bank believes that interest rates are too high, it can instruct its bond traders to purchase additional bonds through open market operations, which inject more liquidity into the financial system, raise bond prices, and lower the short-term rate.[82] This process is also termed "targeting the repo (repurchase) rate," and it is how the South African Reserve Bank (SARB) carries out its inflation targeting (IT) regime. The Central Bank cannot, however, directly influence long-term interest rates. The benchmark for this rate is the long-term bond yield, and it is largely determined by the existing demand for, and supply of, total loanable funds. Therefore, monetary authorities will attempt to shape the long-term rate by influencing arbitrage operations. For example, this type of model predicts that if short-term interests rise as a result of the Central Bank's open market operations, then investors holding long-term bonds with lower rates will sell these instruments and purchase the assets with shorter maturities, thereby causing the price of the ten-year bonds to fall and the yield to rise. Similarly, if short-term rates fall, then it is assumed that investors will sell short-term bond instruments, spiking the yield on these assets, in order to purchase longer-term bonds with higher coupon rates. This process, however, is certainly not guaranteed, and a number of factors can prevent the short-term and long-term interest rates from converging.

In a closed economy, GDP equals consumption and investment (including government consumption and investment), and investment equals savings.[83] However, in an open economy, this equality no longer holds, and the government and the private sector can borrow a given amount of capital that exceeds the domestic savings rate and the level of taxation. This type of policy was exploited by the Reagan Administration in the 1980s, for example, once it was determined by policymakers that the US government could essentially finance its massive deficits and fund domestic programs by tapping into global finance (specifically from the surplus countries such as Japan) by offering a slightly higher rate of return, thereby solving the capital scarcity problem.[84] A similar process is underway in South Africa, though with different implications, since the latter is a developing country. In post-apartheid South Africa, the long-term bond yield has displayed a downward trend because the supply of capital (loanable funds) has matched and exceeded domestic demand. As noted in Chapter 1, this trend is largely related to the carry-trade strategies of global investors, who borrow at low interest rates and invest in securities with higher yields. In fact, regression analysis has shown that the US federal funds rate, which is the interbank rate, is positively correlated with the return on South Africa's ten-year bond, lending corroboration to the notion that speculation is largely driving the decline in the yield.[85] Yet, as noted in this chapter, this downward trend has come at a price. Global investors have demanded a low level of inflation, which is why South African authorities have continued to maintain short-term interest rates within a 3–6% band, and there is also a low tolerance among global investors for high debt/GDP ratio. Thus, on the domestic side, global market integration can serve as an alternative to progressive taxation, and state authorities can borrow on the international capital markets at a lower yield than what would be possible with a closed capital account.

CHAPTER 3

Political Resistance to Neoliberalism: Cracks in the Post-apartheid Corporatist Arrangement

The last two chapters examined the economic and political founda-
tions for the persistence of market orthodoxy throughout South Africa's
post-apartheid trajectory. It was argued that the business community
and policymakers, specifically the large multinational corporations and
technocrats within the Treasury and Reserve Bank, have promoted and
benefitted from economic liberalization. However, this neoliberal growth
model has not gone unchallenged by South African civil society. This
chapter examines an issue of crucial importance; namely, the domestic
resistance that has emerged and evolved against market orthodoxy since
the democratic transition. It also evaluates the political dynamics of corporatism in the country. More specifically, this chapter will look carefully
at the tripartite ruling alliance between the ANC, the South African
Communist Party (SACP), and the Congress of South African Trade
Unions (COSATU), as well as the pressures against orthodoxy emanating
from new opposition parties and the ANC Youth League. As previously
noted, an important question this book has sought to answer is why, in
the context of persistent poverty and social inequality, the ANC has been
able to secure repeated electoral victories throughout the post-apartheid
period. The economic incentives and constraints created by the country's
integration into the global financial markets, and the business sectors'
new accumulation strategies, only tell part of the story. As was discussed

© The Author(s), under exclusive license to Springer Nature
Switzerland AG 2021
S. Ansari, *Neoliberalism and Resistance in South Africa*,
Contemporary African Political Economy,
https://doi.org/10.1007/978-3-030-69766-2_3

in Chapter 2, large swaths of the South African working class and the rural population have continued to lend their support to the ANC. Three factors are responsible for this trend: the integration of much of the organized working class into a corporatist arrangement, the legacy of the liberation movement upon which the ANC continues to capitalize, and certain limited forms of redistribution to impoverished sections of the population.

It will be argued that COSATU and the SACP have continued to promote a strategy that favours incremental change from within the ruling alliance, while refraining from directly and publicly challenging and confronting the ANC's unpopular economic policies. However, discontent from within the umbrella organization has generated a great deal of internal unrest. COSATU's leadership has thus far chosen to address this problem by expelling militant unions from the organization, an example being the National Union of Metalworkers (NUMSA), but this has created a new problem for the ruling alliance: radical opposition to market orthodoxy from outside conventional political channels has begun to grow in South Africa, despite the legacy of the liberation struggle and the disbursement of non-contributory social grants. This poses a serious grassroots challenge to the ANC's implementation of the neoliberal growth model. This challenge emanates not only from specific labour unions, but also from new opposition political parties, such as the Economic Freedom Fighters (EFF), whose electoral victories, though marginal, have begun to slightly erode the ANC's traditional political base. The political unrest generated by these new challenges has created new pressures on the ANC, and the Democratic Alliance (DA) has also seized this as an opportunity to mount relentless attacks against the governing party from the right.

Overall, while the tripartite alliance between the ANC, SACP, and COSATU has come under some strain over the last several years, the latter organizations have thus far chosen to remain within the political coalition and capitalize on the access to political office that their inclusion within the governing alliance affords their members. It will be argued that the persistent stability of this political settlement has helped underwrite the continuation of market orthodoxy throughout the post-apartheid period, despite the opposition that has recently emerged from outside the tripartite alliance against the current economic order. The chapter is divided into two sections. The first part will examine the formation of the tripartite alliance, with an emphasis placed on COSATU and the SACP, as well as the policy implications of this corporatist arrangement. The constraints placed on certain aspects of market orthodoxy by the inclusion of the unions and the SACP in the ruling alliance will be explored. Attention will also be paid to the strains that have recently emerged in the tripartite consensus, as well as the roots behind the expulsion of certain labour unions. This section will also examine the nature of COSATU's collusion with the ANC on certain matters of economic policy, and will further analyse an event that generated a great deal of internal strife within the organization and which led to nationwide protests and wildcat strikes: The Marikana Mining massacre. The second section will examine the rise of the Economic Freedom Fighters, a party founded by Julius Malema, the former President of the ANC Youth League, in order to flesh out the new political challenges this poses for the ANC. The chapter draws on the secondary literature as well as interviews and primary documents, especially press reports. I also draw on certain autobiographical accounts, such as Patrick Craven's recent book, *The Battle for COSATU: An Insider's View.*

3.1   The Tripartite Alliance: Origins, Cracks, and Implications for Policymaking

The tripartite alliance has its roots in the liberation movement and the struggle against apartheid. In the aftermath of the 1960 Sharpeville massacre, the apartheid state launched a repressive assault against both the ANC and the black trade unions, driving the former organization underground for decades and banning the latter. However, with the increasing concentration of black workers at the point of production, which was an outgrowth of segregationist policies which artificially held down black wages through the reserve system and pass laws, the conditions were created for the re-emergence of militant black working class struggles, and in 1973 over one-hundred-thousand black workers in Durban broke the "industrial peace" and engaged in strike actions to demand higher wages.[1]

Following this massive strike, the apartheid state under P. W. Botha moved to neutralize the threat posed by a rising militant South African labour movement. Black trade unions were legalized and coopted through their integration and registration with the National Manpower Commission.[2] This period witnessed the emergence of a pluralistic and competitive dynamic among the trade unions, as the latter sought to confront capital and the state through the employment of strikes, the industrial relations machinery, negotiations, and even the courts to secure better working conditions and higher wages.[3] By the mid-1980s, COSATU had become the dominant federation housing the black trade unions, a development that was largely due to the leadership's decision to facilitate connections with a wide array of social groups as a strategy of mass mobilization against the apartheid state.[4]

The consolidation of COSATU signalled a transition away from pluralism to political unionism. This shift in union strategizing essentially "prioritized the question of national liberation,"[5] and in 1985 the federation issued a joint statement with the ANC that committed the unions to participate in the democratic struggle against apartheid—a commitment that essentially marked the beginning of COSATU's integration into the tripartite alliance. This decision, while a crucial component in the struggle against segregation, also laid the foundation for the consolidation of a corporatist arrangement following the democratic transition. Negotiations with the apartheid government, and the formal transition to democracy, led to a substantive and official shift in labour's strategy in dealing with capital and the state, encapsulated by a movement away from the "politics of resistance to the politics of reconstruction."[6] The democratic transition thus marked the advent of a power-sharing alliance between the ANC, COSATU, and the SACP, as well as a corporatist arrangement that, at least theoretically, incorporated organized labour, capital, and the state into a governance network responsible for macroeconomic policymaking. Viewed from the standpoint of the ANC leadership, the promotion of corporatism was based on a strategic calculation that recognized the party's political and social vulnerability. The ANC was confronted with a strong social movement with the potential for massive mobilization in the context of a political and economic transition—one that was grounded in market orthodoxy and would most likely be unable to address the historic material grievances of the vast majority of South Africans.[7] In this sense, the ANC's embrace of corporatism can be understood as a "response of state elites in times of crisis."[8]

COSATU was also motivated to accept a corporatist arrangement for strategic purposes. However, it is important to note that there was some significant dissent among key leadership personnel regarding the virtues of the tripartite alliance and institutionalized bargaining at the time of the transition. For example, Jay Naidoo, the ex-COSATU's General Secretary, stated in 1994, "We could become trapped in bureaucracy and inaction. Our tradition of organization and struggle could be immobilised."[9]

Nonetheless, other senior trade union officials advocated for "qualified," or even unqualified, support for the tripartite alliance and institutionalized bargaining on the grounds that such a social contract would allow for a period of "transitional stability," which would in turn provide the building blocks for a socialist transformation from within the state's structures of power.[10] Indeed, the union leadership framed their shift away from radical politics and protest as a strategy designed to access the institutions necessary to shape the socio-economic future of their rank and file, even though the collapse of communism, and their adoption of a new discourse of social democracy, was a crucial factor driving their acceptance of corporatism.[11]

During this period, organized labour managed to secure a number of important concessions from the state in the context of a corporatist arrangement. For example, the transition ushered in the 1995 Labour Relations Act, which institutionalized labour relations through the creation of workplace forums, and delegated issues pertaining to wages and working conditions to centralized bargaining councils.[12] This statute was supplemented by the Employment Equity Act (1998), which was designed to eliminate racial discrimination in employment practices, as well as the Basic Conditions of Employment Act (1997), which regulated minimum conditions of employment in order to ensure that unorganized and vulnerable workers were protected under the definition outlined by the International Labour Organization.[13] Most importantly, corporatism led to the creation of the National Economic Development and Labour Council (Nedlac), the forum where capital, labour, and the state are able to discuss and negotiate labour and macroeconomic issues prior to their introduction in parliament. The forum set out the following functions in its founding document:

1. "To reach consensus and make agreements on matters pertaining to economic policy."
2. "The council shall consider all proposed labor legislation."
3. "Nothing in the constitution of the Council should constrain the Council from considering any matter within its terms of reference."[14]

The creation of Nedlac was a clear example of the power of organized labour during this time and its ability to shape the terms of the transition. Nedlac grew out of the National Economic Forum (NEF), a body which was formed at the insistence of COSATU in 1992. Organized labour had become increasingly concerned with the influence of business on the ANC's economic programme, and in 1991, COSATU launched an organized campaign against the introduction of the value-added tax (VAT), demanding the formation of a formal entity to prevent unilateral economic decision-making by business or the government.[15] Although the latter was initially reluctant to consent to the creation of such a forum, the attitude of the Treasury changed once Derek Keys, who came from the business community, took over the post of Minister of Finance. In fact, it was Keys and Alec Erwin, the former Minister of Trade and Industry, who played an instrumental role in facilitating Nedlac's creation.[16] The campaign launched by labour to create such a forum clearly demonstrated COSATU's organizational strength, as the federation was able to bring together a broad coalition of actors in protest against the regressive tax.[17] As a result of this campaign, COSATU managed to win an exemption from VAT for basic foods.[18] More recently, in 2018, negotiations in the forum led to the passage of a National Minimum Wage Law in the country, a significant achievement for labour activists. The passage of the act that created the NEF, and then later Nedlac, was thus quite a significant and important milestone in the liberation movement and the fight against apartheid, as it signalled the real possibility that organized black labour would be able to play a substantive role in the formulation of macroeconomic policymaking in post-apartheid South Africa, and thus could potentially keep the focus on economic redistribution.

However, Nedlac was sidestepped immediately after the transition on matters relating to macro policy formulation and legislation. This became clear when the Treasury unveiled the neoliberal GEAR programme in 1996. The ANC's Finance Minister, Trevor Manuel, announced that proposals set out in the document would be non-negotiable and therefore would not be debated or discussed within Nedlac. This decision frustrated COSATU, especially since the entity had a specific forum, the Public Finance and Monetary Policy Chamber, that was designed to deal precisely with the type of policy issues laid out in the GEAR document. It thus seems likely that government officials understood that COSATU would strongly oppose the market orthodox policies drawn up by the technocrats in the Treasury.[19] Moreover, the decision to drastically reduce import tariffs and duties was simply announced by the Department of

Trade and Industry without being negotiated in Nedlac's relevant policy chamber ahead of time.[20]

Overall, while the creation of Nedlac, and corporatism more generally, increased the power of organized labour at the micro-level through bargaining forums and by institutionalizing the right to strike and minimum wage laws, it has not enabled COSATU to exercise any kind of substantive influence over the direction of macroeconomic policymaking. Additionally, collective bargaining and corporatist arrangements have at times shaped a policy environment that privileges "insiders"—members of organized unions—over "outsiders;" the latter referring to the vulnerable and unorganized workers, as was evidenced by COSATU's strenuous objection to labour broking.[21] Thus, rather than being utilized as a forum to debate and craft macroeconomic measures related to trade, government expenditure, and monetary policies, Nedlac has in recent years become a chamber where issues solely relating to organized labour, such as a national minimum wage and flexible labour contracting, are discussed and negotiated. In fact, the forum's inadequacy as a site for substantive policy formulation has, at times, led the alliance partners to resort to grass-roots mobilization and protest as a strategy to constrain market orthodoxy and private wealth accumulation.

This was illustrated in 2001 during the massive uprisings against the ANC government's proposal for the privatization of state assets. Privatization had initially formed one of the main cornerstones of the neoliberal trajectory in post-apartheid South Africa, and, as noted in Chapter 1, it had begun under the National Party prior to the transition. In August of 2000, the ANC government released a report entitled "An Accelerated Agenda towards the Restructuring of State-Owned Enterprises," which outlined concrete plans for the rationalization of such companies.[22] In response, COSATU tabled a position paper on privatization in July of 2001 in the Nedlac Chamber that vigorously criticized the stance taken by the National Treasury and the Department of Trade and Industry on the privatization of SOEs. The paper stated, in part, that "the market will not meet the social and economic requirements of development, since private companies cannot capture the long-term benefits of developmental measures."[23]

Discussions over privatization reached a deadlock in Nedlac, however, which led COSATU to issue a statement declaring that negotiations on this issue had failed and that the federation would be holding a national strike in August of 2001, with plans for action at the sectoral level also underway.[24] The federation launched a two-day general strike at the end of August that drew tens of thousands of workers in Johannesburg to protest the planned privatization of Eskom.[25] In fact, agitation against privatization continued into 2002, with several provincial protests taking place as well. At the end of the campaign, COSATU declared that they had secured some minor victories, while President Thabo Mbeki labelled the trade union "ultra-leftist."[26] The strikes did succeed in halting the government's plan for the privatization of Eskom. Moreover, opposition by labour to the state's blueprint for the restructuring of SOEs registered other successes as well; for example, transport trade unions managed to convince the government that its proposal to privatize Spoornet, a freight and passenger company, was ill-conceived by demonstrating that such plans would end up thwarting sustainable economic development.[27] In 2005, when the government announced that it planned to divest from Transnet, the state-owned freight logistics company, another strike erupted in March of 2006 that involved 50,000 Transnet workers who were supported by COSATU.[28] Transnet has since remained a government entity. The union's struggle against privatization thus achieved some important victories. SOEs comprise 44% of South Africa's fixed capital stock,[29] and several of the companies that had undergone privatization were soon renationalized.[30]

Privatization was also vigorously opposed by the South African Communist Party (SACP), the third member of the tripartite coalition. The SACP played a crucial role in the struggle against apartheid, mobilizing thousands of members at the grass-roots level to oppose segregation in alliance with the ANC. The Communist Party's integration into the tripartite alliance after the democratic transition has its roots in the specific strategy adopted by the Party leaders during the movement against segregation. Since 1928, the Party has followed a two-stage guide to revolution, which prioritized national liberation over a socialist transition. As a result, the class struggle was subordinated to the issue of racial emancipation.[31] The SACP's strategy for working class liberation was further elucidated in their 2014 position paper, "Going to the Root." In that discussion document, the Party called for a "second phase" in the National Democratic Revolution (NDR), as opposed to a "second stage," since the latter would entail breaking away from the ANC-led alliance. The document also lauded the redistributive gains that had been made since the transition, specifically the social grants currently being delivered to 17 million South Africans, and argued that the next phase of the NDR would have to involve structural transformation of the economy in addition to redistribution, but advocated that this should take place within the confines of the tripartite alliance.[32]

The necessity of remaining within the tripartite alliance was also stressed by Alex Mashilo, the National Spokesperson for the SACP. Mashilo noted that a number of gains were made during the transition and throughout the ANC's tenure in power that were the result of pressure exerted by the SACP, and that breaking away from the tripartite alliance would prevent the Party from being able to secure similar gains in the future. Specifically, Mashilo pointed to the victory won against the privatization drive and suggested that the ANC's reversal of their proposed restructuring of SOEs could be largely attributed to the pressure exerted on the party by the alliance partners, and that this victory would likely have not been possible if the SACP had not been operating from within the alliance.[33] Moreover, the SACP is in a sense locked into the ruling coalition because of the ANC's overwhelming support from the South African population. As Alec Erwin put it, "The SACP never had the kind of political following that would have allowed it to form a separate political party outside of the tripartite alliance after the transition."[34] This point was also made by Mashilo, who stated that the SACP still lacks a mass-based following among the population, and was thus more concerned with cultivating working class consciousness from within the political alliance.[35]

COSATU faced similar issues in the aftermath of the transition and the adoption of GEAR by the ANC government. Firstly, it must be noted that the trade union officials who were elected to parliament in the immediate aftermath of the transition were able to secure victory because they ran primarily as ANC candidates, and not because of their affiliation with COSATU.[36] Secondly, despite the fact that a large number of rank and file members of the trade unions profess to support some form of social movement activism to secure economic gains,[37] it is also the case that the same rank and file are generally loyal to the ANC as the party of liberation, and hence, COSATU and the SACP would have a difficult time attracting voters if either were to splinter off and create an independent worker's party.[38] This support for the ANC should not be underestimated. Indeed, the collapse of many of the independent social movement organizations that sprung up during the privatization debates can be attributed to the fact that a large number of the grass-roots activists who were part of such movements eventually disbanded and were drawn back to the ANC, thereby preventing the forging of an alternative collective identity. These single-issue organizations that emerged in the midst of the ANC's privatization drive included, for example, the Anti-Privatization Forum (APF), the Landless People's Movement (LPM), the Anti-Eviction Campaign (AEC), and the Concerned Citizen's Forum (CCF).[39]

There is also the issue of "business unionism," to cite the SACP, a term which refers to COSATU's vast pension fund investments and the organization's alleged cooptation by the corporate sector.[40] The investment arms of many of the unions under the COSATU federation control a total of R-20 billion, and many of these funds are invested in top South African companies rather than in public housing or infrastructure.[41] This development has created certain "bizarre contradictions," such as when the National Union of Mineworkers (NUM), the largest union belonging to COSATU, negotiated and imposed retrenchments on behalf of a mining house that was controlled by its own investment company.[42] Indeed, it has been reported that trade unions have at times invested in "companies where they organize workers, making it difficult for union leaders to act impartially in their member's best interests."[43] In this respect, organized labour has been integrated into the neoliberal growth model as investors, further dulling the opposition to market orthodox economic policies.[44]

Thus, the corporatist arrangement established after the democratic transition has served to contain popular resistance against neoliberalism over a twenty-five-year period. Nedlac has emerged as a site where union leaders negotiate issues involving wages and flexible labour market policies, but the various chambers are bypassed when it comes to macroeconomic issues such as trade, monetary, and fiscal policies. As noted, COSATU has at times secured important victories, such as against privatization and service charges for certain utilities by bolstering negotiations in Nedlac with public protests and strikes, but overall union leaders have remained wedded to the ANC and hence to market orthodoxy broadly speaking. However, since 2014, a number of large unions have broken off from the federation, and several wildcat strikes have erupted throughout the country as well, creating a real possibility for radical change. Part of the impetus for this new trend was the worst atrocity committed by state forces since the Sharpeville killings, a massacre which occurred in 2012 at Marikana.

3.2 THE MARIKANA MASSACRE AND LABOUR UNREST

The Marikana massacre took place on 16 August 2012. Rock drillers at a platinum mine, operated by the multinational firm Lonmin, went on strike demanding wages equivalent to what the firm paid its Australian workers. Protestors eventually began throwing rocks at the police and refusing orders to disperse, which prompted the police to open fire with automatic rifles, killing thirty-four miners, wounding seventy-eight, and then arresting two hundred and fifty-nine.[45] Several of the miners had been shot in the back, indicating that they were fleeing at the time, and in the aftermath of the killings, it was revealed that the police had tortured several of the detainees at the station in order to extract confessions.[46] The National Prosecuting Authority initially decided to charge the strikers using an apartheid-era legal provision, though this was suspended after public outrage.[47] Following the massacre, several key government ministries, such as the Department of Trade and Industry and the Department of Minerals and Energy, moved to reassure potential international investors that the South African mining industry remained a secure destination for investments.[48] Moreover, the government dispatched a heavy military presence along the Platinum Mining Belt in addition to declaring a temporary state of emergency and suspending the constitutional right of miners to protest and strike.[49]

The massacre was an extremely significant event, and not simply because it involved the state-sanctioned use of force against civilians—the largest since the Sharpeville episode. More importantly, the strike was noteworthy because it was waged outside the authority of the National Union of Mineworkers, and thus was not officially recognized by COSATU. The strikers chose to reject the NUM and accused the union of siding with the platinum company. As a result, Barnard Mokwena, who at the time was the executive vice-president of Lonmin, circulated an internal memo stating that since the strike was taking place outside the authority of the COSATU federation, the company could opt to fire the workers and call in the police to deal with the situation.[50] One of the rebel leaders of the strike, Mgcineni Noki, had reportedly stated that the "NUM is a sellout," and registered with a recent breakaway union—the Association of Mineworkers and Construction Union (AMCU).[51]

In fact, the conflict between NUM and the AMCU contributed to the conditions that led to the massacre. Workers at the Lonmin mine generally felt betrayed by NUM and accused the latter of "abandoning their grassroots concerns" by "focusing instead on politics."[52] NUM officials had a close relationship with the management at Lonmin, and during the strike, the union encouraged workers to break the strike and return to the underground shafts.[53] This type of close relationship between company management and the union bureaucrats is a natural outgrowth of the institutional bargaining structure in South Africa. As a result of the 1995 Labour Relations Act (LRA), centralized bargaining is the norm (with the exception of the platinum sector), with the Chamber of Mines negotiating on behalf of all mining sub-sectors.[54] The absence of bargaining at the firm level has meant that employees at the lower levels of the employment hierarchy have felt alienated by the negotiation process and have often resorted to non-sanctioned strike activity.[55] To add to this instability, and as noted in Chapter 1, during the commodities boom mining companies such as Lonmin chose to distribute their massive profits to shareholders instead of using them for wage increases. NUM, rather than negotiating or pushing for higher wages, adopted a complacent approach in its relationship with management officials at Lonmin.[56]

This perception among workers, that they had effectively been abandoned by their union, was partially responsible for the militant stance that permeated the environment at Marikana. In fact, the rock drillers at Lonmin explicitly rejected representation by NUM on the grounds that the union was plagued with corruption and was unaccountable to its members; additionally, violence was employed against dissenting workers who reported for duty.[57] The strike at Lonmin was not, however, an isolated event. In January of 2012, for example, an unprotected strike broke out at the Impala Platinum mine, as workers downed their tools and demanded a pay increase. NUM had opposed this strike as well, and before a deal was brokered in March that included a salary raise of R9,000, management had dismissed over 18,000 of the striking miners, thereby terminating their union memberships, while another 11,000 had resigned from NUM by the end of March.[58] Following the uprising at Impala, workers engaged in strikes in mines all along the Platinum Belt, and in most cases, the rank and file set up independent worker committees to deal with local management outside of regular institutional channels, though eventually most of them also joined the AMCU after refusing to return to NUM.[59]

In the aftermath of the Marikana killings, it appeared that a new wave of protests and developments within COSATU could seriously threaten the tripartite alliance and potentially undermine the ANC's hegemony. In

2014, following a national strike wave that erupted in the latter part of 2012, 70,000 platinum mineworkers went on strike outside of COSATU and its established industrial negotiating institutions.[60] The workers were demanding a minimum wage of R12,500 a month, a symbolic figure since it was the amount demanded by the striking workers at Marikana. The workers initially faced stiff resistance from management, who, for the first three months of the strike, continued to sell platinum out of accumulated reserves.[61] After six months, the workers emerged victorious with the full support of AMCU, a union which remained outside of the COSATU federation. The wave of strikes that erupted before and after Marikana not only signified growing working class discontent with COSATU, but was also emblematic of increasing conflict within the federation and new strains within the tripartite alliance. Following the massacre, in October 2012, the Zuma administration attempted to contain the fallout by convening an emergency social dialogue session at Nedlac between business, labour, and government officials. The participants then issued an official statement calling on unauthorized strikers to return to work and stating that "the wave of unprotected strikes...could undermine the legal framework of bargaining."[62]

However, despite such pronouncements from organized labour and business, further cracks soon began appearing in the tripartite alliance. In 2014, the National Union of Metal Workers (NUMSA), one of the largest affiliates of COSATU, was expelled from the federation and the ruling alliance. Although NUMSA was excommunicated from the federation, the union essentially made the decision to withdraw from COSATU when it decided to withhold its support for the ANC in the 2014 election, instead pledging to build a strong united movement against neoliberal policies while establishing a political organization that could fight for socialism.[63] Initially, NUMSA's leader, Irvin Jim, had publicly called on COSATU to terminate its alliance with the ANC and instead join a socialist movement consisting of community organizations, churches, and NGOs with the end goal of forming a worker's party that could contest future elections and challenge the ANC's market orthodoxy.[64] In fact, NUMSA did not want to leave COSATU; rather, the leadership simply vocally withdrew its support for the ANC ahead of the election on the grounds that it was no longer the party of workers. COSATU executives, however, voted 33-24 to instead expel NUMSA from the federation, along with the union's 350,000 members, or 15% of COSATU's membership. This expulsion marked a watershed moment in post-apartheid South

Africa's labour relations, with one senior union official describing it as a "struggle for the soul" of the movement.[65]

Patrick Craven, the former National Spokesperson for COSATU who later resigned from the federation, details the events that led to the expulsion in his 2015 autobiography, *The Battle for COSATU: An Insider's View.* Craven points out that NUMSA had convened a Special National Congress in December of 2013 to discuss a number of issues pertaining to the federation's ongoing support for the ANC and COSATU's proposal of specific economic policies. Craven noted that during his attendance he was struck by the active participation of NUMSA's rank and file members (338,000), which, in union business, set it apart from other unions belonging to the federation. During this special meeting, NUMSA further critiqued the ANC's commitment to the neoliberal growth model, issuing a declaration which stated, in part, that "A militant, popular programme [the Freedom Charter] which challenged property relations in South Africa has been replaced by a neoliberal programme which entrenched existing property relations and attacks the working class and the poor in the interests of mining and finance capital."[66] Additionally, the declaration went on to detail the bankruptcy of the alliance partners, arguing that "the SACP leadership has become embedded in the State and is failing to act as the vanguard of the working class."[67]

Craven further documents the response issued against NUMSA's declaration by COSATU's Central Executive Committee. According to the author, at a meeting held by the committee on 10 February 2014, representatives of the federation in leadership positions denounced NUMSA and called for the union's expulsion. Sidumo Dlamini, COSATU's President, cited the federation's charter and argued that NUMSA's decision to terminate its support for the ANC and to recruit members from other unions was "diametrically opposed to that constitution," while other unions, such as the National Union of Mineworkers (NUM), alleged that NUMSA was attempting to destroy the federation from within, and demanded that the union's leadership provide specific reasons as to why they should not be expelled from the federation. According to Craven, the Central Executive Committee was signalling the beginning of a campaign designed to isolate NUMSA and neutralize its rebellion, while reintegrating COSATU's other union affiliates into the federal state structures of corporatism.[68]

A second special meeting was held by the Central Executive Committee on 8 April 2014, and it was attended by members of the ANC Task Team, including the former ANC Deputy President Cyril Ramaphosa (who began his career with the National Union of Mineworkers) and Deputy Secretary General Jessie Duarte. Ramaphosa began his address to the committee by emphasizing the importance of unity ahead of the general election and requested that a ceasefire be put in place and that any decision to expel a union should be, at the very least, postponed. Craven highlighted the relevance of this request in his autobiography by pointing out that the May 7 general elections witnessed the exit of several senior COSATU officials as they were elected to parliament in provincial and national assemblies. Among those elected were Senzeni Zokwana, the President of NUM, Zet Luzipho, COSATU's Provincial Secretary from the Natal region, Joe Mpisi, Deputy President of Nehawu, a COSATU affiliate, and several other officials. Craven revealed that many of the officials who left the federation for parliamentary office had been some of the most vocal critics of NUMSA, and suggested that these officials were not criticizing the union based on ideological convictions, but rather were using the federation as a "stepping stone" to further their careers, which pointed to a material interest in preserving the tripartite alliance and supporting the ANC's electoral campaign.[69] On 7 November 2014, NUMSA's Secretary General, Irvin Jim, gave a three-hour presentation explaining why he believed the union should not be expelled from COSATU. Craven notes that the Central Executive Committee took a vote after spending very little time actually discussing or debating the presentation, and NUMSA then became the first union in the history of the federation to be expelled.[70] The removal of COSATU's largest union from the federation removed a key obstacle to the deepening of corporatism and COSATU's ongoing political support for the ANC.

Since NUMSA's expulsion from the federation, Irvin Jim has increased his populist pronouncements while taking the ANC to task for the party's failure to adequately implement the Freedom Charter, the founding 1955 document that outlined the ANC's plans for the South African post-apartheid economy. At a press conference in Johannesburg, for example, Jim made the following statement to journalists:

> In NUMSA, we have consistently maintained and repeated that the inherited colonial triple crises of poverty, inequality, and unemployment and the colonial status of the African masses in post-1994 South Africa will continue to deepen unless we break new ground in destroying the inherited colonial economy.[71]

Jim has also repeatedly taken aim at the Treasury and Reserve Bank on several occasions, denouncing the "stranglehold of imperialism and white monopoly of South African capital over the National Treasury and the South African Reserve Bank," and accusing all the Finance Ministers of post-apartheid South Africa of serving the interests of finance capital and global ratings agencies.[72] While the breakaway of COSATU's largest union from the federation may signal the beginning of a new movement against market orthodoxy, there are still some formidable challenges that stand in the way of a counter-hegemonic project. Firstly, the majority of the country's unions are still integrated into the country's corporatist framework through their membership in the federation, which, as noted above, supports the ANC. Secondly, as was discussed in Chapter 2, a large segment of the rural population and those in the townships continue to support the ANC as a result of the political capital built up during the liberation movement and the distribution of social grants to the impoverished and unemployed. Indeed, this portion of the South African population has little use for conventional working class politics in the present socio-economic context. As Alex Mashilo put it, "That is why Irvin Jim's project is not going to work."[73]

However, since Marikana and NUMSA's expulsion from the federation, several political developments have also begun to erode the ANC's support in traditional strongholds. Such developments led to the creation of a new radical political party, the Economic Freedom Fighters (EFF), which has taken up the cause of the now abandoned Freedom Charter. The next section will examine the political significance and implications of this new party, as well as the events leading up to its formation and the future implications of the participation of this party's base in the domestic politics of the country.

3.3   NEW POLITICAL RESISTANCE
TO THE NEOLIBERAL GROWTH MODEL

The rise of the Economic Freedom Fighters (EFF) as a viable radical political party has its roots in the politics of the ANC Youth League (ANCYL) and the latter's embattled former leader, Julius Malema. The ANCYL was founded in 1948 as the youth wing of the ANC as part of a strategy to mobilize the masses against apartheid. The ANCYL was to function as an autonomous, but not fully independent, organization, a status that has at times allowed the ANC to deploy the Youth League to take unpopular ideological positions on certain issues. However, this same autonomy had enabled the organization to openly defy its parent body on vital and controversial socio-economic policy issues.[74] Under Julius Malema's leadership, the Youth League became a decisive force within ANC politics. Malema was able to channel the discontent and anger of the mostly male youth from the townships against the socio-economic status quo, often employing fiery and populist rhetoric involving invocations for "revolution" and "militancy."[75]

A deep rift between the Youth League and the ANC emerged, however, over the issue of unemployment and the potential nationalization of the mining industry. In a 2010 discussion document, the ANCYL made the case for the nationalization of the entire mining sector as a means of fulfilling the Freedom Charter's promise to transfer the mineral wealth of the nation to its rightful owners. The document outlined the following benefits that would accrue from the nationalization of the mines:

> a). Nationalization to increase the state's fiscal capacity; b) nationalization as a basis for industrialization; c) nationalization as a means to safeguard sovereignty; d) nationalization as a basis to transform the accumulation path in the South African economy; and e) nationalization to transform South Africa's unequal spatial development patterns.[76]

The Youth League demanded that nationalization be placed on the agenda at the ANC's national general council, prompting President Zuma to declare that the party would research the possibility of a state mining company before the national policy conference in 2012.[77] However, Susan Shabangu, the Minister of the Department of Mineral Resources, dismissed the prospect of nationalization at a conference in Cape Town, stating that in her lifetime "there would be no nationalization," while the chief executive of the Chamber of Mines warned that "nationalization has impoverished countries."[78]

The issue provoked a great deal of discussion and agitation among ANC officials and the ANCYL, and in fact, the momentum it gained led COSATU to eventually throw its support behind the Youth League's call for nationalization. As a result, increasing alarm within the business community over such a prospect generated a decline in foreign direct investment flows in 2010 to just a quarter of what it had been in the previous year.[79] Malema increased his populist pronouncements by demanding that the banks be nationalized alongside the mines.[80] COSATU's support for the programme eventually waned, however, and the position adopted by the federation at this point was that the government should pursue strategic nationalization in conjunction with broader progressive policies. Moreover, there was a general sentiment among certain union officials that the ANCYL was engaging in irresponsible "populist demagoguery," and that the league's drive for nationalization was at least partially being dictated by Malema's alliance with certain beneficiaries of the BEE programme who had suffered significant financial losses in the aftermath of the 2007/8 global crisis, and were thus in need of a state bailout.[81] COSATU established a commission to discuss the prospect of strategic nationalization, but the policy conclusions reached by the committee were suppressed by the ANC.[82]

Nonetheless, the debate on nationalization continued until 2012, accompanied by significant protests led by Malema in Johannesburg, at which point the ANC officially vetoed the proposed policy at the leadership conference in December of 2012—a conference which Malema had been barred from attending—a move which signalled a defeat for left-wing factions within the party and the ANCYL and a victory for the pro-business faction supporting Zuma.[83] The leadership conference also witnessed Zuma's re-election as head of the ANC with 2,983 votes to 991, despite allegations of corruption and protest sparked by Marikana, which did not sway his populist base within the rank and file of the party.[84] In order to appease popular forces, senior party officials also announced that the ANC would consider levying a new tax on the mining industry and the possible formation of a strategic state-owned mining company, though they did not provide detailed commentary on such matters or concrete policy proposals.[85] Although Malema and the ANCL had helped select Zuma at the 2007 leadership conference, his expulsion from the League in March of 2012 was justified on the grounds that he was "sowing divisions and bringing the party into disrepute."[86] The expulsion was ahead of the leadership conference where Malema was expected to mount a challenge against Zuma, and in fact, he had previously stated that Zuma was similar to his predecessor Mbeki for refusing to deviate from the current growth path.[87] The ANC's excommunication of Malema thus neutralized an internal threat that could have potentially derailed Zuma's re-election bid at the 2012 conference.

It was in this context that Malema chose to form a new political party with an electoral platform that incorporated the ANCYL's previous demands for radical redistribution through nationalization. Having failed to transform socioeconomic policy from within the party, Malema sought to challenge the ANC's hegemony from outside. The EFF's Founding Manifesto lays out the party's plan for a future South Africa while also sharply critiquing the ANC's legacy:

> The 20 years of political freedom have not borne much significance to the people of South Africa. This is despite the fact that 20 years should, among other things, entail the intensification of South Africa's political will and its determination to unite the people of South Africa...[88]

The EFF's appeal was initially limited to the Platinum Mining Belt and Malema's home province of Limpopo. Malema was involved with the striking miners in this region both before and after the Marikana massacre; in fact, Malema and his communications officer were the first political and public figures to arrive at the scene after the killings, were embraced by the families of the killed miners as their only political representatives, and soon began to employ the memory of the massacre as a means of highlighting everything corrupt and morally degenerate about the ANC.[89]

The party managed to secure 6.4% of the national vote in the 2014 elections, with twenty-five MPs at the national level and thirty elected to provincial legislatures, a rather impressive feat for a party that was formed not too long before the election and had very limited financial resources.[90] This modest success could be attributed to several factors, which highlight the limited, though gradually increasing, discontent with the ANC among the population and former party officials. Firstly, in the provincial elections, the EFF exclusively ran former ANC party officials as their candidates, including Dali Mpofu, who had a long association with the ANC and had served on the Farlam Commission investigating Marikana on behalf of the miners.[91] Secondly, unlike previous "radical" parties, the EFF was able to incorporate other left-wing movements into its support structure and thus avoid competition while also buttressing its own image. The Socialist Party of Azania as well as the Black Consciousness Party officially joined the EFF and ran candidates during the election.[92] Moreover, the National Congress of Trade Unions, a union federation separate from COSATU, officially endorsed the EFF a month before the election, thereby bolstering the party's credentials as a viable left-wing alternative to the ANC.[93] It is also important to note that, contrary to claims made by certain ANC officials and pundits that the EFF's support base was made up entirely of marginalized, unemployed youth, pre-election surveys found that the party's supporters consisted largely of males between the ages of 25 and 49, and that the majority of such supporters held a post-secondary education.[94]

The ANC has also consistently lost electoral ground to the Democratic Alliance (DA) party. The DA was essentially formed as a party for racial minorities and white capitalists in a democratic South Africa; however, it was not until the National Party disbanded, and the latter's support base embraced the DA, that the party was able to secure the majority of white and non-black votes in multiple elections.[95] In recent years, the DA has also sought to recruit black members into its ranks and won the provincial election in the Western Cape. The party also espouses a very different ideology from the ANC, arguing that the latter has fostered a culture of dependency through social grants and state intervention, and that the solution to the country's poverty and unemployment problem is to deepen market structures and enable citizens to support themselves by promoting free enterprise.[96] As a DA member of parliament stated, "The ANC has made it their business to foster dependency on the state and they will always play that card—stating that their opponents won't give you that."[97] This party official also predicted that the DA had a good chance of winning at the national level in the next several years, suggesting that the glow and legacy of the liberation movement would eventually subside.[98] However, the 2019 nation wide elections ended with the ANC securing another majority, although both the DA and the EFF again gained ground in terms of the national popular vote. Whether ANC dominance continues into the future will depend to a large extent on the nature of the political coalitions that emerge to substantively challenge neoliberal orthodoxy in the future. A brief examination of the events leading to the removal of former President Mbeki could lend some insight into this matter.

3.4   ZUMA'S INITIAL ASCENSION TO POWER AND THE LEFT-WING POLITICAL COALITION

Zuma's victory at the 2007 leadership conference can only be understood in the context of the opposition among the alliance members that had built up against Mbeki since the transition. Mbeki was one of the architects and supporters of the GEAR macroeconomic programme which, as noted, had been formulated without consulting the alliance members and had been initially denounced by leading officials within COSATU and the SACP. Since 2002, there was a growing perception among the more left-leaning elements within COSATU that Mbeki was attempting to formulate a strategy designed to isolate the democratic elements within the ANC alliance and prevent them from informing the policymaking process. Particularly vocal in this area was the former Secretary General of COSATU, Zwelinzima Vavi, who authored a report detailing the history of the elite transition and the manner in which the isolation of democratic forces was accomplished. The crystallization of support behind Zuma was thus the expression of COSATU's opposition to Mbeki and the latter administration's ongoing support for the neoliberal growth model.[99]

Zuma, as the deputy president under Mbeki, had the task of representing the ANC at meetings with COSATU and SACP delegates, and several leading officials within both organizations began to view him as a potential ally of the left.[100] In 2005, the courts determined that Zuma had engaged in corrupt business practices by accepting a pension from a company, Thomson-CSF, in exchange for government contracts. In response to the finding, Mbeki removed him from his post as deputy president, a decision which angered both COSATU and the ANCYL, who viewed the action as an attempt to marginalize a left-leaning member of the ANC cabinet.[101] A political coalition thus began forming among the ANC's left allies and Zuma, which culminated in Mbeki's removal as the leader of the ANC at the 2007 conference when delegates overwhelmingly cast their vote for Zuma. This crystallization of a left-wing political coalition that formed behind Zuma consisting of COSATU, the SACP, and the ANCYL was partially a reflection of the internal machinery within the ANC. The party maintains a ban on internal factionalism, which makes it quite difficult for delegates to campaign in favour of a candidate prior to the leadership conference. As a result, only organizations such as COSATU, the SACP, and the ANC Youth League could serve as independent caucuses where a challenge could be mounted against a party incumbent well in advance of the leadership conference.[102]

These organizations, as well as COSATU's Secretary General at the time, Zwelinzima Vavi, who was a strong critic of GEAR and the neoliberal growth path, saw in Zuma a potential ally who could potentially challenge certain aspects of market orthodoxy. In fact, Vavi's radical stance pitted him against other establishment figures within COSATU. Thus, it was not surprising that, amid allegations of sexual misconduct levelled against Vavi by an acquaintance, the Central Executive Committee moved to suspend Vavi from the federation, though this decision was eventually overturned in court.[103] A public feud had also broken out between Vavi and Mbeki over the role of the state in stimulating employment, with the former stating that the government should adopt a far more interventionist role. Mbeki responded by informing Vavi that COSATU was not the government or in charge of policymaking. This was followed by a massive strike on June 27, which encouraged Vavi's militancy.[104]

It is also undeniable that Zuma's ascendance to Mbeki's position followed a massive grass-roots campaign against specific elements of the neoliberal trajectory as well as general civil society resistance against the ANC's adherence to market orthodoxy. A 2006 survey of 2,500 inhabitants in a Soweto township, for example, found that there was a strong correlation between material deprivation and support for Zuma in the township, even among inhabitants who were not members or general supporters of the ANC.[105] Moreover, Mbeki had generated massive discontent among the unemployed and impoverished citizens with his adherence to market measures; in fact, in 2005, there were over 881 incidents of unrest involving protests triggered by service and delivery charges as well as the high rates of poverty in the country, and some of the uprisings turned violent.[106]

Despite the array of left-wing actors that initially rallied around Zuma, as is now known, his ascension to power did not lead to a significant deviation from the neoliberal growth path. Firstly, the pact made between the alliance partners and Zuma generated a greater distribution of cabinet seats for the SACP and COSATU.[107] Yet, given the corporatist structures previously discussed, this did not substantively generate a greater degree of autonomy over economic policymaking for these organizations. Secondly, while Zuma's election in 2009 was accompanied by a cabinet reshuffle, as well as the exit of several government officials, a number of state bureaucrats who held tenure under Mbeki were nonetheless retained for strategic purposes. For example, Trevor Manuel, another architect of the GEAR policies, was convinced by Kgalema Motlanthe, who had temporarily taken Mbeki's place as president before the 2009 general elections, to remain in his post as Finance Minister in order to assuage the concerns of international investors and the business community.[108] Additionally, in an address to SACP officials during a policy meeting, Zuma signalled a certain degree of continuity with Mbeki's economic programme by highlighting the necessity of creating viable work opportunities and combating crime.[109] Clearly, Mbeki's defeat was not followed by a radical transformation within the ANC. It should also be noted that Mbeki's concentration of executive power laid the basis for specific aspects of political corruption that later transpired under Zuma, namely the episode of "state capture" that has largely come to define his governance. This issue will be examined in greater detail in the final chapter.

It should be noted that had NUMSA entered the national elections it would have been quite possible that, in conjunction with the EFF and the DA, the ANC might have been deprived of a majority for the first time since the democratic transition, forcing the party to form a coalitional alliance in parliament. In 2016, however, Irvin Jim declared that NUMSA would remain a labour union and thus would not transform itself into a socialist party. Instead, he stated that "all our shop stewards and officials should maintain an activist role" and that they would "work with Marxist forces everywhere, including those who are traditional ANC allies."[110] This decision signified the removal of a potential electoral challenge to the ruling party. Despite rhetoric, it is clear that COSATU and the SACP are more interested in employing the threat of protests and strikes to check the excesses of neoliberalism from within the tripartite alliance as opposed to mobilizing South Africans to transform the existing accumulation regime. Moreover, Cyril Ramaphosa, despite his credentials as a labour leader, is firmly integrated into the neoliberal regime and the circuits of MEC capital.

Overall, while the resistance to the neoliberal growth path in South Africa over the past twenty years has not yet succeeded in altering the current developmental trajectory of the governing party, there is no doubt that grass-roots resistance, labour unrest, and spontaneous protests and strikes have slowly begun to chip away at the ANC's post-transition popularity. However, while their share of the national vote has slowly declined in recent years, opposition parties have thus far been unable to force a coalition government in parliament. Nonetheless, growing voter dissatisfaction and unrest in civil society could very possibly force the ANC to substantively alter the neoliberal model, despite the present stability of the tripartite alliance and the social welfare payments to the rural and urban impoverished. In fact, there is precedent to suggest that when societal pressure and the perception of public opinion are strong enough on a particular issue, then popular preferences are reflected in government decision-making. One such episode involved the attempts by the

International Monetary Fund (IMF) and the World Bank to exert decisive influence over macroeconomic policymaking in a democratic South Africa. This topic will be explored carefully in the next chapter.

Notes

1. Edward Webster, "The Promise and the Possibility: South Africa's Contested Industrial Relations Path," *Transformation: Critical Perspectives on Southern Africa* 81 (2013), p. 212.
2. Adam Habib, "From Pluralism to Corporatism: South Africa's Labour Relations in Transition," *Politikon* 24, 1 (1997), p. 58.
3. Ibid.
4. Sakhela Buhlungu, *A Paradox of Victory: COSATU and the Democratic Transformation in South Africa* (University of KwaZulu-Natal Press, Durban, 2010), pp. 69–71.
5. Lambert and Webster, cited in Adam Habib and Ashwin Desai, "COSATU and the Democratic Transition in South Africa: Drifting Towards Corporatism?" *Comparative Studies of South Asia, Africa and the Middle East* 15, 1 (1995), p. 29.
6. Adam Habib and Ashwin Desai, "COSATU and the Democratic Transition in South Africa," p. 30.
7. Adam Habib, "From Pluralism to Corporatism," p. 71.
8. Stepan, cited in Adam Habib, "From Pluralism to Corporatism," p. 72.
9. Jay Naidoo, cited in Gregory Gall, "Trade Unions and the ANC in the New South Africa," *Review of African Political Economy* 72 (1997), p. 204.
10. Ibid., p. 208.
11. Adam Habib, "From Pluralism to Corporatism," p. 72.
12. Franco Barchiesi, "Labour, Neoliberalism and Democratic Politics in Nigeria and South Africa: A Comparative Overview," *Labour, Capital, and Society* 30, 2 (1997), p. 200.
13. Edward Webster, "The Promise and the Possibility: South Africa's Contested Industrial Relations Path," p. 215.
14. Government of South Africa, "Nedlac: Founding Documents and Protocols" (Nedlac, Johannesburg), p. 7. https://new.nedlac.org.za/wp-content/uploads/2015/09/Founding-documents-and-protocols-20151.pdf.
15. Nicoli Natrass, "Politics and Economics in ANC Economic Policy," *African Affairs* 93 (1994), p. 351.
16. Raymond Parsons, "The Emergence of Institutionalized Social Dialogue in South Africa," *South African Journal of Economics* 75, 1 (2007), p. 7.
17. Edward Webster, "The Promise and the Possibility: South Africa's Contested Industrial Relations Path," p. 213.

18. Nicoli Natrass, "Politics and Economics in ANC Economic Policy," p. 351, n. 57.
19. Raymond Parsons, "The Emergence of Institutionalized Social Dialogue in South Africa," p. 13.
20. Adam Habib and Ashwin Desai, "COSATU and the Democratic Transition in South Africa," p. 34.
21. Ann Bernstein, "South Africa's Key Challenges: Tough Choices and New Directions," *The Annals of the American Academy of Political and Social Science* 652 (2014), p. 30.
22. Edward Webster and Dinga Sikwebu, "Tripartism and Economic Reforms in South Africa and Zimbabwe," in L. Fraile (ed.), *Blunting Neoliberalism* (Palgrave MacMillan, London, 2010), p. 194.
23. "COSATU Position Paper on Privatization" (Nedlac, July 30, 2001).
24. "South Africa: Action Will Follow Deadlock at Nedlac on Privatization Issue," *All-Africa*, August 2, 2001.
25. Weizmann Hamilton, "South Africa's Anti-privatization Strike," *Socialism Today*, October 2001. https://www.socialismtoday.org/60/south_africa.html.
26. Nixon Kariithi and Peter Kareithi, "A Critical Discourse Analysis of Media Coverage of the Anti-privatization Strike in South Africa in October 2002," *Journalism Studies* 8, 3 (2007), p. 477.
27. Edward Webster and Dinga Sikwebu, "Tripartism and Economic Reforms in South Africa and Zimbabwe," p. 194.
28. Nixon Kariithi and Peter Kareithi, "A Critical Discourse Analysis of Media Coverage of the Anti-privatization Strike in South Africa in October 2002," p. 478.
29. R. Rumney, "Who Owns South Africa: An Analysis of State and Private Ownership Patterns," in Daniel et al. (eds.), *State of the Nation: South Africa 2004–5* (Human Sciences Research Council, Cape Town), p. 406.
30. Anne Pitcher, "Was Privatization Necessary and Did It Work? The Case of South Africa," *Review of African Political Economy* 39, 132 (2012), pp. 243–260.
31. P.D. Thomas, "The South African Communist Party (SACP) in the Post-apartheid Period," *Review of African Political Economy* 34, 111 (2007), p. 123.
32. "Going to the Root," *African Communist* 4, 187 (2014), p. 5.
33. Personal Interview, National Spokesperson, SACP (Johannesburg, December 28, 2016).
34. Personal Interview, Former Senior Official, DTI and SACP (Cape Town, January 10, 2017).
35. Personal Interview, National Spokesperson, SACP (December 28, 2016).
36. Adam Habib and Ashwin Desai, "COSATU and the Democratic Transition in South Africa," p. 34.

37. Pauline Dibben, Geoffrey Wood, and Kamel Mellahi, "Is Social Movement Unionism Still Relevant? The Case of the South African Federation COSATU," *Industrial Relations Journal* 43, 6 (2012), pp. 494–510.
38. Mark Harcourt and Geoffrey Wood, "Is There a Future for a Labour Accord in South Africa?" *Capital & Class* 79 (2003), p. 85.
39. Carin Runciman, "The Decline of the Anti-Privatization Forum in the Midst of South Africa's Rebellion of the Poor," *Current Sociology* 63, 7 (2015), p. 968.
40. "Business Unionism' Destroying Union Movement," *Business Report*, July 16, 2016.
41. Matuma Letsoalo, "Business Unionism the Cause of Cosatu's Factional Battles," *Mail & Guardian*, July 10, 2015.
42. Geoffrey E. Schneider, "Neoliberalism and Economic Justice in South Africa: Revisiting the Debate on Economic Apartheid," *Review of Social Economy* 61, 1 (2003), p. 43.
43. *Mail & Guardian*, July 10, 2017.
44. Stefan Andreasson, "The African National Congress and Its Critics: Predatory Liberalism, Black Empowerment and Intra-Alliance Tensions in Post-apartheid South Africa," *Democratization* 3, 2 (2006), p. 310.
45. Rajendra Chetty, "The Marikana Massacre: Insurgency and Counter-Insurgency in South Africa," *New Labor Forum* 25, 2 (2016), p. 63.
46. Mia Swart, "Politics Gone Cancerous: Why the Marikana Massacre should be Prosecuted as an International Crime," *Social Dynamics* 41, 2 (2015), p. 347.
47. Vishwas Satgar, "Beyond Marikana: The Post-apartheid South African State," *Africa Spectrum* 47, 3 (2012), p. 34.
48. Ibid.
49. Ibid.
50. Nick Davies, "Marikana Massacre: The Untold Story of the Strike Leader Who Died for Worker Rights," *The Guardian*, May 19, 2015. https://www.theguardian.com/world/2015/may/19/marikana-massacre-untold-story-strike-leader-died-workers-rights.
51. Ibid.
52. Rajendra Chetty, "The Marikana Massacre: Insurgency and Counter-Insurgency in South Africa," p. 64.
53. Ibid.
54. Ross Graeme Harvey, "Why Is Labour Strife So Persistent in South Africa's Mining Industry?" *The Extractive Industries and Society* 3, 3 (2016), pp. 3–4.
55. Ibid., p. 4.
56. Ibid., p. 65.
57. Crispen Chinguno, "Marikana: Fragmentation, Precariousness, Strike Violence and Solidarity," *Review of African Political Economy* 40, 138 (2013), p. 641.

58. Luke Sinwell, "AMCU by Day, Worker's Committee by Night: Insurgent Trade Unionism at Anglo Platinum Mine, 2012–2014," *Review of African Political Economy* 42, 146 (2015), p. 594.
59. Ibid., p. 599.
60. Leonard Gentle, "What About the Workers? The Demise of COSATU and the Emergence of a New Movement," *Review of African Political Economy* 42, 146 (2015), p. 667.
61. Ibid.
62. Ibid., p. 669.
63. Devan Pillay, "Worker's Control, Marxist-Leninism, and the Revitalization of Working Class Politics in South Africa," *Capital and Society* 45, 2 (2012), p. 6.
64. "Workers of South Africa Disunite! A Split in the Main Union Federation Presages a Realignment," *The Economist*, November 14, 2015. https://www.economist.com/news/middle-east-and-africa/216 32639-split-main-union-federation-presages-realignment-workers-south.
65. Ibid.
66. Cited in Patrick Craven, *The Battle for COSATU: An Insider's View* (Bookstorm, Johannesburg, 2015), Chapter 14.
67. Ibid.
68. Ibid., Chapter 15.
69. Ibid.
70. Ibid., Chapter 18.
71. "Irvin Jim Lays Xenophobia at ANC's Door," *Mail & Guardian*, April 23, 2015. https://mg.co.za/article/2015-04-23-irvin-jim-lays-xenoph obia-at-ancs-door.
72. Irvin Jim, "Global Capitalism is in Terminal Crisis—And the Alliance Is in Irreversible Decline," *Daily Maverick*, September 15, 2016. https://www.dailymaverick.co.za/opinionista/2016-09-15-global-capitalism-is-in-terminal-crisis-and-the-alliance-is-in-irreversible-decline/#.WSYTG4 WcHIU.
73. Personal Interview, National Spokesperson, SACP (Johannesburg, December 28, 2016).
74. Deborah Posel, "The ANC Youth League and the Politicization of Race," *Thesis Eleven* 115, 1 (2013), p. 64.
75. Ibid., p. 65.
76. ANCYL, "Towards the Transfer of Mineral Wealth to the Ownership of the People as a Whole: A Perspective on Nationalization of Mines," August 2010. https://www.ancyl.org.za/show.php?id=5502.
77. Robb M. Stewart, "South Africa to Study State Role in Mines," *The Wall Street Journal*, September 24, 2010.
78. Ibid.

79. Devon Maylie, "South Africa Considers Nationalization," *The Wall Street Journal*, July 2011.
80. Ibid.
81. Personal interview, Former Advisor to the Minister of Economic Development (EDD), and Strategies Coordinator at COSATU (June 22, 2017).
82. Ibid.
83. Geoffrey York, "South Africa's ANC Vetoes Plan to Nationalize Mining," *The Globe & Mail*, December 20, 2012. https://www.theglobeandmail.com/report-on-business/international-business/african-and-mideast-business/south-africas-anc-vetoes-plan-to-nationalize-mining/article6611394/.
84. *The Guardian*, "South Africa: Jacob Zuma Sweeps to Victory in ANC Leadership Election," December 18, 2012. https://www.theguardian.com/world/2012/dec/18/jacob-zuma-south-africa-anc.
85. Ibid.
86. *The Guardian*, "ANC Expels Head of Youth League," March 1, 2012. https://www.theguardian.com/world/2012/mar/01/anc-african-national-congress-southafrica.
87. Ibid.
88. Economic Freedom Fighters, "Founding Manifesto: Radical Movement Towards Economic Freedom in Our Lifetime" (EFF National Assembly, July 27, 2013).
89. J. Robinson, "The Economic Freedom Fighters: Birth of a Giant," in Roger Southall and C. Shultz (eds.), *Election 2014 South Africa: The Campaigns, Results, and Future Prospects* (Jacana Media, Johannesburg, 2015), p. 74.
90. Roger Southall, "The South African Election of 2014: Retrospect and Prospect," *Strategic Review for Southern Africa* 36, 2 (2014), p. 90.
91. J. Robinson, "The Economic Freedom Fighters: Birth of a Giant," pp. 76–77.
92. Ibid., p. 76.
93. Ibid.
94. Ibid., p. 83.
95. Roger Southall, "The South African Election of 2014: Retrospect and Prospect," p. 84.
96. Ibid., pp. 86–87.
97. Personal Interview, Stevens M. Shadow Minister for Human Settlements (Cape Town, September 30, 2013).
98. Ibid.
99. Personal interview, Former Advisor to the Minister of Economic Development (EDD), and Strategies Coordinator at COSATU (June 22, 2017).

100. Tom Lodge, "The Zuma Tsunami: South Africa's Succession Politics," *Representation* 45, 2 (2009), p. 127.
101. Ibid., p. 128.
102. Ibid., p. 132.
103. Patrick Craven, *The Battle for COSATU: An Insider's View*, Chapter 11.
104. Claire Ceruti, "African National Congress Change in Leadership: What Really Won It for Zuma?" *Review of African Political Economy* 35, 115 (2008), p. 111.
105. Ibid., p. 108.
106. Ibid., p. 110.
107. Leonard Gentle, "What About the Workers? The Demise of COSATU and the Emergence of a New Movement," p. 668.
108. Tom Lodge, "The Zuma Tsunami: South Africa's Succession Politics," p. 139.
109. Ibid., p. 140.
110. Emsie Ferreira, "Numsa Commits to Independent Labor Federation, Socialist Party," *IOL News*, December 15, 2016. The news story further pointed out that while Irvin Jim pledged that Numsa would not transform itself into a political party, he did nonetheless urge officials to help form a separate Marxist socialist party for the future.

CHAPTER 4

Early Forms of State Resistance to Neoliberalism: The International Monetary Fund in South Africa

This chapter breaks down the international financial institutions' (IFI) early interactions with the ANC in the immediate aftermath of the democratic transition, focusing specifically on the International Monetary Fund (IMF). It will be argued that the ability of the Fund to influence South Africa's policy trajectory has been quite negligible, and that ANC officials preferred to adopt a "home-grown" structural adjustment programme during the early years of the transition in order to induce private capital inflows and avoid long-term dependency on IMF lending. Moreover, it will be shown that while ongoing policy dialogue between officials in the Treasury, the Reserve Bank, and the Fund during Article IV consultations may have bolstered certain aspects of market orthodoxy during the post-apartheid period, the main channels of influence shaping the policy trajectory in South Africa remain the global capital markets and the business sector's financialized accumulation regime. Indeed, if Fund officials did have any success in influencing the trajectory of economic policy-making in post-apartheid South Africa, it was not due to any leverage they held as a result of an external debt or even due to superior technocratic expertise. As was discussed in Chapter 1, the ANC chose to reject the MERG and accept a version of market orthodoxy based on the pro-liberalization position held by the National Party, as well as the internalization of neoliberal arguments by party officials within the

S. Ansari, *Neoliberalism and Resistance in South Africa*, Contemporary African Political Economy, https://doi.org/10.1007/978-3-030-69766-2_4

Department of Economic Planning (DEP). In this context, the Fund and World Bank may have bolstered pre-existing policy positions; yet, as will be shown, even under these circumstances these multilateral organizations faced stiff resistance from party leaders in the domain of policymaking. The chapter will begin by briefly reviewing the literature on the key arguments concerning debt negotiations between the IMF and sovereign governments, as well as the imposition of conditionality. The second portion will then examine the history of the IFI's involvement in South Africa's economic policymaking and how the Fund's influence has evolved since the transition from apartheid to liberal democracy. A key take-away of this chapter is that the ANC does possess sufficient autonomy to resist globalizing forces when necessary, especially in the context of sufficient political pressure. Additionally, the chapter highlights the fact that, contrary to popular conventional wisdom, the IMF and the World Bank often lack sufficient power or leverage to facilitate economic policy shifts in emerging market economies where resistance and state autonomy are moderately strong, as evidenced by the post-apartheid case study.

4.1   The Policy of the International Financial Institutions in South Africa During Apartheid

The imposition of conditionality on sovereign governments, and the implementation of stabilization measures and structural adjustment policies in emerging market economies, has been the subject of significant debate and controversy among scholars and analysts of the IMF. A number of authors, for example, have argued that the Fund's central purpose in the developing world is to impose, with the help of domestic elites, macroeconomic policies that negatively impact growth, redistribute income to the upper classes, and primarily benefit Western capitalist nations.[1] Additionally, certain scholars have sought to demonstrate that Fund decision-making is primarily a reflection of the organizations' dominant shareholders, as opposed to the technocrats in the bureaucracy who conduct the negotiations and formulate the letters of intent.[2] Important scholarship has also documented how targeted dialogue between Fund technocrats and state officials in Central Banks and National Treasuries can facilitate policy shifts in member countries by facilitating the empowerment of specific policy networks.[3] For instance, it has been argued that the debt crisis of the 1980s led to the creation of tightly knit transnational policy networks between multilateral organizations. The establishment of such policy networks is said to have enabled the multilaterals to influence policymaking by engaging relevant state officials in dialogue, even in countries where such organizations had little to no leverage, such as Chile.[4]

This shift in strategy by the IFIs, employing dialogue as opposed to conditionality, is partially attributable to the alternative commercial sources of finance that developing countries have been able to draw on since at least the early 1990s, especially as capital markets have become increasingly integrated on a global scale. Moreover, as noted in Chapter 2, emerging market economies have begun accumulating large amounts of foreign exchange reserves in order to defend and stabilize their currencies in the event of significant capital outflows. In this sense, developing countries are able to safeguard their policymaking autonomy even in the context of financial crises and mild recessions. As a result of this development, it is not surprising that the IFIs have increasingly resorted to policy dialogue in their dealings with member states, specifically in the form of technical advice to domestic authorities. Regarding South Africa, several authors have argued that the IFIs played a decisive role in influencing top ANC officials in the area of economic policymaking in the years leading up to the democratic transition.[5] Patrick Bond, for example, has argued that a number of brainstorming events and corporate scenarios were aimed at cementing a social contract between the ANC, the National Party, and the IFIs in order to secure the transition to conventional supply side economics in the post-apartheid setting. Bond further argued that, in conjunction with elite policy planning scenarios and exercises, the World Bank succeeded, through economic policy publications and their general diffusion of developmental knowledge to key policymakers such as Finance Minister Trevor Manuel, in fostering the belief that there was no real alternative to neoliberalism given the realities of economic globalization.[6] Moreover, Bond points to an $850-million-dollar loan that was issued by the IMF to the Transitional Executive Committee (made up of members of the National Party and the ANC prior to the official democratic transition) in December of 1993 for the purpose of drought relief. The loan came with certain specific conditions, as detailed in *Business Day,* which included tariff reduction and cut backs in public expenditure.[7]

However, while some analysts have argued that this loan from the Fund placed certain policy constraints on the incoming ANC government, a few points must be noted. Firstly, as was discussed in the introduction, ANC officials were also engaged in informal discussions with the business community, and it was the latter that played a crucial role in facilitating a shift away from heterodox, redistributive policies. Secondly, as noted in Chapter 2, there is evidence that during this period several ANC leaders were far more concerned with whether the incoming government would be able to access the global capital markets on favourable terms, and thus faced far greater constraints from the latter than from the IFIs. Perhaps most importantly, regarding the 1993 850-million-dollar loan to the ANC, the resources disbursed to the government by the Fund were not predicated on a binding agreement linked to conventional conditionality. In fact, based on an evaluation of little known data and official reports from both the National Treasury and the IMF, Vishnu Paday-achee and Ben Fine have shown that this early loan did not have any substantive impact on the economic policy trajectory within the ANC in the immediate aftermath of the transition.[8] It was noted by the authors that the loan, which was accompanied by the Fund's Letter of Intent outlining a slew of recommended policies from inflation targeting to trade and exchange control liberalization, represented only 45 per cent of South Africa's own borrowing reserves at the Fund at a time when the country owed no debt to the organization.[9] Additionally, the Fund's Article IV mission in 1993 indicated that the Letter of Intent was being prepared at a time when the National Party was still in power, casting serious doubt on the notion that the ANC "sold-out" in exchange for hard currency.[10] Thus, if the IMF had any leverage to influence ANC policymaking, it would have to be found through a mechanism other than through official conditionality. Briefly delving into the Fund's history in the country will help flesh out this issue.

During the apartheid era South Africa enjoyed a privileged relationship with the IMF, largely because of the strategic position the country occupied in the region for the United States and other Western powers during the Cold War. The first loan was granted by the Fund to South Africa in 1957/58, and was offered without any imposed conditionality. This was done despite the fact that during this period the IMF was not in the habit of disbursing funds to developing nations without demanding the implementation of specific macroeconomic policies, as evidenced by its relationship with Latin American countries.[11] An IMF delegation had advised the South African authorities to implement capital controls in the aftermath of the Sharpeville massacre in order to stem the outflow of capital triggered by investor panic. The Fund disbursed several other loans to South Africa in the 1970s as well. In 1982, the IMF approved 1.07 billion dollars in funds to the apartheid government despite a UN

General Assembly resolution calling for the termination of additional credits to Pretoria. American and European voting power in the IMF was crucial in enabling South Africa to secure the 1982 loan, and the funds permitted the authorities to cover the country's deepening balance of payments deficit, caused largely by declining gold prices, as well as navigate the economic recession.[12] The strategic role played by the apartheid government during the Cold War, and the privileged relationship the state enjoyed with the IMF throughout this period, was an important variable in determining the degree of influence that the multilateral organizations could exercise in shaping domestic economic policy within the country. To begin with, in the absence of a large sovereign external debt the multilaterals could not employ conditionality as a mechanism to bolster policy dialogue with domestic authorities.[13] In other words, a small external debt set South Africa apart from other borrower countries, such as India or those in Latin America, where the Fund and the Bank often employed the "hard sell" tactic of conditionality in conjunction with targeted dialogue as a means of bolstering the organization's influence over domestic macroeconomic policy decisions.[14] Additionally, South Africa's role as a strategic asset to the United States during the Cold War meant that the apartheid government could pursue a number of highly nationalist and protectionist economic policies even while drawing on IMF resources when necessary.

Furthermore, South Africa's relatively small sovereign external debt meant that the ANC government was accorded a significant level of policy autonomy during and immediately after the democratic transition. As noted, South Africa's position was, in this sense, rather unique among emerging market economies despite the fact that private external finance had always been an important component for the functioning of the economy, especially due to the absence of a domestic capital goods industry. For instance, the apartheid government was forced to declare a debt moratorium in 1985 because $14 billion in short-term liabilities could no longer be serviced as a result of the refusal of private creditors to issue new loans. It is noteworthy that the debt was held entirely by domestic banks which had borrowed on the short-term international money markets in order to lend to the private sector.[15] Even during this period, South Africa's strategic importance to the international economy was evidenced by the fact that a consortium of international bankers was willing to reschedule debt payments on short-term interbank credits. Not only was this decision extremely rare, but the international creditors did not even consider freezing the assets that South Africa held abroad in these banks in response to the moratorium, despite the fact that such asset freezes would have repaid the debt.[16] The nature of South Africa's private debt during this period was connected to the stigmatization of the apartheid regime and the pressure foreign governments and banks faced in terms of their lending practices to the country. Since transactions on the interbank market are not published it provided the perfect disguise for Western banks seeking to lend to the apartheid government; however, the short-term nature of this debt also rendered it highly unstable. This also explains why, in comparison with other emerging market economies, there was relatively little reliance on medium- or long-term financing from the multilateral organizations during this period.[17]

In light of this history between the multilateral organizations and South Africa, it is reasonable to ask whether targeted dialogue and policy networks between the IFIs and South African authorities have served as one of the variables in the persistence of market orthodoxy during the post-apartheid period. This question is especially crucial since, as noted in the introduction, neoliberal orthodoxy failed to meet its policy objectives in several vital areas. Thus, the continued implementation of such orthodox policies over several ANC administrations by various Finance Ministers and Reserve Bank governors requires an explanation, especially if the influence of external actors is largely responsible for such persistence. Earlier chapters have argued that the global capital markets and the business community have been crucial actors driving the reproduction of the neoliberal growth model. However, an alternative possible explanation is that such policies and ideas have been reproduced over time by the bureaucratic and technocratic officials within the Treasury in order to win political favour with early finance ministers such as Trevor Manuel, who was an early proponent of fiscal restraint because of decisive influence from multilateral organizations. It has indeed been posited that the continuity of specific policies flows from the transmission, and then eventual ownership, of such ideas by national governments. According to this argument, the intervening variable between technical advice and the economic policy shift, which conditions the development of the internalization of neoliberalism over the long-run, is internal coalition formation. In other words, "Building a domestic consensus in favour of neoliberal strategies of growth is a far more complex process of consolidating political support for those policies than the one-way imposition of ideas."[18] Put differently, the dissemination of a specific economic ideology emanating from external actors, such as the Fund, is eventually internalized by political elites and state bureaucrats. However, this type of analysis does not adequately explain how external actors, specifically the multilateral organizations, have been able to decisively influence a cluster of bureaucratic policymakers over successive administrations in a manner that would allow market orthodoxy to be reproduced in a systemic fashion in South Africa. In fact, the legacy of the liberation movement, and the ideologies it was steeped in, generated stiff resistance by top ANC officials to early Fund influence. The next section will proceed to flesh out this argument through an examination of the Fund's evolving role and tactics in the country in the twenty-five years following the transition.

4.2 THE IMF: EVOLUTION
AND INVOLVEMENT IN SOUTH AFRICA

The 1980s, when international banks decided to stop rolling over the debts of a number of emerging market economies, marked a significant turning point in the evolution of the Fund's role in managing financial and economic crises.[19] Throughout the 1970s, major banks had recycled OPEC surpluses into sovereign debt in certain developing countries where there was a higher risk-adjusted rate of return. The debt crisis, triggered by higher spreads, raised the possibility of a devaluation or default, and hence led to IMF involvement in large Latin American debtor countries. It is noteworthy that several years after the Fund's intervention private banks in South Africa also defaulted on their external debts. However, in the case of South Africa, the Fund could not facilitate a concerted lending project because international sanctions and public opinion precluded additional public funding, thus closing off one avenue of IMF involvement and the potential for future intervention. Nonetheless, as noted in further detail below, the Fund also began to evolve with regard to its policy of financial surveillance of member countries, and this development is relevant for post-apartheid policymaking in South Africa. Although the Fund has practised some form of surveillance as specified in its Articles of Agreement since 1978, the concept has evolved since that period to include a number of areas which historically have not fallen under the purview of the IMF. In the 1990s, the Fund expanded its activities from policy advice on matters related to macro-stabilization programmes to include structural issues, such as labour and product markets, and also began to devote attention to activities aimed at identifying the necessary economic conditions that tended to be present in the period preceding a financial crisis.[20] This expansive role was crucial in enabling the Fund to convince domestic government authorities to adopt certain policies regardless of whether or not the country was suffering from a balance of payments crisis and actually needed to draw on IMF resources.

James M. Boughton, a former historian of the IMF, served as the Assistant Director in the Strategy, Policy and Review Department from 1992 to 2012. His publications on the role of the IMF in emerging market economies, as well as the evolution of the Fund's outlook in response to global conditions, are an invaluable primary resource on IMF intervention in the developing and developed world, especially his monograph entitled *Tearing Down Walls: The International Monetary Fund 1990–1999*. The following pages draw heavily on this resource, especially when discussing the Fund's interaction with South African government officials in the early years of the transition. The primary purpose of financial surveillance since its inception has been to enhance the Fund's influence over the policies of member countries.[21] However, in the 1980s the Article IV consultations with member countries were generally not effective at identifying policy inconsistencies with IMF prescriptions because Article IV was initially drafted in a manner that rendered its main import quite vague. As Boughton points out, although current account and currency convertibility was uncontroversial within the Fund and for domestic policymakers in most emerging market economies, the issue of capital account liberalization was far less straightforward. In fact, among all the economic policies included within the Washington Consensus, capital account regulations were excluded and the Fund was willing to adopt far more flexibility in its official policy on trans-border capital flows at the time.[22]

The above noted evolution in the Fund's approach to macroeconomic policy and financial surveillance coincided with South Africa's transition from apartheid to liberal democracy. This development was significant because it clearly influenced the IMF's involvement in the sphere of policy dialogue, or "soft sell," with post-apartheid policymakers. Nonetheless, despite the shifts in the Fund's internal protocols and the evolution in IMF surveillance tactics, conditional lending has remained a crucial component of the Fund's overall strategy of policy influence in emerging market economies. At the time of the democratic transition, South Africa was suffering from a lack of capital inflows, high private sector debt, and low foreign exchange reserves. The Treasury and the Reserve Bank were interested in tapping external sources of finance; however, such sources were limited since creditor nations were unwilling to lend to the Transitional Executive Council (TEC) until after international sanctions were lifted and the transition was completed.[23] In the immediate aftermath of the formal shift to democracy, the IMF was perfectly positioned to exploit South Africa's recessionary economy and issue a conditional loan which, as previously noted, was in fact agreed to and disbursed in 1994 as a means of coping with temporary shocks such as the declining gold price and an agricultural drought.

However, it is noteworthy that even at this crucial stage of the transition, and despite the precarious position of the South African economy, Fund officials encountered a fair amount of resistance from the domestic authorities on the issue of conditionality, loans, and general policy formulation. For example, the policy advice offered by the Fund during this early stage of the democratic shift followed the standard prescriptions of fiscal austerity and monetarism, with the Executive Board concluding that "fiscal policy was constrained by the already large deficit, while monetary policy was constrained by the weakening exchange rate and the need to overcome investor's doubts about macroeconomic stability."[24] Boughton recounts that when the Government of National Unity (GNU) was formed after the 1994 elections, Fund Director Michael Camdessus sent the Deputy Managing Director, Alassane Ouattara, to Cape Town to meet with Mandela and discuss the possibility of further IMF assistance. During the visit, Ouattara discovered that the core leadership of the ANC was still highly critical of Fund practices, and a second visit by First Deputy Managing Director Stanley Fischer also failed to secure an agreement for future IMF lending.[25]

An especially telling episode, which illustrated the tension between the Fund and the new democratic government, occurred in 1996 in the midst of the currency crisis. When investors began to attack the rand amid rumours of Mandela's health and redistributive policies, Camdessus flew to Johannesburg and met with Mandela and Finance Minister Trevor Manuel. As the financial crisis deepened, official foreign exchange reserves declined to less than a few weeks' worth of imports, and Camdessus informed the domestic authorities that the Fund was ready to offer a multibillion-dollar arrangement provided that the government was willing to continue with, and accelerate, the economic policies outlined in the

GEAR document.[26] Mandela and Camdessus reached a tentative agreement on the terms for an IMF loan in October of 1996, which provided for a multibillion-dollar arrangement conditional upon a pledge by the ANC to persist with the liberalization reforms outlined in the GEAR document. However, later that same day the proposal was vetoed by senior party officials, and although negotiations between the Fund and the senior domestic political authorities persisted for several months, no agreement was ever reached and no additional IMF funds would be disbursed following the initial 1993 loan.[27]

This decision by the ANC, to jettison official IMF assistance at this early stage of the democratic transition, is significant for a number of reasons. First, it is noteworthy that during the negotiations between Camdessus, Mandela, and Trevor Manuel, the Fund made it clear that in exchange for the loans the Executive Board simply expected the South African authorities to continue with the implementation of the policies already outlined in the official ANC documents. Yet, despite the absence of official conditionality, senior party officials chose to reject the offer in order to avoid even the perception that external actors were guiding or shaping the domestic policy agenda. Thus, it is apparent that even though there was a substantial degree of interaction between the IFIs and the ANC prior to the transition, the senior party officials were unwilling to trade even a modicum of policy independence in exchange for an official loan, which calls into question the overall effectiveness of technocratic dialogue as a method of influencing policy in the South African context. Interviews with two former senior ANC officials during the period of the transition lend corroboration to the above point as well. Alec Erwin has stated that during this period the ANC was quite sensitive to the notion that the IFIs were, in some quarters, believed to function as agents of Western economic power, and that senior party officials had decided during this period, in the sprit of the liberation movement and public perception, that the Fund's "cure was worse than the disease."[28] Alan Hirsch also downplayed the possibility that the Fund might have played a significant role in facilitating a change in policy during this period. Specifically, it was asserted by Hirsch that the decision to liberalize the capital account could be attributed to the pressures emanating from the business community, and not the IFIs.[29]

One point that buttresses the above assertion has to do with the timing of capital account and trade liberalization, as well as the history of IFI involvement in South Africa. The Fund had previously sent its advisors to Pretoria in the late 1980s, during the period when the National Party had begun to experiment with certain neoliberal policies as a response to economic stagnation.[30] The Fund advised the government to adopt specific aspects of market orthodoxy such as high interest rates, a value-added tax (VAT), and privatization. However, despite these changes, capital controls and tariffs remained in place. As discussed in previous chapters, the ANC opened the capital account for non-residents and liberalized trade to facilitate private capital inflows and to permit the conglomerate corporations to expand beyond South Africa's borders. By refusing conditional aid at the early stage of the democratic shift, the ANC deprived the Fund of significant leverage that it could have exercised over the Treasury and the Reserve Bank at a later date. In fact, given the absence of official sovereign external debt in South Africa, owing largely to this initial decision by the South African authorities to eschew Fund financing, any influence over the Treasury and Reserve Bank by the IMF would have to be exercised solely through the shaping of dominant ideas via technical advice and other forms of consultation. Although unusual, this would certainly be compatible with the Fund's previously discussed evolution from a mere lender of last resort to an organization devoted to consensus building and long-term crisis management through enhanced forms of financial surveillance.

As noted, the Article IV consultations take place annually between the IMF's South African Bureau, key representatives within the country's government departments, and certain civil society representatives. A review of these documents could shed light on the extent to which the Fund's recommendations have been followed by South Africa's domestic political authorities, and whether there has been additional tension between government policymakers and the Fund staff. It will be shown that although there is little evidence that the IFIs played a decisive role in affecting economic policy during the transition, in recent years ongoing dialogue between the Fund and officials within the Treasury and Reserve Bank, as well as certain activities by the World Bank in conjunction with IFI reports, have nonetheless served to reinforce the economic worldview already prevalent within the Central Bank and Finance Ministry.

The IMF's 2014 Article IV report on South Africa provides some insight into the dealings between the Fund staff and the domestic authorities. The findings of this particular mission are significant because they highlight several structural economic problems South Africa was grappling with during a period of heightened public rhetoric of a developmental state, and offer a window into the Fund's relationship with state authorities and the organization's policy universe. The report notes the importance of the ANC's infrastructure expansion programme, as outlined in the New Development Plan (NDP), and again draws attention to the structural challenges constraining economic growth, such as bottlenecks in the energy sector, the 25 per cent unemployment rate, and declining productivity gains[31] However, the Fund's staff report also noted that the government was operating within a constrained fiscal space because of the rising public sector debt, and recommended that the total debt/GDP ratio be reduced to below 50 per cent by 2020. The Fund further advised that over the long-run a "tight fiscal stance" would have to be implemented in order to bring total public debt below 40 per cent of GDP.[32]

Moreover, the 2014 report lists the Fund's proposed policy responses, within its Risk Assessment Matrix (RMA), to potential events that could further jeopardize growth. Noteworthy here is the Fund's proposed response in dealing with financial market volatility and potential capital flow reversals: "Provide FX liquidity if dollar shortages appear; Increase policy rate to ensure adequate fiscal and external financing." In addition, it is stated that authorities "may also need to tighten fiscal policy further if financing becomes problematic." On the one hand, the Fund recognized that South Africa's stagnating growth is attributable to structural factors such as low skill development, sluggish public sector investment in crucial infrastructure, and the persistence of unemployment and poverty. However, the Fund's primary recommendation to South African authorities as a solution to the problem, namely increased infrastructural development and increased investments in education, is largely incompatible with the IMF's prescriptions pertaining to monetary and fiscal policy. For example, the recommendation of a targeted inflation monetary policy would increase the cost of capital and thus potentially thwart increases in private sector investment, which the Fund acknowledges is necessary to lower the unemployment rate. In addition, the call for debt stabilization and the reduction of government expenditure to below 40 per cent of GDP over the long-run is incompatible with the goal of increasing public investment in infrastructure and education, and the policy recommendation of bolstering foreign exchange reserves, as opposed to regulating the capital account, would clash with the aim of increased capital spending. The most interesting piece of information to be gleaned from the 2014

Article IV report, however, is that the Fund staff and the South African authorities were generally in agreement on the broad macroeconomic issues, though the report does mention that policymakers voiced some minor disagreement on certain issues, such as the strategy for debt sustainability. Yet on issues such as monetary policy and fiscal sustainability, the report illustrates that there is a shared economic worldview among the domestic authorities and the Fund officials.

It is also important to note that the Fund is able to influence the volume and terms of private capital inflows into South Africa by sending a signal to private investors through its reports and statements. This factor alone could influence the convergence of interests between Fund officials and state authorities. As the president of the South African Chamber of Commerce and Industry (SACCI) stated, "We do not borrow from the IMF, but the Fund can make a lot of noise about certain policies which sends a signal to investors."[33] In this sense, Fund officials are able to play an indirect role in shaping economic policymaking in post-apartheid South Africa by influencing the global capital markets and creditors, a point that has been highlighted in general by certain authors.[34] Indeed, in the 2019 Article IV Staff Report, the concluding remarks raise serious concerns about the state of the South African economy. For instance, Fund officials pointed out that the country's economic growth rate was dismal, and that the debt/GDP ratio was well above that of other emerging market economies. Moreover, it was pointed out that the State-Owned-Enterprises (SOEs) remained highly inefficient and burdened with liabilities, and that debt buildup, and interest payments on the debt, continue to pose a significant risk in terms of crowding-out productive public and private investment. Such public pronouncements do indeed adversely impact the perception of credit-rating agencies and investors.[35]

Furthermore, although the South African domestic authorities have not received technical advice (TA) on the subject of capital account liberalization, such official consultation has been sought from the Fund by the Treasury with regard to fiscal policy. Indeed, the 2014 Article IV report noted that the IMF South African team, led by the mission chief, has been coordinating their efforts with the World Bank country leader since September of 2014 in the areas of macro-structural issues as well as fiscal and debt sustainability. Add to this the fact that there is also a shared worldview among World Bank and Fund staff and officials in the Treasury and Reserve Bank, which is partially attributable to the shared ideology permeating the institutions, and it becomes clear that coercion and conditionality are not even necessary to influence the ANC's commitment to orthodoxy. As Patrick Bond put it, "In reality, Pretoria and Washington have constructed a revolving door...of bureaucrats who move seamlessly between the World Bank, the Department of Finance, and the Johannesburg Banks."[36]

In fact, the Bank has been active in consultations with the Reserve Bank to improve their management of foreign currency reserves and in aiding the Treasury in the preparation of the debt management strategy.[37] The IMF's Fiscal Affairs Department has been providing technical advice (TA) to the Treasury since 2010, and in 2013 the FAD and the Treasury's Fiscal Policy Unit (FPU) conducted a joint workshop on the subject of fiscal risks. In 2014, several FAD missions were sent to Pretoria for the purpose of providing technical advice on the subject of expenditure reviews and the value-added tax (VAT) gaps.[38] In addition, the World Bank has been active in providing long-term loans, in the amount of 3.75 billion, in order to increase electricity generation capacity through the Eskom Investment Support Project, and has also provided advice on the issues of land reform and the township economy. It is also significant that the Bank has been engaged in dialogue with the Department of Basic Education regarding the possibility of promoting private sector educational programmes, specifically in the area of vocational training, in order to enhance labour productivity.[39] The World Bank's International Finance Corporation is involved in many of the long-term loan projects.

The Bank's involvement in long-term infrastructural projects and macro-structural issues has better positioned the organization to influence the direction of policymaking by leveraging its control over crucial resources. Thus, technical advice on specific developmental priorities, such as education and land reform, as well as ongoing dialogue between the domestic authorities and Bank officials, likely carries greater force when buttressed by large international loans and hence has a greater probability of influencing long-term development strategies while placing constraints on viable alternatives. Additionally, Bank officials have access to a far larger number of government departments and key policymakers, while the Fund, with the exception of the Article IV meetings which include civil society representatives, generally focuses its energy on key officials within the Reserve Bank and the Ministry of Finance, thereby limiting the range of its potential influence over domestic policymaking. The Fund, however, has had to rely solely on targeted dialogue as a means of steering macroeconomic policymaking in a certain direction. As noted, this type of strategy is dependent on the construction and maintenance of viable policy-networks among the domestic authorities and various Fund officials. While this type of ongoing dialogue has helped buttress a dominant economic programme that has been in place since the transition, it would be a mistake, however, to view such interactions as the decisive factor driving the reproduction of market orthodoxy in South Africa. For example, an interview with a senior economist in the Fund's South Africa Bureau, who was a member of the 2014 Article IV staff mission, confirmed that TA has a number of limitations when it comes to influencing policy formulation, especially in the context of an independent bureaucracy in a country with a low external debt. This senior official thus reiterated that in the absence of conditionality, formal dialogue between the Fund and the domestic authorities is limited to those specific areas in which advice is specifically requested, and the element of coercion does not enter the dynamic in any manner.[40]

The IMF has also been active in sponsoring informal workshops and informational sessions in which participants, including Fund officials and specific policymakers from the Treasury and the Reserve Bank, are able to exchange ideas on relevant economic issues. These types of workshops are similar to the brainstorming scenarios that were sponsored by the corporate elite in South Africa during the period leading up to the democratic transition, the purpose of which was to mould economic agency through consent. The former head of the Fund's South Africa Bureau stated that the IMF continues to sponsor such informational seminars in Washington for the domestic authorities in the Treasury and Reserve Bank.[41] This point was corroborated by a former Fund official in the IMF's Fiscal Affairs Department who had also served as a member of the South Africa desk. He stated that in order to avoid the "potential stigma" associated with official technical advice (TA), dialogue with the South African domestic authorities had increasingly taken "the form of joint workshops and seminars," during which time general information was disseminated but specific policy recommendations were avoided.[42]

Overall, however, such tactics have not been a crucial variable responsible for the persistence of the specific cluster of neoliberal reforms such as monetarism and capital account liberalization. Although the activities of the IFIs in South Africa have helped buttress the policies emanating from specific government departments, the type of intervention exercised primarily through surveillance, dialogue, and information seminars has served as neither a necessary or sufficient condition in the reproduction of neoliberal orthodoxy. In assessing the impact of the IMF's influence in shaping policy in post-apartheid South Africa, heavy emphasis must be placed on the absence of any official loans after 1994. As previously noted, Boughton's account of the Fund's initial attempt to gain leverage over the early stages of the policymaking process during the period immediately preceding the democratic transition was met with scepticism and a good deal of hostility from the senior party leaders within the ANC, many of whom had bitter memories of the Fund's involvement with the apartheid regime and were generally loath to provide a footing for multilateral organizations that were perceived to be complicit with neocolonialism.

This early dynamic between the ANC and Fund officials, as well as the absence of official loans, has had important implications for the present relationship between the IMF and the National Treasury and Reserve Bank. In other national contexts, such as India, external donors, especially the World Bank, relied on hard loans at times to reward the efforts of the pro-market reformers in the 1980s, a tactic which served to strengthen their position over the internal policymakers committed to the regime of statist controls.[43] Additionally, although the Bank eventually shifted to the employment of "soft sell" in India as the predominant tactic in the 1980s, both strategies were used throughout the 1960s, and in fact the consolidation of soft sell was dependent on the provision of a major IMF loan in 1981 which paved the way for a series of important negotiations between Fund officials and the domestic authorities by helping to create a political climate of "greater mutual cooperation and trust."[44] More importantly, however, the paradigmatic shift to neoliberal orthodoxy in India in 1991 took place against the backdrop of a severe balance of payments crisis which necessitated additional IMF loans which could serve as the catalyst for the transition. A combination of "hard sell" and "soft sell" was employed by the Bank in several Latin American countries as well,[45] which is in stark contrast to the situation in South Africa where, as noted, the ANC leadership was recalcitrant on the issue of loans from the multilaterals, despite the outbreak of periodic financial crises. Indeed, in recent years the flow of funds has moved in the opposite direction.[46]

The World Bank, unlike the Fund, has been active in the disbursement of loans for large economic and macro-structural projects. It must be noted, however, that the Bank does not engage in much dialogue with Treasury or Reserve Bank officials, thereby placing certain policy issues, such as those pertaining to the capital account and inflation targeting, beyond their jurisdiction. In areas such as housing, land reform, and infrastructural projects including education, health, and factor productivity, the Bank has, as noted earlier, far greater influence. Yet, of crucial significance is the fact that the loans issued by the Bank were not part of a broader programme of conditionality. In fact, the repayment schedule attached to the loans was not at all onerous, and in the absence of the type of constraints imposed by conditionality Bank officials have lacked a crucial ingredient in the South African context that historically has accompanied their policy dialogue. In other words, dialogue alone may bolster certain policy models that have already emerged and are dominant, but it is unlikely that by itself such a strategy will be able to prevent the internal generation of alternative economic models within influential domestic policy circles. The question, therefore, is whether alternative models have been seriously considered by the South African domestic authorities since the transition, and whether their failure to emerge as dominant can be attributed to IFI intervention.

The above question leads us to a second point of crucial importance when evaluating IFI influence over domestic policymaking in South Africa. In other national contexts where the tactic of "soft sell" was employed, most notably India, there was a long tradition of a statist and protectionist regime that resisted the encroachment of market orthodoxy for several decades prior to any decisive economic transition. The paradigm shift materialized in India in 1991 only after the balance of payments crisis and was preceded by a long period of policy dialogue during which time the market radicals were groomed by World Bank technocrats and supplied with the data and information necessary to emerge victorious over their opponents who favoured the statist regime of selected controls. In other words, the state was fragmented and fractured along ideological lines, and the serious challenge that state interventionism faced from the new market radicals created an environment whereby certain external actors could insert themselves into the domestic policy arena in order to facilitate the victory of one cluster of core bureaucratic policymakers over another.[47] In post-apartheid South Africa, however, the domestic authorities who supported some form of aggressive state interventionism and economic controls after the GEAR document was unveiled in 1996 were minimal and quickly neutralized by the Treasury. This is especially true with regard to the composition of the Finance Ministry and the Reserve Bank. As noted in Chapter 2, it was in these government departments that a group of decision-makers, who supported the ideological stance of Trevor Manuel, came to dominate the policy-making space in the post-apartheid period. Moreover, in South Africa the shift to market orthodoxy took place almost immediately after the democratic transition. The consolidation of a neoliberal programme, and the marginalization and exclusion of those elements of the bureaucracy and policymakers who were aggressively pushing for implementation of the Keynesian RDP programme, was thus accomplished early during the transition by the Treasury.[48]

In general, South Africa's early experience with the Fund highlights the importance the ANC appeared to place on maintaining a public image compatible with the goals of the liberation movement. This was demonstrated by the fierce resistance key politicians exercised against Fund attempts to intervene in and direct the policy process during the early phases of the democratic transition. It has been effectively argued by various scholars that when politicians within the executive want to implement unpopular economic policies that could potentially generate popular protests, officials will then have an incentive to bring in international organizations such as the Fund in order to deflect political responsibility for austerity programmes.[49] In South Africa, however, we have seen that there was a perception among the ANC leadership that bringing in the Fund to implement market orthodoxy would have had serious repercussion in the context of the liberation struggle and popular opposition. Thus, ANC leaders implemented a "home-grown" structural adjustment programme to placate the large firms within the business sector and to access private capital through the global financial markets, thereby maintaining the perception of autonomy and safeguarding the political capital that had been accumulated throughout the liberation struggle. In this context, Baldev Nayar's comment on the Fund's influence in India in 1991 is more fitting for the case of post-apartheid South Africa: "If the IFIs were pressing for their policy preferences, they were pressing against an already open door."[50]

The legacy and politics of the liberation movement necessitated that ANC leaders avoid public allegations of collusion with certain international organizations, specifically those that could be charged with acting on behalf of Western capitalist interests. As a result, state officials chose to facilitate private capital inflows by imposing a home-grown structural adjustment programme. Thus, while the multilateral organizations did not play a decisive role in shaping the initial shift to market orthodoxy in 1996, there is some indication that the IFIs have been responsible for the persistence of neoliberal policies in the country since that period. By engaging Treasury and Reserve Bank officials in policy dialogue, and through the revolving door that has been established between the organizations since the transition, the IFIs have been able to bolster and reinforce the neoliberal trajectory that the ANC has been following since 1996. The next chapter will offer a comparative analysis of industrial policy in emerging market economies and will further examine whether the current economic and political impediments to a truly inclusive developmental state in South Africa can be overcome.

NOTES

1. See L.J. Mueller, "Drinking the Kool-Aid: The IMF and Global Hegemony," *Middle East Critique* 19, 2 (2010), pp. 93–112; James Vreeland, *The IMF and Economic Development* (Cambridge University Press, Cambridge, 2003); Michel Chossudovsky, *The Globalization of Poverty: Impacts of IMF and World Bank Reforms* (Zed Books, London, 1997); Cheryl Payer, *The Debt Trap: The IMF and the Third World* (Monthly Review Press, New York, 1974).
2. James Vreeland, Jan Egbert Sturm, and A. Dreher, "Politics and IMF Conditionality," *Journal of Conflict Resolution* 59, 1 (2015), pp. 120–148; Michael Breen, "IMF Conditionality and the Economic Exposure of Its Shareholders," *European Journal of International Relations* 20, 2 (2012), pp. 416–436; B. Momani, "American Politicization of the International Monetary Fund," *Review of International Political Economy* 11, 15 (2004), pp. 880–904.
3. Mitu Sengupta, "Making the State Change Its Mind—The IMF, the World Bank, and the Politics of India's Market Reforms," *New Political Economy* 14, 2 (2009), pp. 181–210; Judith Teichman, *The Politics of Freeing Markets in Latin America: Chile, Argentina, and Mexico* (University of North Carolina Press, Chapel Hill, 2001).
4. Judith Teichman, "Multilateral Lending Institutions and Transnational Policy Networks in Mexico and Chile," *Global Governance* 13, 4 (2007), p. 565.
5. Ian Taylor and Paul Williams, "Neoliberalism and the Political Economy of the 'New South Africa,'" *New Political Economy* 5, 1 (2001), p. 27.
6. Patrick Bond, *Elite Transition: From Apartheid to Neoliberalism in South Africa* (Pluto Press, London, 2014), p. 178.
7. Ibid., p. 68.
8. Ben Fine and Vishnu Padayachee, "The Role and Influence of the IMF on Economic Policy in South Africa's Transition to Democracy: The 1993

Compensatory and Contingency Financing Facility Revisited," *Review of African Political Economy* 46, 159 (2019), pp. 157–167.

9. Ibid., p. 161.

10. Ibid., p. 162.

11. Vishnu Padayachee, "Debt, Development, and Democracy: The IMF in Post-Apartheid South Africa," *Review of African Political Economy* 21, 62 (1994), p. 589.

12. H.M. Beri, "IMF Loan to South Africa," *Strategic Analysis* 6, 9 (1982), p. 549.

13. Antoinette Handley, "Business, Government, and Economic Policymaking in the New South Africa, 1990–2000," *Journal of Modern African Studies* 43, 2 (2005), p. 222.

14. Mitu Sengupta, *The Politics of Market Reform in India—The Fragile Basis of Paradigm Shift* (University of Toronto, Unpublished Doctoral Dissertation, 2004), Chapter 6.

15. Lawrence Harris, "South Africa's External Debt Crisis," *Third World Quarterly* 8, 3 (1986), p. 794.

16. Ibid., p. 816.

17. Ibid., p. 807.

18. James Hentz and Margaret Hanson, "Neocolonialism and Neoliberalism in South Africa and Zambia," *Political Science Quarterly* 114, 3 (1999), p. 480.

19. James M. Boughton, *Tearing Down Walls: The International Monetary Fund, 1990–1999* (International Monetary Fund, Washington, 2012), p. 284.

20. Ibid., p. 108.

21. Ibid., p. 110.

22. Ibid., p. 131.

23. Ibid., p. 692.

24. Ibid., p. 695.

25. Ibid.

26. Ibid., p. 697.

27. Ibid.

28. Ibid.

29. Personal Interview, Alan Hirsch (Cape Town, January 10, 2017).

30. James Hentz, "The Two Faces of Privatization: Political and Economic Logics in Transitional South Africa," *The Journal of Modern African Studies* 38, 2 (2000), pp. 203–223.

31. International Monetary Fund, Article IV Staff Report (Washington DC, 2014), pp. 5–6.

32. Ibid., pp. 17–18.

33. Personal Interview, Alan Mukoki, CEO, SACCI, (Johannesburg, December 7, 2017).

34. James Vreeland, *The IMF and Economic Development*, p. 53; R. Stone, *Lending Credibility: The International Monetary Fund and the Post-Communist Transition* (Princeton University Press, New Jersey, 2002), p. 4.

35. International Monetary Fund, Article IV Staff Report (Washington DC, 2019).

36. Patrick Bond, *Elite Transition*, p. 143.

37. IMF, Staff Report Informational Annex, p. 6.

38. Ibid., p. 5.

39. Ibid., pp. 6–7.

40. Personal Interview, Senior Economist, IMF South Africa Bureau (December 9, 2014).

41. Personal Interview, IMF Mission Chief for South Africa (December 12, 2014).

42. Personal Interview, IMF Official, Fiscal Affairs Department (January 8, 2014).

43. Mitu Sengupta, *The Politics of Market Reform in India—The Fragile Basis of Paradigm Shift*, p. 246.

44. Ibid.

45. Judith Teichman, *Politics of Freeing Markets in Latin America: Chile, Argentina, and Mexico* (University of North Carolina Press, Chapel Hill, 2001).

46. The announcement of this loan, which was part of a general BRIC country commitment of $72 billion, was met with a good deal of controversy in South Africa. Deputy President Kgalema Motlanthe defended the loan in parliament, stating that it was in the "national interest to strengthen IMF resources," and Jacob Zuma argued that the loan would help "avoid further global instability." Although the loan received support from numerous ANC and DA politicians, it was strongly opposed by the trade unions. See The Africa Report, "IMF loan in South Africa's 'National Interest.' https://www.theafricareport.com/Southern-Africa/imf-loan-in-south-africas-qnational-interestq.html.

47. Mitu Sengupta, *The Politics of Market Reform in India—The Fragile Basis of Paradigm Shift*, Chapter 2.

48. Sargie Narsiah, "Neoliberalism and Privatization in South Africa," *Geojournal* 57 (2002), p. 5.

49. R. Vaubel, "A Public Choice Approach to International Organization," *Public Choice* 51, 1 (1986), p. 43; see also L.K. Remmer, "The Politics of Economic Stabilization: IMF Standby Programs in Latin America, 1954–1984," *Comparative Politics* 19, 1 (1986), pp. 1–24; James Vreeland, *The IMF and Economic Development*, p. 13.

50. Baldev Nayar, "Globalization and India's National Autonomy," *Commonwealth and Comparative Politics* 41, 2 (2003), p. 25.

CHAPTER 5

Forging a Developmental State in Post-apartheid South Africa: A Comparative Analysis of the Structural and Political Barriers to Industrialization

As previous chapters have shown, the persistence of the neoliberal growth model and the absence of a truly viable developmental state—one predicated on industrial diversification and social inclusion—are largely responsible for post-apartheid South Africa's dire economic situation. This chapter unpacks the various social and economic barriers that have prevented the emergence of effective state intervention in democratic South Africa over a twenty-five-year period. The chapter is rooted partially in a historical analysis of developmental states, with an emphasis on effective policies, and also focuses on the structural and institutional factors that promote or hinder the emergence of developmental states. It argues that the absence of a viable industrial programme in the country can be attributed to ineffective economic and financial policies emanating from the Treasury and Reserve Bank, as well as the structure of the post-apartheid corporate landscape. Specifically, the dominance of multinational and transnational companies in the mining and manufacturing sectors, in conjunction with a specific labour market, has meant that there is very little political support for the type of protectionist economic policies that were successfully adopted by developmental states in East

© The Author(s), under exclusive license to Springer Nature Switzerland AG 2021
S. Ansari, *Neoliberalism and Resistance in South Africa*, Contemporary African Political Economy, https://doi.org/10.1007/978-3-030-69766-2_5

Asia and, to a lesser extent, in Latin America. Moreover, the industrial strategies that the governing party has adopted post-1995, such as the Department of Trade and Industry's Automotive Development Programme, have had limited success because these policy clusters have been shaped by an economic environment predicated on trade liberalization and deregulated capital outflows. The argument offered here is situated within the broader thesis of financialization and coalitional politics put forward throughout this monograph.

The focus on the industrial policies adopted by other developing countries is meant to highlight, through a comparative analysis, the potential trajectory that post-apartheid South Africa could have embarked upon had policy-makers implemented a heterodox programme such as the MERG. Indeed, the examination of some of the other countries in this chapter will illustrate that several of the key prescriptions outlined in MERG and rejected by the ANC, such as nationalization of the Central Bank, were precisely the type of policies that have enabled certain countries to successfully embark on inclusive development. Additionally, an examination of the specific social conditions prevailing in these countries during the period of state-led industrialization will allow us to potentially identify, through the method of comparison, the political and socioeconomic barriers hindering effective industrial policies in post-apartheid South Africa.

The chapter will be divided into three sections. It will begin with an examination of the type of policies that different developmental states have adopted, along with an analysis of why some countries were able to overcome the political and economic obstacles to inclusive development. The second section will then evaluate South Africa's attempts to forge a developmental state in the post-apartheid period. The overall effectiveness and limitations of the policies and programmes implemented since the transition will be critically examined and situated within the current neoliberal growth model. This portion of the analysis will focus specifically on the country's motor vehicle industrial programme and its many limitations. The third section will then contextualize South Africa's developmental trajectory through an examination of the country's current corporate profile, with an emphasis placed on the structure of production and distribution within the economy. Since a great deal of recent political rhetoric has focused on the alleged dominance of "White Monopoly Capital" in the post-apartheid period, it will be necessary to unpack the accuracy of this assertion in order to determine whether oligopolistic structures do, in fact, currently serve as the central barrier to inclusive development and the emergence of a viable developmental state. This portion of the book will not deal with issues related to state capacity, since the topic was examined in Chapter 2, and will be further analysed in the conclusion. Suffice to say, the case studies surveyed in this chapter will illustrate that even with lower levels of bureaucratic competence and expertise, it is possible for state actors to achieve a modicum of inclusive development and social protection with the appropriate policies.

5.1   STATE-LED INDUSTRIALIZATION
IN THE GLOBAL SOUTH: POLICY DIVERGENCE
AMONG THE LATE-INDUSTRIALIZERS

Among the post-war industrializing countries, South Korea stands out as perhaps the most successful example of inclusive economic advancement in the developing world. Numerous scholars have by now analysed the various political and economic factors responsible for the country's rapid industrial upgrading. These include the impact of Japan's colonial-era policies on Korea's bureaucratic structures, as well as the formation of the industrial enterprises linked to Japan's economic dominion over the country.[1] Additionally, a comprehensive and progressive land redistribution programme initiated during the US military occupation, which was largely a response to peasant mobilization and the threat from Communist agitation, succeeded in alleviating rural poverty and inequality prior to the country's industrial drive.[2] While there is thus no doubt that Japan's colonization of the country, as well as broader Cold War geopolitical considerations, played an important role in laying the foundation for future industrialization, the mix of policies adopted during both the Rhee and Park dictatorships was an indispensable component of the nation's developmental trajectory.

Firstly, it is important to note that South Korea's strategy for industrialization was predicated on the stimulation of both the agricultural and manufacturing spheres. Social welfare provisioning and consumer and input credits were provided to farmers in the 1960s and 1970s through the National Agricultural Cooperatives Federation (NACF).[3] State expenditure on education, health care, and infrastructure drove down the rural illiteracy rate from the 1945 level of 78 per cent to 10 per cent in 1979, and by 1975, rural income was approximately 80 per cent higher than the rate prevailing in the 1930s.[4] In terms of industrialization, an import-substitution-industrialization (ISI) drive was initially implemented under the Rhee dictatorship. Inclusive development was achieved largely by targeting employment generating manufacturing industries. For example, the Korean working class grew from approximately 8 per cent in 1960 to over 31 per cent by 1980, while the share of manufacturing employment as a whole increased from only 6.8 per cent in 1960 to 21.7 per cent by 1980.[5] Moreover, the share of manufacturing in the country's exports in the 1980s stood at 90 per cent, and the share of heavy industry accounted for 38 per cent of this number.[6]

South Korea's impressive industrial upgrading over three decades was, in contrast to the arguments put forward by conventional neoclassical economics, firmly grounded in selective policy incentives and heavy state protection and intervention. Industrial strategy in the country was premised specifically on identifying, and then favouring, high productivity sectors. The overarching goal was to construct comparative advantage in globally competitive industries. In fact, in the first Five-Year-Plan (FYP), state bureaucrats highlighted cement, fertilizer, and oil refining as "basic industries."[7] From 1967 to 1971, the second FYP then identified chemicals and steel as the new strategic industries to be developed. In 1973, the South Korean state announced the beginning of the Heavy-Chemical-Industries (HCI) programme, which designated shipbuilding, electronics, semiconductors, chemicals, and machinery as the new "priority" sectors.[8] South Korean enterprises were able to establish a strong global foothold in such industries, and by the early 1980s, 10 of the top 500 non-US multinational corporations were domiciled and based in the country. Moreover, during this same period, South Korea ranked 9th among the countries possessing the largest number of transnational corporations, with Korean firms conducting international operations in key sectors such as petroleum, industrial machinery, chemicals, and shipbuilding.[9]

South Korea's industrialization trajectory is especially impressive because it was not simply based on an export promotion drive. The latter was a development strategy already being pushed by US officials and multilateral organizations in emerging market economies. Rather, post-1963, the country's development initiative was in fact anchored to a programme of "export-led" development (ELD). Although the difference may appear trivial, the distinction is in fact crucial for understanding the country's economic success story. Export promotion can be understood as a policy instrument that simply seeks to integrate production for export into an already existing development paradigm, often times as a means of alleviating excess productive capacity. Export-led development, on the other hand, centres exports as the primary aim of economic planning and industrial strategy, thereby enabling the state to allocate resources and credit based on a firm's performance in global export markets.[10] This type of programme is unique in that it can potentially influence and alter the investment strategies of private enterprises. Indeed, within a year of the programmes' official implementation, the magnitude of South Korea's exports impressed even the American advisors.[11]

What accounts for the rapid success of the ELD strategy in the Korean context? In addition to the legacy of Japanese colonialism and the US-supported post-war land redistribution noted earlier, South Korea's highly efficient industrial upgrading programme can be attributed to three other crucial factors. Firstly, there was the nationalization of banks and private finance following the military coup that ushered General Park to power in 1961. Public control over the financial market was an extremely important institutional modification that greatly contributed to the construction of a South Korean developmental state. It essentially created a "quasi-internal capital market," whereby the bureaucracy was able to allocate large quantities of funds to multi-divisional enterprises in the context of very specific developmental goals.[12] Control over finance by the Park regime thus provided authorities with the leverage they needed to reward the performance of individual firms. Companies that did not meet the target requirements could be disciplined by having their access to funds on favourable terms severely limited or even denied.[13] The second factor driving South Korea's economic success story was the emergence of the *Chaebol*, the multi-divisional South Korean conglomerate firm often headed by a single family. The *Chaebol* was created and nurtured under the dictatorship of Syngman Rhee through the sale and consolidation of Japanese property in conjunction with state protection.[14] The concentration of economic power within this group of companies enhanced their ability to compete in international export markets. In fact, the South Korean state would often engineer mergers and acquisitions among firms in order to increase scale economies and avoid "competitive waste."[15] This latter point is quite significant for the current analysis of developmental states in general since, as will later be discussed, South Africa's economic stagnation is often attributed to the structures of inefficient monopoly capital dominating the country.

The third factor driving South Korea's economic success, often over-looked in the literature on developmental states, was the close alliance forged between Japanese and Korean firms in 1965. This collaboration was a crucial determinant of the country's rapid export expansion. During the period of the country's industrialization drive, Korea lacked the type of entrepreneurial and marketing skill set that would have enabled South Korean manufacturing firms to break into highly competitive interna-tional markets, even with the incentives and subsidies provided by the state.[16] The partnership between Korean and Japanese enterprises, driven by Japan's desire to outsource the production of light manufactured goods to low-wage regional environments, thus facilitated the emergence of a "triangular system of trade." Under this system, producer goods and intermediate products were imported from Japan and then employed to manufacture labour-intensive commodities, which in turn were exported to the United States.[17] In fact, joint-ventures with Japanese firms drove Korean exports during the 1970s, and it was Japanese trading companies, which possessed the marketing skills and buyer contacts, that provided South Korea with access to the extremely lucrative and competitive US export markets throughout this period.[18] With the ELD accumulation regime firmly in place, the South Korean bureaucracy could then enhance the process by utilizing a series of financial rewards and punishments. In the absence of this Japanese-Korean alliance, business confidence would have likely declined over the long-run. Such a scenario would have caused a steady drop in investment demand, meaning that any supply-side attempts by the Park regime to stimulate production would have floundered on the rocks of a private investment strike.[19] Eventu-ally, after the exhaustion of the labour-intensive exports to the US, the state succeeded in shifting the economy towards the production of the Heavy-Chemical-Industries, and the government expanded social protec-tion measures throughout the 1970s to mitigate the rise in inequality triggered by this shift.[20] The policy was successful, evidenced by the fact that even though the Gini coefficient had initially risen with the transi-tion to capital-intensive sectors, by the mid-1990s it had again declined to 0.29.[21]

South Korea employed additional developmental policies as well, such as the creation of strategic public enterprises, heavy trade protec-tion combined with selective liberalization, and investment subsidies to newly developed firms and industries.[22] Amsden has argued that the

South Korean case belongs to a category of late-industrializing countries that extend even beyond East Asia. Such states include Argentina, India, Brazil, and Mexico, all of which employed similar interventionist measures and possessed certain commonalities in terms of their labour markets.[23] However, the South Korean example was especially noteworthy in terms of the extent and speed with which the state achieved its industrial upgrading and export success. In light of this fact, the country can be employed as a benchmark both to evaluate the successes and failures of other emerging market economies along a developmental spectrum, and to isolate the variables responsible for the divergence in their industrial trajectories. This will also provide a solid foundation to later examine post-apartheid South Africa's developmental shortcomings. The economic path adopted by the post-colonial state in India, one of the case countries mentioned by Amsden, offers a useful comparison with which to begin. The country's developmental trajectory also bears some resemblance to South Africa, since both adopted a form of ISI in the mid-twentieth century and then switched to a neoliberal model in the 1990s—though in the case of India, the Bretton Woods institutions played a far greater role in facilitating the initial transition to market orthodoxy.[24]

From the nineteenth century until the end of the First World War, India's economy was structured around the British doctrine of *laissez-faire* and free trade. This policy primarily reflected Britain's economic interests, specifically the empire's requirements for raw materials. British colonial authorities would often engage in "discriminating interventionism" in order to maintain the stability of this trade regime.[25] In the aftermath of the First World War, it was recognized that the country was in need of a stronger industrial base and military capacity, and thus, a programme based on selective industry protection was initiated. This ISI process was again, however, premised on the principle of "discriminating intervention." The programme was anchored to a colonial Tariff Board that would evaluate applications for protection and make a final decision based on issues related to efficiency, cost to the consumer, "natural advantage," and export earnings.[26] After independence in 1947, the Nehru government embarked on a far more comprehensive, and non-discriminatory, programme of domestic industrialization based on heavy state protection. Although Indian industry had expanded even prior to the First World War, political officials during the post-colonial period imposed a series of tariffs that, on average, exceeded 100 per cent, along with several other regulations such as restrictions on FDI and exchange controls. It is important to note that this shift in policy, which was supported by industrialists and national economists, was driven primarily by the desire to create an indigenous Indian capitalist class, and that issues linked to efficiency were to be subordinated to this broader aim.[27] This politically motivated ambition propelling indiscriminate protection would have implications in terms of the productivity and competitiveness of India's domestic manufacturing industry.

Despite the fact that heavy state protection was granted across the board to multiple firms in each sector, growth rates were disappointing. From 1971 to 1975, India's GDP grew at a rate of 2.4 per cent, from 1976 to 1980 at a rate of 3.4 per cent, and then at a rate of 5.4 per cent from 1981 to 1990.[28] Meanwhile, Singapore grew at a rate of 9.4 and 8.5 per cent during the 1970-5 and 1976-80 periods, and Malaysia's GDP expanded at a rate of 7.2 and 8.6 per cent throughout the same time frame.[29] More importantly, unlike South Korea, the type of industrialization that did take place in India during the post-colonial period was not in the vein of inclusive development. For instance, even though the share of agricultural activities in GDP declined from 55 per cent in 1960 to below 18 per cent by 2011, the proportion of the population employed in this sector dropped by only 24 per cent during the same period.[30] The manufacturing industry also succumbed to stagnation throughout the 1990s, and the vast majority of employees remained relegated to low-productivity sectors and the informal sphere, strong indicators that India's economic development was marked by essentially jobless growth.[31]

The absence of inclusive industrial development in India can, in part, be attributed to the type of growth model adopted by the post-colonial political authorities. Unlike South Korea, where economic development was predicated on ELD, Indian political elites and the state bureaucracy implemented a form of ISI that was inherently flawed in terms of its potential to incorporate steady productivity increases and global competitive advantages. Firstly, recall that in South Korea state managers utilized financial repression and their control over the credit system to influence microeconomic investment decisions at the firm level. In contrast, Indian bureaucrats employed a licensing system to limit firm investment and the number of companies operating in specific industrial sectors. This industrial licensing strategy protected the early entrants from competition and ensured that high profits kept flowing to a select number of firms. The companies that benefitted from this system were often those with the right political contacts, and over time the policy promoted oligopolistic rent-seeking in contrast to cost-cutting and productivity increases.[32] This in turn led to a sub-optimal level of technological innovation and expansion. Additionally, the 1969 Monopolies and Restrictive Trade Practices Act sought to limit economic concentration by preventing firms from expanding and utilizing their excess capacity. The effect of this policy was to thwart economies of scale as well as industrial diversification and rationalization, which generated inefficiencies and waste and prevented incumbent firms from capturing global market share.[33] These type of regulations led to low rates of employment and private sector investment. Note that the Indian political elite's restriction of industrial capacity expansion and economies of scale was in direct contrast to the policies promoted by the South Korean bureaucracy, which engineered mergers and directly sought to impede excessive competition in specific strategic industries in order to enhance firm competitiveness at the global level.

What accounts for this notable divergence between the developmental trajectory followed by the two countries? A key difference was that India's industrial programme was, as noted, highly influenced by a domestic class that was primarily interested in nurturing its own privileged position within the national socioeconomic hierarchy. These interests were reflected in several of the policy instruments adopted. For instance, sectors that had received heavy state support in the initial periods of the ISI initiative continued to receive excessive tariff protection well after their comparative advantage had been established. This policy, which was partially designed to enhance regime stability through the cultivation of state/society alliances, was in direct contradiction to the standard infant industry prescriptions which highlighted the necessity of eventually exposing sheltered industries to global competitive pressures.[34] While this variant of ISI did manage to increase output in some heavy industry and durable consumer goods sectors, Indian companies never managed to reach the productivity levels achieved by South Korean firms, a pattern that was particularly notable among the steel producers.[35]

The ability of agrarian and industrial elites to penetrate the Indian state apparatus, and in turn distort the country's developmental path, was linked to the social structure prevailing at the time of independence. Post-colonial India, in contrast to South Korea, was not the beneficiary of a comprehensive land reform programme in the post-war period. The persistence of land concentration and agrarian inequality had important implications for economic development in the country.

Unequal patterns of land distribution meant that investments in agricultural productivity remained low, since in this social context agrarian elites preferred to simply exploit small peasant cultivators through usurious interest rates and excessive land rents. This type of economic exploitation had the effect of stifling the domestic market for industrial and consumer goods.[36] Additionally, the post-independence pact between the traditional landowning class and the domestic industrialists thwarted progressive taxation policies and linked industrialization to continuing state investment and expenditure. However, in an economic environment marked by continuous wasteful subsidies to the agrarian elites and industrial oligopolies, this policy eventually came up against inflationary barriers and contributed to stagnation.[37] It should also be noted that India did not have the benefit of close collaboration with Japanese industrial firms and trading companies, nor did state elites receive anywhere near the same quantity of US military and industrial aid.

Economic liberalization measures were introduced in India in 1991 in the midst of a balance of payments crisis. The programme was implemented with the purported aim of reducing private sector inefficiencies and correcting the distortionary effects of decades of statist policies. The dismantling of the license system and trade liberalization did in fact lead to higher growth rates and macroeconomic stability. GDP grew at an average rate of 7 per cent from 2000 to 2012, while industry value added averaged 7.4 per cent during this same period, up from an average of 5.8 during the decade of the 1990s.[38] Gross savings as a percentage of GDP averaged an impressive rate of 31.8 per cent from 2000 to 2012. This was an important achievement, since it allowed investment to be funded through the utilization of internal resources. As a result, growth did not require a rising external debt burden.[39] However, these macroeconomic improvements were not accompanied by a concomitant increase in employment levels. In fact, economic development in India throughout the neoliberal period has continued to take the form of "jobless growth," an industrial pattern driven primarily by advances in the service industry and capital-intensive high-tech sectors.[40] This peculiar aspect of the country's post-1991 development trajectory has led some analysts to suggest that India could, potentially, skip the stage of industrialization centred on manufacturing exports and instead propel itself forward through rapid progress in advanced technology areas such as pharmaceuticals and software.[41] However, this type of economic strategy would certainly not succeed in absorbing the masses of unemployed or those who continue to labour in the agricultural sector. Overall, India's divergence from the developmental path followed by South Korea was rooted in a difference in state policies, external alliances, and the distribution of resources prevailing at the time of independence.

Important lessons regarding developmental policy can also be drawn from the Brazilian case. Brazil's developmental trajectory was, in certain respects, similar to the South African path. Beginning in the 1930s, both countries adopted a variant of ISI policy with a close symbiosis between the state and domestic capital, both were aligned with the United States as junior partners during the Cold War, and both countries experienced a period of economic stagnation in the 1980s. Additionally, each country was confronted with agitation from labour organizations pushing for democratic reform.[42] Moreover, the political leadership in each country, in response to internal and external economic pressures, implemented some variant of neoliberal orthodoxy in the 1990s. Additionally, the dominant socioeconomic class in Brazil, much like in South Africa, drew its political and economic influence from access to the land and their control over primary commodities. In fact, industrialization in Brazil was very heavily tied to the state's ability to siphon off a portion of ground rent and channel the resources into industrial activities.[43] Targeted developmental strategies were initiated first by the Goulart regime, then accelerated in the 1960s under the tutelage of the military dictatorship, and yielded some impressive industrial and export successes in sectors such as automobiles, steel, chemicals, mining, and even aircraft. Yet, unlike the case of South Korea and other East Asian economies, Brazil never managed to embark on a sustained, systematic shift towards the production of high technology products for export on international markets.[44] This shortcoming would have significant consequences in terms of the long-term viability of the developmental model adopted.

A crucially important component of Brazil's industrialization path was the triangulated collaboration between the state, local capital, and multinational corporations. This alliance was responsible, to take one significant example, for the emergence and rapid development of the petrochemicals industry in the country. In the early 1960s, Brazil's output in plastics essentially matched that of other less developed countries. By the early-mid-1970s, however, the Brazilian petrochemical industry had reached a stature similar to that obtained by the United States and Britain in 1962.[45] The impetus for this venture initially came entirely from local industrialists. In the aftermath of the 1964 Military Coup, and assurances from the new government that petrochemicals would be an industry reserved for private capital, multinational firms were willing to participate in the project. Local capitalists were of course happy to collaborate so long as the state, through its own refinery company Petrobras, stepped in to ensure the steady supply of inputs.[46] The alliance with multinational firms was fostered by the state as a mechanism for securing high grade technology that could eventually be replicated by domestic capital.[47] Participation by public enterprises was also crucial in this respect. In fact, much of Brazil's developmental success can be attributed to the role played in the process by SOE's, many of which provided important technological spin-off effects and political support to private sector domestic firms in strategic industries.[48]

However, the Brazilian development model was not without its own contradictions and economic drawbacks. To begin with, the country's industrial path was underwritten by a shifting coalition of actors and socioeconomic classes, including workers, populists, urban professionals, and domestic and foreign firms. Additionally, as noted earlier, the ISI process was largely driven forward by diverting revenue from ground rent into industrial endeavours. This combination generated a fundamental instability, since this crucial source of income fluctuated in accordance with world market demand. Thus, when commodity prices fell in the aftermath of the Korean War, the Brazilian state turned to foreign capital inflows to fill the gap. However, when these proved to be insufficient, worker's wages were suppressed.[49] In conjunction with the prolonged economic crisis, extremely high inflation, and a rapid decline in foreign investment flows, this event culminated in the 1964 military overthrow of the populist Goulart government—a coup backed by the landowners, local capitalists, and the multinational firms represented by the US government.[50] The new dictatorship did usher in a period of double-digit growth and succeeded in increasing exports, and the sub-period of 1968–73 has since been referred to as the "Brazilian Miracle."[51]

It must be noted, however, that even during the years of accelerated economic expansion under military rule, Brazil's industrial success was predicated on contingent and unstable factors. Firstly, the deepening of the industrialization process, carried out by the technocrats appointed by the generals, was not based on an inclusive model of development. From the early 1960s, and throughout the period of the "miracle," Brazil ranked behind several other large Latin American countries in terms of standard human indicators. In the 1960s, for example, Brazil's infant mortality rate was nearly double the rate in Mexico, Cuba, and Argentina, and the country also had fewer hospital beds per capita when compared to Chile and Argentina.[52] This was combined with a general rate of inequality, measured by the proportion of national income flowing to the top 5 per cent, which was the largest in all of Latin America.[53] Additionally, this was a period of rapid "denationalization" as foreign, mostly US based, TNCs increased their control as dominant shareholders in the country's 300 largest manufacturing enterprises by the early 1970s.[54] Brazil's export success during the late 1960s-early 1970s must be interpreted precisely within this context of foreign dominance. Foreign control over the economy was reflected in the fact that from the beginning of the miracle to 1972, nearly three-fourths of the exports from TNC's operating in Brazil were intra-company sales between subsidiaries—a striking component of its much heralded export performance, and one which illustrates the extent to which investment and trade decisions were under the control of foreign enterprises as opposed to domestic capital or the government.[55] Furthermore, in contrast to South Korea, Brazil lacked the institutional innovations that would have allowed the state to adequately evaluate the export performance of companies in order to make a comprehensive transition from an ISI to an ELD model.[56] Thus, the country's dependence on agricultural and primary commodity exports was never fully shaken. The economy was also extremely vulnerable because the industrialization drive of the early 1970s was largely financed through debt accumulation, and by 1979, 63 per cent of export earnings were being diverted to service these obligations.[57]

The "Brazilian Miracle" was therefore unsustainable. The second oil shock generated a contraction of primary commodity prices (aside from oil) and a rise in interest rates. This caused Brazil's economy to enter into a period of stagnation, which prompted a reduction or elimination of the generous subsidies to industry in addition to the devaluation of the national currency.[58] From 1985 to 1990, Brazil implemented the first neoliberal package under the stewardship of the Democratic Movement Party (PMDP). This initial programme involved stringent monetary policy to curb inflation along with a slew of privatizations of SOEs.[59] An element of market orthodoxy was maintained even after the election of the Brazilian Labor Party in 2003 to keep inflation in check.[60] This period was also marked by a modicum of inclusive development.

Under Lula da Silva's administration, for instance, not only were inflationary tendencies kept under control, but state intervention increased in
certain areas and the privatization of state enterprises was terminated.[61]
Moreover, social services were expanded and accompanied by increased
spending on health care and education, while formal sector employment
grew at an annual rate of 5.8 per cent. There was also a steady rise in
real wages from 2004.[62] Yet, there were limits to this form of redistribution in terms of industrial deepening and growth. The increase in
the minimum wage and rising government transfers to poor households,
which included cash-transfer payments and other redistributive measures,
fuelled aggregate demand and in turn stimulated production in the wage-
goods sector. However, these industries were generally characterized by
low levels of productivity, and the redistributive strategy generated cost-
push inflation over time. Moreover, it was combined with a policy mix
that included indiscriminate industry subsidies as well as high short-term
interest rates (inflation targeting) to attract foreign capital, which had the
effect of appreciating the exchange rate and weakening the balance of
payments over the long-run.[63] Thus, in the absence of a comprehensive
and targeted industrial programme, this type of inclusive development
through redistribution was also unsustainable. In 2019, in the midst of
an economic crisis, the PT was replaced with the far-right regime of Jair
Bolsonaro. The Brazilian "Miracle" was thus short-lived.

It is also possible to evaluate the industrialization successes of other
developing countries, as well as their prospects for inclusionary development, by roughly positioning them on the continuum occupied by the
concrete case studies discussed above. Indonesia, for instance, was able
to achieve impressive targets for poverty reduction by channelling profits
from the petroleum sector into agricultural development and industry.
Mexico, in contrast, implemented ISI policies that increased manufacturing exports and GNI per capita, but was less successful in lowering
inequality in the country.[64] As was noted in Chapter 1, South Africa
implemented a racialized and rather limited ISI programme that facilitated a degree of industrialization but also generated stagnation over
the long-run. Overall, several important lessons regarding developmental
policy and industrial upgrading can be extracted from the examples
surveyed. First, it must be noted that successful industrialization is, to
a certain degree, dependent on fortuitous events. For example, under
normal circumstances, it is highly unlikely that developing nations today
could replicate the global variables partially associated with South Korea's

developmental success. Specifically, the alliance with highly experienced Japanese enterprises and the generous US military and economic aid that flowed into the country were structural factors largely outside the control of state authorities. While the implementation of comprehensive land reform is certainly possible, it should be kept in mind that this type of policy requires a great deal of political will on the part of rulers.

However, it is also undoubtedly the case that certain policies and programmes have a far greater track record than others when it comes to sustainable industrial diversification and inclusive development. To start, it is clear that when implementing protectionist measures the state must, first and foremost, be willing to discriminate on the basis of both firm performance and their positioning within carefully selected strategic sectors. The developmental successes of South Korea, as well as some of the failures in India's programme, make this clear. As noted, the former country was able to climb the value-added production chain relatively quickly by employing policy instruments grounded in financial repression and credit allocation. This policy innovation enabled technocrats to reward/punish companies that were meeting/failing export quotas, and to facilitate investment and scale economies in crucial industries. In India, where the state bureaucracy utilized a licensing system to regulate production, industrialists resorted to unproductive oligopolistic rent-seeking that obstructed the emergence of scale economies and industrial diversification, policies which eventually led to economic stagnation. Moreover, the case of Brazil illustrates that initial export success must be combined with a coherent policy based on industrial upgrading in order to be successful over the long-run. To this end, the cases also demonstrate that self-sufficient development must involve inclusivity. State expenditure on education, health care, and general human capital formation are crucial components of successful industrialization. Investments in education and skill development are also an important aspect of industrial upgrading, particularly when making the shift to high value-added technology goods. Again, the South Korean case clearly highlights the type of developmental successes that this approach can yield. The Brazilian experience also shows that redistribution and inclusive development in the absence of a comprehensive industrial programme have limitations in terms of long-term sustainability. This point is also relevant for other developing countries. In fact, there is evidence to suggest that the redistributive, consumption-oriented policies of the Allende regime in Chile stoked inflation and contributed to the business revolt that led to the military coup.[65]

The problem of redistribution in the absence of comprehensive inclusive development and industrial upgrading thus holds important implications for the future sustainability of South Africa's cash-transfer programme as well.

Finally, the nationality of core firms and enterprises—whether they are foreign or domestically owned—clearly matters. The benefits of a nationally based class of capitalists who control strategic companies and, with the support of the state, can shape accumulation and productive investment while establishing an international presence have been well documented in reference to the *Chaebol* in South Korea. Alice Amsden has convincingly argued that the conventional notion that there is no substantive difference between Foreign-Owned-Enterprises (FOEs) and a domestic Privately-Owned-Enterprise (POE) is premised on the neoclassical assumption of perfect markets and competition. This position, however, is fundamentally flawed. In fact, when confronting the global reality of monopolistic industries and production, POEs are far better suited at cultivating nationally based managerial talent while facilitating technological spin-offs and strategic investment.[66] China is so far, with the exception of Singapore, the only developing country that has been able to achieve a specific form of economic and developmental success while relying to a large extent on the operations of TNCs. This decision was partially based on the Chinese Communist Party's (CCP) desire to focus on FDI as a driver of growth and exports, mainly as a mechanism to limit the formation of a domestic socioeconomic class that could potentially challenge totalitarian rule.[67] In the context of a labour market characterized by abundant reserves and massive repression, China has succeeded in achieving impressive growth rates and export volumes by fully integrating into the production and assembly ends of geographically dispersed global value chains, thereby benefitting from American-led economic globalization.[68] While joint-ventures with foreign firms can certainly yield important benefits in terms of capturing market share and replicating advanced technology, as was shown in the case of South Korea and partially in Brazil, the unravelling of the "Brazilian Miracle" also illustrates the dangers of overreliance on foreign capital as a means of industrial upgrading. Having reviewed the effective elements behind comprehensive inclusive development, the next section will examine South Africa's attempts to forge a successful developmental state.

5.2   Attempting to Forge a Developmental State in Post-Apartheid South Africa: Minor Successes Amid Institutional Failures

In Chapter 1, it was argued, in line with Fine and Rustomjee and other heterodox economists, that South Africa's developmental trajectory was shaped according to the evolution of the Minerals-Energy-Complex (MEC), both in terms of the emergence of manufacturing sub-sectors serving the mining industry and as a system of accumulation. Seeraj Mohamed argues that production centred around the MEC was a crucial factor that explains why large South African firms have historically avoided investment in downstream high-value manufacturing. Private funds, Mohamed points out, were primarily channelled into processing and manufacturing activities focused on minerals beneficiation, coal processing, and petroleum production.[69] Yet, it is also true that post-war South Africa did manage to accomplish several important feats associated with conventional developmental states. Bill Freund, in his recent study entitled *Twentieth-Century South Africa: A Developmental History*, argues that it was during the apartheid era that South Africa came the closest to approximating the ideal model of state-led developmental success. Freund points to the creation of SOEs specializing in steel and chemicals production (Iscor and SASOL), the formation of strategic state institutions such as the International Development Corporation (IDC), and the cultivation of close linkages between Afrikaner political elites and business leaders as important indicators.[70] To be sure, Freund also notes that many of the features associated with successful developmental states were lacking or inadequately developed throughout this period, including institutions to promote manufacturing for export, the establishment of a centralized planning ministry (which, as noted in Chapter 2, remains a problem, especially in light of Treasury's dominance), and the creation of a national bank linked to industrial interests and investments.[71] Moreover, with the official shift to neoliberal orthodoxy, much of the developmental state apparatus that had been built up during the apartheid years was dismantled. Iscor and SASOL, the two SOEs producing heavy industrial goods, for example, were privatized leading up to the democratic transition. Additionally, a number of factories that could have employed low-wage workers to produce labour-intensive commodities for export, such as textiles, collapsed with the removal of trade protection.[72]

Nonetheless, in the post-apartheid period, the ANC has continued to champion the principles of redistribution and inclusive development through official political discourse. For example, the party has repeatedly referenced the developmental state in the National Development Plan (NDP) document. The NDP was formulated by experts in the National Treasury, as well as academics from multiple disciplines, and the programme was officially launched in 2012. The committee in charge of drafting the document, the National Planning Commission, was chaired by the former Minister of Finance Trevor Manuel, who has already been discussed in previous chapters. The NDP was selected by the ANC over the New Growth Path (NGP). The latter was a developmental programme drafted by the Economic and Development Department (EDD) in collaboration with the Department of Trade and Industry (DTI).[73] This decision marked a decisive moment in terms of the country's developmental path. The NGP anchored its developmental goals to specific policies promoting infrastructural development, profitability, export-led growth, and the sustainability of services. The NGP emphasized the importance of private sector investment as a mechanism for growth and employment generation, whereas the NDP focused largely on improving service delivery and reducing poverty.[74] Nonetheless, it is noteworthy that even the NGP was largely silent on the issue of financialization in South Africa and its impact on capital flight, thus failing to substantively break with the GEAR document. Indeed, it is telling that the document is silent on the issue of Reserve Bank independence, which was a key point of contention during the MERG debates.[75]

The NDP programme, on the other hand, employs the type of language that is compatible with a developmental state, but does not outline a strong component of state intervention in the economy. The blueprint does call for the implementation of policies designed to increase skills training and expand education; however, the document does not aim to accomplish all of this through state intervention. In fact, much of the projected expansion of educational facilities is predicated on the assumption that private investment will pick up the slack where the state is unable to do so.[76] This is why the programme is consistent with deficit reduction, a debt ceiling, the inflation targeting regime (IT), and other elements of market orthodoxy. In short, the NDP is fully compatible with the principles of the neoliberal growth model, which limit its potential developmental success. In fact, a concrete example of the

shortcomings of an industrial strategy predicated on neoliberal orthodoxy and integration into transnational production circuits, at the sectoral
level, is South Africa's 1995 Motor Industry Development Programme
(MIDP). The MIDP, which was rebranded and slightly altered to become
the Automotive Production and Development Programme (APDP) in
2013, was developed by the Department of Trade and Industry (DTI)
as a programme to increase investment, production, and exports in
the automotive industry. This was to be accomplished through tax-free
cash-grants, import duty rebates, and other government allowances and
incentives.

The South African automotive sector was established in the 1920s by
Ford and General Motors under high tariff walls. The industry continued
to develop under heavy state protection and local content requirements,
with production geared solely for the domestic market. The primary
aim behind the establishment of local content was to generate foreign
exchange savings, and by 1960, automobile production in South Africa
reached 87,000 units, which at the time was the highest volume produced
by any developing country.[77] A new phase in the government's industrial
strategy was initiated in 1989 with the aim of increasing exports by easing
local content requirements. The programme was eventually transitioned
into the MIDP as a result of ongoing criticism of the unproductive nature
of state protection of the industry.[78]

The APDP has been lauded by its proponents as a successful case of
targeted development, as well as an example of how "picking the winners"
can generate gains in value-added exports and private investment.[79] It is
certainly true that South Africa's automotive programme has succeeded
in raising the absolute volume of automobile exports and private investment in the country. However, several points must be taken into account
when evaluating the overall success of this industrial initiative. First, it
is important to note that the MIDP and its successor the APDP have, as
mandated by the WTO, operated within the context of a free trade regime
and the abolishment of local content requirements. In conjunction with
trade liberalization, the APDP provides automotive firms with industrial
incentives in the form of import rebates issued by the DTI. These certifi-
cates, which can also be sold on the market, allow companies to avoid
import duties in proportion to a certain percentage of the value of their
exports. This carries significant implications for the industry, specifically
the components suppliers. With the shift to globalization, component
manufacturers are increasingly integrated into the operations of their

parent companies, and suppliers who cannot meet the latest technological, design, and pricing requirements are either relegated to the after-markets or crowded out by more competitive imports.[80] This is a trend which has clearly materialized in post-apartheid South Africa under the MIDP and APDP.[81] The internationalization of the industry, in conjunction with import penetration, has thus negatively impacted employment growth in the sector.

In 2000, the DTI introduced the Productive Asset Allowance (PAA) as an additional mechanism to induce private investment in the auto-motive sector. The PAA required that auto-manufacturers increase scale economies by reducing their number of models. In exchange for this effort, they would receive 20 per cent of the value of their productive investments over a five-year period at 4 per cent annually. The incentive, which is generally offered in the form of additional import rebate certifi-cates, was designed to improve rationalization, lower average production costs, and increase employment in the productive sector. The PAA did succeed in raising investment in productive capacity while reducing the quantity of models and increasing the total volume of vehicles produced. However, investment in R&D activities, which is a good measure of industry innovation, remained low from 2000 to 2005, with the majority of firms (51 per cent) failing to allocate any funding for such activities.[82] The low levels of research and innovation in the country can largely be attributed to the fact that the vehicle assemblers in South Africa consist of multinational firms, and that these companies tend to strategically locate R&D operations at their home headquarters.[83] Recall that this feature of the internationalization of production—which involves crucial economic decision-making being centralized outside of the nation's national bound-aries—was one factor responsible for the eventual demise of Brazil's export miracle.

The multinational nature of South Africa's automotive industry, as well as the fact that under the MIDP the government has lavished companies in the sector with cash grant subsidies, import rebates, and investment incentives, has led some to argue that the industrial programme bares all the hallmarks of a "business nanny state."[84] The latter refers to a situation where the state supplies industry with generous subsidies but has very little control over the coordination of investment and innova-tion—the opposite of a truly effective developmental state. Prior to the democratic transition, the vehicle manufacturers in South Africa in the 1980s were domestically owned but operating under licensing agreements with foreign firms. With the lifting of economic sanctions in the 1990s, these firms were reincorporated into their parent companies' ownership structure and production apparatus, so that the seven auto-companies producing vehicles in South Africa began producing as subsidiaries of European, American, and Japanese multinational corporations by 1995.[85] As a result of this reestablishment of foreign ownership over the industry, it is not just R&D that has been largely removed from the control of subsidiary producers. The R billions worth of subsidies that the DTI has handed to the automotive firms succeeded in raising company profits from 1995 through 2012. Yet, the rate of investment declined from 2005 to 2010, despite the fact that the profit rate continued an upward trajectory during this period, suggesting that these multinational companies were not ploughing profits back into productive capital investment in the country.[86]

It should also be noted that as an automotive producer, South Africa is in competition with numerous other emerging market economies for investment in productive capacity. To take one example, Thailand has carved out a significant automotive space based on FDI inflows. However, Thai authorities have employed a far more comprehensive and effective mix of industrial measures to increase exports. These include limits on the quantity of assemblers (in line with the general South Korean industrial strategy of limiting "competitive waste") in order to facilitate economies of scale and mass production, local content requirements which were in place until 1998, and lower wage costs.[87] Such policies have enabled the Thai government to more effectively bargain and negotiate with foreign multinationals.[88] Moreover, Thailand offers a far more protectionist environment to auto-producers in the form of higher tariffs. In combination with the other policies outlined, such protectionist measures have succeeded in creating a trade surplus of automotive products along with rising investment levels and some R&D activities.[89] In sum, the MIDP has not, in the context of a neoliberal growth model, managed to create a truly competitive automotive hub within South Africa in terms of exports, employment, and innovation. In fact, on a macro-level, the industry has not succeeded in lowering the country's unemployment rate or closing the trade deficit. The failures and shortcomings of industrial policy within the automotive sector, and more generally on a macroscale, raise important questions as to whether South Africa's economic structure and corporate landscape are conducive for the emergence of a truly interventionist developmental state. The next section will provide some answers to this question.

5.3   The Post-Apartheid Economic Landscape: Monopoly Capital or Foreign Ownership as a Barrier to State-Led Inclusive Development and Growth?

During the Zuma administration, the phrase "White Monopoly Capital" entered South Africa's political discourse. Since that period, the term has been employed to highlight the stark economic inequalities in the country and the dominance of white big business. As noted in Chapter 3, Irvin Jim, leader of the National Union of Metal Workers (NUMSA), has repeatedly invoked the slogan to highlight economic disparities in South Africa and the failed promises of the ANC. Although the phrase may carry some descriptive and rhetorical appeal as a method of drawing attention to the persistent social and economic injustices of the post-apartheid era, the term could also conceal far more than it illuminates. Specifically, on the issue of the barriers preventing the emergence of a South African developmental state, statements alluding to "monopoly capital" need to be substantively investigated. There are, however, two distinct interpretations of this rhetorical device. One understanding of the term could be that it is simply a useful way of describing the persistence of economic racial hierarchies in the post-apartheid period. The second interpretation actually focuses on the "monopoly capital" descriptor as an accurate snapshot of the country's current corporate landscape and economic structure. This section will focus primarily on the second view. In order to adequately evaluate the merits of this claim, it is necessary to examine the origins of the term and the economic theories surrounding it.

Although the prevalence of oligopoly and market power is generally accepted within most schools of economic thought, the monopoly capital theory of investment and profit emerged as a very specific variant of the Marxian model of accumulation in the mid-twentieth century. A number of post-Keynesian and neo-Marxist authors, including Josef Steindl, Paul Baran, Paul Sweezy, and Harry Magdoff, employed the terms, and developed the framework associated with the label, to highlight the shifting profit-making strategies of increasingly large and powerful private firms in the aftermath of the transition from competitive capitalism to general oligopoly. According to the classical Marxian law of value, capitalist firms—driven by competitive pressures—will adopt labour-saving technology in order to raise productivity and capture market share through a dynamic process that leads to concentration and the centralization of capitals.[90] Certain companies and sectors may temporarily reach a level of market power that denotes oligopoly, but it is a fleeting state; investment will, over the long-run, continuously flow between different industries in order to disrupt equilibrium in their search for the highest profit rate.[91] The monopoly capital school of thought completely revises the orthodox Marxist theory of firm competition and price formation in order to account for developments in twentieth-century capitalism. Kalecki specifically argued that excess capacity and the degree of monopoly determined the pricing power of individual firms. In this context, an increase in variable costs would translate into a higher price markup based on the decisions of the price leader and the prevailing degree of monopoly for the sector as a whole.[92] Baran and Sweezy further developed this model into a general theory of accumulation and stagnation within a neo-Marxist framework. The authors, building not just on Kalecki but also on Steindl and some of the earlier work put forward by Sweezy on oligopoly and demand, argued that in a capitalist economy the monopoly sectors could avoid profit squeezes through their ability to persistently mark up prices above costs (subject to certain constraints imposed by the "price leader in the industry").[93] Within this model of accumulation, economic stagnation emerges as the normal state of affairs. The price markup necessitates excess capacity and a reduction in output, all of which curtails investment and transfers income to capitalists, who have a lower propensity to consume than workers.[94] Accordingly, new sources of surplus absorption must emerge to counteract stagnation. These new investment outlets include the sales and advertising effort as a new form of inter-firm competition, and, most importantly, military expenditure.

The above theory of accumulation and stagnation could, theoretically, be applied to post-apartheid South Africa to explain the low rates of growth and productive investment, as well as the persistently high unemployment rate. In fact, much of the monopoly capital school of thought posits that under conditions of widespread oligopoly financial activities emerge as a specific form of waste to absorb the rising surplus. This in turn generates asset price inflation and, periodically, financial crashes.[95] As was noted in Chapter 1, the post-apartheid South African economy can be characterized by heightened levels of financial activity, including asset and equity inflation, despite low levels of economic growth and high unemployment. It was also noted in Chapter 1 that several sectors in South Africa remain oligopolistic, even in the aftermath of corporate unbundling. Therefore, it might be fair to conclude that monopoly capital is indeed one variable influencing the absence of consistent employment generating private sector investment throughout the post-apartheid period. Moreover, the inflation of asset prices in the context of domestic stagnation in the post-transition era is also consistent with the monopoly capital theory of accumulation and crisis. For instance, corporations wielding market power could be compelled to channel surplus funds into unproductive endeavours in order to avoid an expansion of industrial output that could disrupt informal cartel arrangements and end up lowering prices.

However, there are several underlying economic assumptions associated with the original monopoly capital school of thought that render the theory ill suited to fully explain stagnation and high unemployment in the South African national context. To begin with, recall that in the aftermath of trade liberalization in 1996, smaller firms collapsed when faced with global competitive pressures. While this type of event could have led to the consolidation of larger companies and enhanced their control over the South African market, it is also important to note that the emergence and survival of large firms does not, on its own, imply the negation of competition. For instance, national and international markets, as centres of competition, do not necessarily remain constant and static over a period of several decades, in which case measures of economic concentration may not capture the extent to which different firms are able to acquire market share over their competitors across specific time-trends.[96] Moreover, international trade is an important variable that could independently disrupt monopoly conditions in national economies. The revival of Japan and European economies in the 1960s, for example, eventually led to the saturation of global export markets, which negatively affected the ability of incumbent US firms to mark up prices above costs.[97] Adherents of the monopoly capital school of thought tend to argue that international trade has a minimal impact on oligopolistic markets, because a rising proportion of exports/imports are in fact based on intra-firm trade between monopolistic companies.[98] While this is certainly true, it is also the case that import penetration, whether the result of intra-company trade or not, impacts the ability of domestic firms to mark up prices by increasing the supply of goods in a given economy, thereby reducing market power.[99]

The above economic indicators are useful for determining the degree of monopoly prevailing in post-apartheid South Africa. Firstly, some studies have shown that the level of oligopoly that exists within the manufacturing industry is due to barriers of entry that are temporary in nature. For example, the degree of monopoly in several manufacturing sectors, as measured by the price markup, was higher in the 1970s and 1980s than it was in the 2010–2012 period, which suggests that trade liberalization has reduced the market power wielded by numerous industrial companies operating in South Africa.[100] Secondly, the tendency towards stagnation that the monopoly capital approach posits is a natural outgrowth of market power and oligopoly might be ill suited to explain the prevalence of slow growth and income distribution in the post-apartheid environment. According to this school of thought, the price markup transfers income to capitalists, who have a lower propensity to consume, thereby depressing aggregate demand and contributing to economic stagnation. However, as discussed in Chapter 1, the South African economy remains centred around the Minerals-Energy-Complex, which is fundamentally premised on the extraction of primary commodities for export. Since the goods produced in this industry and its various sub-sectors are not wage goods, and since pricing is largely determined by the market and commodities/index, then the standard monopoly capital mechanism pertaining to income transfer and stagnation would not be germane in this context.[101]

Finally, even if oligopolistic structures do exist in the post-apartheid period, this would not on its own serve as a sufficient variable to generate structural unemployment and stagnating investment rates. As was noted earlier in the chapter, economic concentration and the formation of cartels was a crucial aspect of South Korea's economic strategy of industrial catch-up. In an environment marked by heavy state guidance and intervention, market power exercised by strategic industrial firms can enable late developers to reap advantages in global export markets by facilitating economies of scale and limiting domestic resource waste. Indeed, as was discussed above, this was the essence of the economic strategy of South Korea's *Chaebol*. Moreover, the barriers to entry that make oligopolistic control and market power possible in the first place have, historically, existed only as temporary roadblocks which rival firms and countries eventually overcome in their quest for the highest profit rates.[102] Thus, in light of these economic facts, the monopoly capital school of thought may not be an adequate framework with which to trace the origins of skewed income distribution and stagnation during the post-apartheid period.

In fact, the actual source of South Africa's contemporary barriers to inclusive industrial development is to be found not in firm concentration levels within specific sectors, but rather in the ownership structures of the private economy. It was pointed out earlier in the chapter, in reference to the work of Amsden and other heterodox political economists, that nationally owned firms are better equipped to construct comparative advantage and secure the domestic economic rewards of technological spin-offs and innovation than foreign-owned enterprises (as noted, exceptions to this rule include China and Singapore; the latter will briefly be discussed in the conclusion). Yet, the South African economy is largely dominated by multinational corporations. It was highlighted in the previous section that the seven automobile manufacturers operating in the country are foreign transnational automotive firms, with investment as well as R&D operations controlled by company headquarters outside of South Africa. A 2017 report by the Department of Finance also showed that 38 per cent of the JSE, measured by market capitalization, was owned by foreign investors.[103] Moreover, several of the large corporations domiciled in South Africa nonetheless possess ownership structures that relegate control to dominant foreign shareholders.[104]

It is precisely this type of foreign ownership of the South African economy that has created a form of "dis-embedded autonomy," to paraphrase a term coined by Peter Evans, between the state and a large section of the private economy. In general, the large multinationals involved in mining, finance, and automobile production have little use for a developmental state that intervenes aggressively to promote and implement industrial policies. In fact, Business Leadership South Africa (BLSA), a business lobby representing many of the multinational companies operating in South Africa, has actively lobbied against interventionist industrial policies. In 2007, for example, the BLSA publicly voiced its opposition to a proposal put forward by the DTI to diversify the country's export basket through targeted forms of intervention, such as trade tariffs and taxes levied on mineral commodity exports. Instead, the organization argued in favour of targeting the exchange rate, stating that "the most effective tool in the industrial policy makers' toolkit is exchange rate manipulation."[105] As noted in Chapter 2, the Treasury has adopted a similar stance on the issue of state intervention and industrial development.

Thus, it follows that if the central barrier to diversified employment generating investment and development in South Africa is not oligopoly and market power, then the government solution is not to be found in competition policy. Rather, the state should focus on nurturing strategic domestic companies that have an incentive to favour further state intervention and protection, while also fostering collaborative developmental projects with multinationals. This would have to be coupled with strategic industrial policies, including limited exchange controls, an expansionary monetary policy, as well as productive state expenditure and massive investments in human capital. Moreover, if the South Korean case serves as an example of inclusive development, South Africa must also attempt to implement a comprehensive land reform programme in order to raise agricultural productivity and lower wealth inequality. It must also be noted that the feasibility and effectiveness of such policies from a developmental perspective have been recognized by certain bureaucratic centres in South Africa. Chapter 2 examined some of the inter-bureaucratic conflicts over economic policymaking in the post-apartheid period. The DTI has, on several occasions, recommended and drafted heterodox policy proposals predicated on targeted intervention (similar to MERG), industrial clusters, and capital controls, yet such a programme, which has consistently been opposed by Treasury officials, has not been implemented.

While some might argue that the post-apartheid state lacks the capacity to implement such ambitious programmes, it is important to keep in mind that the ANC has already intervened effectively to alter, in a limited fashion, distribution and investment patterns within the business community. In Chapter 1, we analysed the ANC's "Black Economic Empowerment" (BEE) scheme, a programme designed to transfer equity ownership to black South African entrepreneurs and foster a strong party support base among aspirant domestic capitalists. Even though the programme has not succeeded in stimulating employment generating private investment, it did nonetheless entail a combination of state discipline of, and concessions to, the large multinationals, specifically in the mining industry. Future state industrial programmes could thus build on this precedent by implementing policies premised on the collaboration between domestic and SOEs with foreign enterprises that actually generate employment, technological spin-offs, and innovation. However, given the ANC's current commitment to the neoliberal growth model and the country's integration into global financial markets, this type of state-led programme will likely require sustained pressure from below.

While this type of state transformation may seem daunting, the protests and resistance against market orthodoxy outlined in Chapter 3 offer a hopeful outlook regarding the potential for a post-apartheid model of inclusive development driven by popular democratic pressure.

NOTES

1. Timothy C. Lim, "The Origins of Societal Power in South Korea: Understanding the Physical and Human Legacies of Japanese Colonialism," *Modern Asian Studies* 33, 3 (1999), pp. 603–633.
2. Judith A. Teichman, *The Politics of Inclusive Development* (Palgrave Macmillan, New York, 2016), pp. 135–136.
3. Ibid., p. 137.
4. Ibid., p. 139.
5. Ibid., p. 135.
6. Charles A. Barone, "Dependency, Marxist Theory, and Salvaging the Idea of Capitalism in South Korea," *Review of Radical Political Economics* 15, 1 (1983), p. 47.
7. Ha-Joon Chang, "The Political Economy of Industrial Policy in South Korea," *Cambridge Journal of Economics* 17 (1993), p. 142.
8. Ibid.
9. Charles A. Barone, "Dependency, Marxist Theory, and Salvaging the Idea of Capitalism in South Korea," p. 49.
10. Vivek Chibber, "Building a Developmental State: The Korean Case Reconsidered," *Politics & Society* 27, 3 (1999), p. 328.
11. Ibid.
12. Chung h. Lee, "The Government, Financial System, and Large Private Enterprises in the Economic Development of South Korea," *World Development* 20, 2 (1992), p. 192.
13. Vivek Chibber, "Building a Developmental State: The Korean Case Reconsidered," p. 336.
14. Jiyoung Kim, "Corporate Financial Structure of South Korea After Asian Financial Crisis: The *Chaebol* Experience," *Journal of Economic Structures* 6, 24 p. 1.
15. Ha-Joon Chang, "The Political Economy of Industrial Policy in South Korea," p. 140.
16. Robert J. Castley, "Korea's Export Growth: An Alternative View," *Canadian Journal of Development Studies* 28, 2 (1997), p. 193.
17. Ibid., p. 194.
18. Ibid., p. 202.
19. Vivek Chibber, "Building a Developmental State: The Korean Case Reconsidered," p. 337.

20. Judith A. Teichman, *The Politics of Inclusive Development*, p. 141.
21. Ibid., p. 134.
22. Dani Rodrik, "The 'Paradoxes of the Successful State,'" *European Economic Review* 41 (1997), p. 424.
23. Alice H. Amsden, "Like the Rest: South-East Asia's 'Late' Industrialization," *Journal of International Development* 7, 5 (1995), p. 491.
24. See Mitu Sengupta, "Making the State Change Its Mind—The IMF, the World Bank, and the Politics of India's Market Reforms," *New Political Economy* 14, 2 (2009), pp. 181–210.
25. Basudev Chaterjee, "The Political Economy of 'Discriminating Protection:' The Case of Textiles in the 1920s," *The Indian Economic and Social History Review* 20, 3 (1983), p. 241.
26. Ibid., p. 248.
27. Tirthankar Roy, "The Origins of Import Substituting Industrialization in India," *Economic History of Developing Regions* 32, 1 (2017), pp. 71–95.
28. Sarosh Kuruvilla, "Linkages Between Industrialization Strategies and Industrial Relations/ Human Resource Policies: Singapore, Malaysia, the Philippines and India," *Industrial and Labor Relations Review* 49, 4 (1996), p. 642.
29. Ibid.
30. Jayati Ghosh, "Growth, Industrialization, and Inequality in India," *Journal of the Asia Pacific Economy* 20, 1 (2015), p. 45.
31. Ibid., pp. 46–47.
32. Ashutosh Varshney, "Strategy in Industrial Development: India and South Korea," *India International Centre Quarterly* 20, 4 (1993), p. 5.
33. Ibid., p. 6.
34. Mona Lyne, "Bringing the Structure Back in: Limited Access Orders, 'Extreme' ISI and Development," *Revista de Estudios Sociales* 68, p. 30.
35. Ashutosh Varshney, "Strategy in Industrial Development: India and South Korea," p. 4.
36. P. Patnaik, "On the Political Economy of Liberalization," *Social Scientist* 13, 7 (1985), p. 7.
37. Ibid., p. 8.
38. Rahul A. Sirohi, "Alternate Paths to Economic Development: A Comparative Analysis of Brazil and India in the Era of Neoliberalism," *Brazilian Journal of Political Economy* 37, 2 (2017), p. 307.
39. Ibid.
40. Ibid., p. 308.
41. T.N. Srinivasan, "China and India: Economic Performance, Competition, and Cooperation: An Update," *Journal of Asian Economics* 15 (2004), p. 624.
42. Janis Van der Westhuizen, "Comparing the Rise and Fall of the Authoritarian Developmental State in Brazil and South Africa," *Journal for Contemporary History* 41, 2 (2016), pp. 106–107.

43. Nicolas Grinberg, "From Populist Developmentalism to Liberal Neo-Developmentalism: The Specificity and Historical Development of Brazilian Capital Accumulation," *Critical Historical Studies* 3, 1 (2016), pp. 65–104.
44. Ben Ross Schneider, "The Developmental State in Brazil: Comparative and Historical Perspectives," *Revista de Economia Politica* 35, 1 (2015), p. 115.
45. Peter Evans, "Multi-Nationals, State-Owned Corporations, and the Transformation of Imperialism: A Brazilian Case-Study," *Economic Development and Cultural Change* 26, 1 (1977), p. 45.
46. Ibid., pp. 48–49.
47. Ibid., p. 55.
48. Ben Ross Schneider, "The Developmental State in Brazil: Comparative and Historical Perspectives," p. 116.
49. Nicolas Grinberg, "From Populist Developmentalism to Liberal Neo-Developmentalism: The Specificity and Historical Development of Brazilian Capital Accumulation," p. 79.
50. Ibid., p. 80.
51. Peter T. Kilborn, "Brazil's Economic 'Miracle' and its Collapse," *The New York Times* (November 26, 1983): 1.
52. Peter Evans, "The Military, the Multinationals, and the 'Miracle': The Political Economy of the Brazilian Model of Development," *Studies in Comparative International Development* 9 (1974), p. 35.
53. Ibid.
54. Ibid., pp. 40–41.
55. Peter Evans and Gary Gereffi, "Transnational Corporations, Dependent Development, and State Policy in the Semi-Periphery: A Comparison of Brazil and Mexico," *Latin American Research Review* 16, 3 (1981), p. 53.
56. Ben Ross Schneider, "The Developmental State in Brazil: Comparative and Historical Perspectives," p. 118.
57. Rahul A. Sirohi, "Alternate Paths to Economic Development: A Comparative Analysis of Brazil and India in the Era of Neoliberalism," p. 311.
58. Nicolas Grinberg, "From Populist Developmentalism to Liberal Neo-Developmentalism: The Specificity and Historical Development of Brazilian Capital Accumulation," p. 84.
59. Virgilio Caixeta Arraes, "The Brazilian Business World: The Difficult Adaptation to Globalization," *Revista Brasileira de Politica Internacional* 53, 2 (2010), p. 200.
60. Ibid., p. 202.
61. Rahul A. Sirohi, "Alternate Paths to Economic Development: A Comparative Analysis of Brazil and India in the Era of Neoliberalism," p. 312.

62. Ibid., p. 313.
63. See Pedro Mendes Loureiro, "Class Inequality and Capital Accumulation in Brazil, 1992–2013," *Cambridge Journal of Economics* 44 (2020), pp. 181–206.
64. Judith A. Teichman, *The Politics of Inclusive Development*, p. 67.
65. Sebastian Edwards and Rudiger Dornbusch, "Macroeconomic Populism," *Journal of Development Economics* 32 (1990), pp. 247–277.
66. Alice Amsden, "Does Firm Ownership Matter? POEs vs FOEs in the Developing World," in R. Ramamurti and J.V Singh (eds.), *Emerging Multinationals in Emerging Markets* (Cambridge University Press, Cambridge, 2009), pp. 64–78.
67. David Harvey, *A Brief History of Neoliberalism* (Oxford University Press, Oxford, 2007), p. 123.
68. Sean Starrs, "Can China Unmake the American Making of Global Capitalism," *Socialist Register* 55 (2019), pp. 186–187.
69. Seeraj Mohamed, *The Political Economy of Accumulation in South Africa: Resource Extraction, Financialization, and Capital Flight as Barriers to Investment and Employment Growth* (University of Massachusetts Amherst, 2019), Chapter 3.
70. Bill Freund, *Twentieth-Century South Africa: A Developmental History* (Cambridge University Press, Cambridge, 2018).
71. Ibid., p. 81.
72. Ibid., p. 192.
73. Devan Pillay, "Worker's Control, Marxist-Leninism, and the Revitalization of Working Class Politics in South Africa," *Capital and Society* 45, 2 (2012), p. 15.
74. Sheryl Hendricks, "South Africa's National Development Plan and New Growth Path: Reflections of Policy Contradictions and Implications for Food Security," *Agrekon* 52, 3 (2013), pp. 9–10.
75. Aurelia Segatti and Nicolas Pons-Vignon, "Stuck in Stabilisation? South Africa's Post-Apartheid Macroeconomic Policy Between Ideological Conversion and Technocratic Capture," *Review of African Political Economy* 40, 138 (2013), p. 546.
76. Personal Interview, Former Senior Policymaker, (Pretoria, October 3rd, 2013).
77. Anthony Black, "Globalization and Restructuring in the South African Automotive Industry," *Journal of International Development* 13, 6 (2001), p. 781.
78. Ibid., p. 782.
79. Justin Barnes, Raphael Kaplinsky, and Mike Morris, "Industrial Policy in Developing Economies: Developing Dynamic Comparative Advantage in the South African Automobile Sector," *Competition & Change* 8, 2 (2004), pp. 153–172.

80. Justin Barnes and Raphael Kaplinsky, "Globalization and the Death of the Local Firm? The Automobile Components Sector in South Africa," *Regional Studies* 34, 9 (2000), p. 806–809.
81. *Ibid.*
82. Martin Kaggwa, Anastassios Pouris, and Jasper L. Steyn, "South Africa Government's Support of the Automotive Industry: Prospects of the Productive Asset Allowance," *Development South Africa* 24, 5 (2007), p. 687.
83. Ibid., p. 688.
84. See David Masondo, "South African Business Nanny State: The Case of the Automotive Industrial Policy Post-Apartheid, 1995–2010," *Review of African Political Economy* 45, 156 (2018), pp. 203–222.
85. Justin Barnes and Raphael Kaplinsky, "Globalization and the Death of the Local Firm? The Automobile Components Sector in South Africa," pp. 798–799.
86. David Masondo, "South African Business Nanny State: The Case of the Automotive Industrial Policy Post-Apartheid, 1995–2010," p. 212.
87. Justin Barnes, Anthony Black, and Kriengkrai Techakanont, "Industrial Policy, Multinational Strategy, and Domestic Capability: A Comparative Analysis of the Development of South Africa's and Thailand's Automotive Industries," *European Journal of Development Research* 29, 1 (2016), pp. 40–41.
88. Ibid., pp. 40–41.
89. Ibid., pp. 50–52.
90. Anwar Shaikh, "Political Economy and Capitalism: Notes on Dobb's Theory of Crisis," *Cambridge Journal of Economics* 2, 2 (1978), pp. 233–251.
91. Anwar Shaikh, "Neo-Ricardian Economics: A Wealth of Algebra, a Poverty of Theory," *Review of Radical Political Economics* 14, 2 (1983), p. 77.
92. Michel Kalecki, *Theory of Economic Dynamics: An Essay on Cyclical and Long-Run Changes in Capitalist Economy* (Allen and Unwin, London, 1954), pp. 12–14.
93. Paul Sweezy and Paul Baran, *Monopoly Capital: An Essay on the American Economic and Social Order* (Monthly Review, New York, 1966), p. 72.
94. Paul Sweezy, *The Theory of Capitalist Development* (Monthly Review Press, New York, 1942), p. 80.
95. Hans Despain, "Sweezyian Financial Instability Hypothesis—Monopoly Capital, Inflation, Financialization, Inequality and Endless Stagnation," *International Critical Thought* 5, 1 (2015), pp. 67–79.
96. Paul Auerbach and Peter Skott, "Concentration, Competition, and Distribution—A Critique of Theories of Monopoly Capital," *International Review of Applied Economics* 2, 1 (1988), p. 44.

97. Robert Brenner, "The World Economy at the Turn of the Millennium Toward Boom or Crisis?" *Review of International Political Economy* 8, 1 (2001), pp. 6–44.
98. Keith Cowling and P. R. Tomlinson, "Globalization and Corporate Power," *Contributions to Political Economy* 24, 1 (2005), p. 41.
99. Paul Auerbach and Peter Skott, "Concentration, Competition, and Distribution—A Critique of Theories of Monopoly Capital," p. 42.
100. Johannes Fedderke, Nonso Obikili, and Nicola Viegi, "Markups and Concentration in South African Manufacturing Sectors: An Analysis with Administrative Data," *South African Journal of Economics* 86, 1 (2018), p. 128.
101. Adam Aboobaker, "Visions of Stagnation and Maldistribution: Monopoly Capital, 'White Monopoly Capital' and New Challenges to the South African Left," *Review of African Political Economy* 46, 161 (2019), p. 520.
102. Robert Brenner, "Competition and Class: A Reply to Foster and McNally," *Monthly Review* 51, 7 (1999), pp. 24–44.
103. Cited in Seeraj Mohamed, *The Political Economy of Accumulation in South Africa: Resource Extraction, Financialization, and Capital Flight as Barriers to Investment and Employment Growth*, p. 144.
104. Ibid.
105. Business Leadership South Africa, "Déjà vu? The Department of Trade and Industry's National Industrial Policy Framework" (Occasional Paper Number 2, 2007), p. 8.

CHAPTER 6

Conclusion: Incentives for 'State Capture' and Dis-Incentives for Industrialization

This book has been primarily concerned with the coalitional and class dynamics driving the persistence of neoliberal orthodoxy in post-apartheid South Africa. This conclusion will focus on two tasks. Firstly, I intend to explore the incentives that, historically, have driven states to form coalitions with societal actors in order to construct developmental states and intervene into economies to stimulate industrialization. Note that this initiative is rather different from the subject of the last chapter, which examined the structural and economic barriers currently hindering the establishment of a developmental state in South Africa. This concluding chapter will now attempt to outline precisely which factors compel and motivate state officials to actively attempt to surpass such barriers and construct the institutional capacity required to facilitate industrial upgrading. This will allow us to roughly gauge the likelihood that South African state authorities might in the near future actually abandon the neoliberal prescripts that have shaped the economy over the last two and a half decades. Put differently, this final section asks the following questions: How is bureaucratic and institutional capacity constructed in the first place, and why has post-apartheid South Africa thus far failed to discipline and incentivize private actors to cooperate with state authorities in accordance with an industrial model predicated on inclusive development? The second part of the chapter will further unpack some of these

© The Author(s), under exclusive license to Springer Nature
Switzerland AG 2021
S. Ansari, *Neoliberalism and Resistance in South Africa*,
Contemporary African Political Economy,
https://doi.org/10.1007/978-3-030-69766-2_6

questions through an examination of the "state capture" phenomena that occurred under the Jacob Zuma Presidency. This episode is telling not only because it highlights the concrete manifestations of state corruption in post-apartheid South Africa, but also because it illustrates the manner in which a specific form of predation and neopatrimonialism has dovetailed with market orthodoxy.

6.1   INCENTIVE STRUCTURES DRIVING STATE-CAPACITY

In a journal article published in 2017 I argued, in line with a growing body of scholarship that unpacks the convergence of economic and political interests among state actors and socioeconomic classes, that the divergent industrial trajectories followed by advanced and developing nations can primarily be attributed to the varying incentive structures that state authorities have faced in the nineteenth and twentieth centuries.[1] The nature of the different incentives—political, economic, or military—is a useful starting point for not only explaining why certain developmental states emerged while others remained weak and non-interventionist, but also why state-led development and industrialization have assumed very different forms and practices within specific national contexts. This approach is beneficial for several reasons. Firstly, by analyzing the convergence of interests among state and non-state actors it highlights the importance of the formation of coalitional alliances in driving economic policy and state-led industrialization (a recurring theme in this book). Secondly, rather than simply employing the concept of state capacity as a pre-existing necessary condition for the emergence of developmental states, the argument based on incentives assumes that bureaucratic expertise is itself a dependent variable that must be explained. This is a significant component of the model, since such an approach could potentially enable us to identify the type of incentive structure necessary to compel South African state authorities to formulate economic policies that undermine the current neoliberal trajectory. Thirdly, shifting the focus to incentives and the construction of state capacity highlights some of the flaws in the "no alternative" to globalization discourse. Indeed, contemporary arguments that developmental states are unique to specific regions of the world or are no longer feasible in the present era of transnational capital flows, are all predicated on an idealization of the historical form of the developmental state.

One potential problem with attempting to identify which cluster of policies or sets of institutions give rise to efficient interventionist states and industrial achievements is that it is often difficult to disentangle the developmental concept from the actual outcome. In other words, the very concept of a developmental state can potentially devolve into a tautology, "since evidence that the state is developmental is often drawn deductively from the performance of the economy."[2] One way to avoid this type of tautology would be to frame the notion of a developmental state as primarily an ideology; which is to say, a set of overarching developmental goals either embodied within a document or espoused as a hegemonic project by state leaders.[3] Framing the concept of a developmental project as an ideological commitment to industrial upgrading by state officials thus allows for the possibility of "failed" developmental states, thereby avoiding the tautological pitfall. However, one problem with this approach is that it assumes that the pronouncements of political elites will always be genuine in this area. Yet there is no reason to assume this, nor is it always necessarily the case that elected officials are even fully aware of the type of developmental outcomes interventionist states have historically sought to achieve. Additionally, such an approach does not explain how state capacity might be constructed in the first place; or, if it is assumed to exist, it does not explain why a developmental state would be motivated to embark on an employment generating project of industrial upgrading as opposed to one based on wealth extraction for personal gain.

One fruitful strategy that avoids the problem of circularity, and which might enable us to identify the conditions and factors necessary for efficient state intervention, is the comparative method. After establishing the type of outcomes that qualify as examples of successful industrialization and inclusive development, we can then identify via the process of elimination precisely which variables were present in the successful country cases. For our purposes, a successful developmental outcome refers to employment generating industrial upgrading and diversification on the value-added hierarchy of products in conjunction with inclusive development (a reduction in social and economic inequality). Note that according to this definition South Korea would qualify as a successful developmental state, while India would not—despite the fact that the latter country has managed to climb the value-added ladder of sophisticated technological goods, as discussed in the last chapter. The task now is to identify which variables were present in the highly successful developmental states that could explain not simply their industrial outcome but the establishment of state capacity as well.

As noted previously, one common answer that if often put forward in the developmental literature is the degree of bureaucratic and technical expertise possessed by the successful late industrializers. However, there is a problem with this argument, as it rests on an idealization of the type of state capacity that was possessed by some of the developmental states under examination. For instance, while South Korea is held up as an example of what a highly disciplined, capable, and expertly trained bureaucracy can accomplish, it is also the case that the political administration of Syngman Rhee was plagued with corruption. In fact, despite the legacy of Japanese colonialism and bureaucratic structures, it was not until after the military coup that ushered General Park to power that South Korea began to accelerate its industrialization process. The question, therefore, is why capacity and state discipline would suddenly increase during this period? This is precisely where the analysis of political and economic incentives can allow us to make sense of the timing of the Korean developmental process, as well as the emergence of strong state capacity. For example, Kang has argued that the unpredictability of US military aid to South Korea, in conjunction with the ongoing military threat from the North, compelled state authorities to construct the domestic capacity necessary to develop a diversified industrial base to enhance economic development as well as military independence and superiority.[4]

This approach allows us to make sense of why the Park regime, which was also blessed with the good fortune of inheriting a budding Japanese business alliance and comprehensive land reform, was actually motivated to reign in unproductive corruption and embark on a programme of industrial upgrading. The Nixon Doctrine of 1969, which outlined the planned withdrawal of US troops from Asia, created a sense of urgency and panic within the Park regime, especially in light of North Korean incursions into the South.[5] Faced with this reality, the Park regime and the technocrats within the Economic Planning Board had to devise an industrial strategy to ensure military independence, and this required investments in technical education and a highly skilled labour force. The Park regime integrated the *Chaebol* into this militarized industrial strategy, which entailed not only the subsidization of dual purpose (military and civilian) technologies, but also the construction of bureaucratic capacity that would allow for the regular state surveillance of industrial plants receiving contracts for military production.[6] Thus, as a result of this pressing need in the context of scarce resources, capacity was built. Moreover, even during Park's reign there were examples of state corruption and rents; for example, allegations that state contracts were given to certain *Chaebols* based on personal ties with state officials.[7] The necessity of militarized production has been credited with kick-starting industrial development in several other late industrializers as well, including Germany and Japan, with the two latter developmental cases being termed "revolutions from above."[8] Indeed, it has been argued that even in South Africa early state efforts towards industrialization were motivated by the Boer government's desire to stimulate heavy industry as a protective mechanism against potential British military aggressions.[9]

In a 2005 article, Richard F. Doner et al. further developed the argument linking institutional and economic development to incentives. The authors focused on the industrial successes of the newly industrializing countries, South Korea, Taiwan, and Singapore (NICs), and compared these cases with the partially successful, though less impressive, Southeast Asian examples of Malaysia, Indonesia, Thailand, and the Philippines. Although the latter countries were able to secure some impressive gains in economic growth and industrial diversification, they differed from the former set of nations in one significant respect: their performance was not extensively rooted in export led development combined with industrial deepening, innovation, and shifts along the value-added hierarchy of global value production chains—all of which constitute the hallmarks of industrial upgrading.[10] What factors might explain this divergence? The authors posit that the answer lies in the type of coalitional alliances that emerged in the two sets of country cases. In the NICs, broad coalitions crystalized in the context of credible security threats, which prompted state authorities to generate economic rents in order to avoid resource conflicts. However, since it was important that such side payments not detract from the military budget, state authorities were compelled to embark on a process of industrial deepening and inclusive economic development to generate additional resources.[11] Thus, according to Doner et al., the presence of "systemic vulnerability" is what separates successful developmental states from those with less bureaucratic capacity. "Systemic vulnerability," however, is in turn triggered by the interaction of three conditions: (1) Broad coalitions; (2) Resource scarcity; (3) Credible military threats.[12] All three were present in South

Korea, Taiwan, and Singapore. If even one of these variables is missing, however, then, according to the authors, institutional development and the construction of state capacity will be limited, as in the Southeast Asian examples.

This structural account of industrial up-grading is useful for at least three reasons. First, the emphasis on incentives illustrates that economic rents, which are often interpreted as a form of "corruption" within the worldview of neoclassical economics, are not always detrimental to development and industrialization. In fact, as Doner et al. argue, the necessity of securing rents in the context of broad coalitions played a productive role in driving forward state-led industrialization. In other words, not all rents are created equally; in social contexts where the business sector and government have incentives to cooperate and are able to generally balance one another out in terms of power, then coalitions can lead to the generation of "productive" rents as opposed to predatory extraction.[13] This point is significant because it indicates that the mere presence of corrupt behaviour on the part of state authorities is not necessarily a barrier to the construction of state capacity; moreover, the analysis suggests that even just pockets of bureaucratic expertise might be sufficient for the emergence of a developmental state given the appropriate coalitional alliances and incentives, as noted in Chapter 2.

Secondly, the above theoretical model implies that the type of developmental state that eventually crystalizes in any given national context will be largely shaped and determined by the nature of the coalitional alliances from which it emerged. The notion of a developmental state has been applied rather loosely over the last two decades. For instance, even though the United States has historically been categorized as a liberal free market capitalist state, scholars have noted that many of the country's industrial policies have targeted strategic sectors in a fashion that bears some of the crucial hallmarks of aggressive developmental states.[14] While it is certainly true that the US state has intervened in a comprehensive fashion to the benefit of technologically sophisticated industries, the fundamental nature of state-led industrial policy pursued by various administrations is what distinguishes the United States from the historically conventional developmental states in Northeast Asia. In fact, American industrial policy was designed to "push the high-tech frontier," an ambition which was in line with an overall strategy predicated on a global quest for military and technological superiority.[15] This overarching goal was especially important during the Cold War, and it shaped the manner in which US policymakers selected specific industries and companies as worthy of state support. The relevance of this factor for South Africa will be discussed further below. Thirdly, and perhaps most importantly, the structural analysis puts to rest the notion that African countries are simply incapable of constructing the type of bureaucratic expertise necessary for the establishment of viable developmental states. For too long, analysts and commentators have dismissed the prospects of a successful interventionist state in African nations on flimsy grounds. Much of this dismissal was based on highly flawed comparisons between an idealized conception of successful developmental states and African countries during periods of crisis, as well as a false belief that any form of patrimonialism was incompatible with state capacity.[16]

Applying this framework of incentives to post-apartheid South Africa generates some crucial insights. First, and as previously noted, it highlights the fact that less than ideal state capacity and bureaucratic expertise in the present is not a hindrance to future industrial upgrading. Additionally, the focus on coalitional alliances allows us to highlight the structural and political factors that have served as barriers to inclusive state-led development throughout the post-apartheid period. As noted earlier, Doner et al. put forward the case that if even one of the three structural variables they outlined is missing in a particular national context, then that will impede the emergence of the type of comprehensive and highly capable developmental state found in the NICs. Indeed, if we closely examine the cases surveyed in Chapter 5, the successful examples of inclusive development and industrial up-grading can be distinguished from the less successful ones by the absence of one or more of the specified variables. For instance, India has achieved some notable successes in advanced-technology goods, such as IT and pharmaceuticals, and the country has faced a number of external security dilemmas. Yet, the narrow nature of the post-independence political coalition, which essentially excluded the peasantry but involved the landholding class, has meant that much of the country's development has remained non-inclusive. The same point could be made about Brazil.

Developmental policy in South Africa is also currently constrained when viewed through the lens of this framework. Resource scarcity— one of the conditions of "systemic vulnerability"—is certainly present in South Africa. The post-apartheid state does not have a monopoly over crucial primary commodities, such as oil, that would enable authorities to generate high rents despite low levels of industrial diversification. Yet, the second condition of a "broad coalition" has largely been absent in South Africa over the last twenty-five years. As discussed in Chapters 2 and 3, a narrow coalition between the ANC and COSATU has allowed political elites to essentially lock-in neoliberal orthodoxy, while an informal economic coalition between the Treasury and mobile internationally-oriented investors has allowed for the disbursement of social welfare transfers to much of the impoverished population. This latter component of the current political alliance in South Africa is what has allowed the ANC to meet its side-payment obligations to a section of the population without embarking on structural economic transformation. As discussed in Chapter 2, this raises significant questions regarding the long-term economic impact of a developing countries' integration into the global capital markets. According to neoclassical economic doctrine, integration into the international financial markets should create efficiency through a neutral allocation of resources predicated on symmetrical information. Over time, this is supposed to enhance developmental opportunities. Yet, if access to global capital markets enables state officials to distribute rents to marginal sections of the population, then, as we have seen, financial liberalization could serve to cement extremely narrow political and economic coalitions which exclude the vast majority of the population from the benefits that could be reaped through inclusive development and industrial upgrading.

However, as has also been discussed, there is a growing possibility that social unrest might force a shift in this limited coalition, forcing the ANC to incorporate the marginalized classes into the ruling alliance through the formulation of economic policies that reduce income and wealth inequality. Social and civil unrest is also relevant in terms of the third component of "systemic vulnerability;" namely, a credible security dilemma. Doner et al. define this rather narrowly, to include mainly external military threats. It is certainly true that, when defined in such a fashion, this element of vulnerability is missing in post-apartheid South Africa. However, if "security" is defined loosely to include the type of social instability arising from popular protests and wild-cat strikes, then the post-apartheid state may indeed face a credible security dilemma, one which could potentially compel the construction of state capacity and inclusive industrial up-grading. In fact, during the periods of segregation and apartheid, the state was compelled to produce a domestic military sector amid international sanctions and boycotts in order to suppress domestic unrest. Thus, if radical opposition parties (such as the

EFF) gain increasing ground in future elections, and if economic and social inequality continue at an increasing rate, then it is entirely possible that the ANC may begin to interpret "security" rather differently. This possibility would make for a fruitful avenue to be explored in future research.

There are, of course, certain limits to the type of developmental trajectory the post-apartheid state can impose on society. For example, as the economist Philippe Burger has noted, the structure of the South African labour market is vastly different from the type existing currently in China or, historically, that has existed in other East Asian economies. Labour repression in the pursuit of growth, even during the early phase of industrial upgrading, is simply unfeasible in post-apartheid South Africa where unions are strong, and in fact the National Development Plan (NDP) precludes lowering wages as a development strategy.[17] Yet, as Burger further points out, while certain elements of the East Asian developmental model are unavailable to South Africa, there are other appealing trajectories that could be pursued. Building on previous literature, the author highlights two other economic models, the "transfer welfare state" and the "social investment state." As discussed in previous chapters, South Africa currently most closely resembles the "transfer welfare state," where social grants are distributed to impoverished citizens due to inefficient investment in and cultivation of education, healthcare, and infrastructure—deficiencies which prevent the emergence of the type of social investment model existing in Scandinavian countries.[18] This type of trajectory could be a promising path for inclusive development; in fact, Singapore, despite a heavy presence of foreign capital in the country, was able to upgrade precisely through strategic investments in human capital, technology, and skills development.

However, whichever developmental model the post-apartheid state adopts, the construction of capacity and bureaucratic expertise is crucial, as is a large degree of investment in the country's manufacturing base. A recent comparative study on wealthy, developed nations and developing countries found that manufacturing employment shares, in contrast to output, is a strong predictor of future prosperity and inclusive industrial development.[19] This finding clearly highlights the problems a country could encounter in attempting to bypass the manufacturing stage of development and establish a presence in sophisticated service and technological goods, a strategy that India seems to be pursuing. While the study also notes that it is more difficult to establish a competitive manufacturing base with a high employment share in the present era compared to previous periods, this should not deter South Africa from attempting to develop a manufacturing base as a strategy for reducing unemployment. The main focus of policymakers and party elites should be around constructing the type of state capacity and technical expertise that would make such a feat possible. Since extreme levels of state predation could potentially thwart the institutionalization of such capacity, it would be useful to examine the manifestation of political corruption in the post-apartheid period. The next section will thus analyze the roots and consequences of "state capture" under the Zuma administration, and contextualize the event by situating it within the neoliberal growth regime.

6.2   Zuma, State Capture,
and Economic Transformation

The term "state capture" entered the political discourse in South Africa during President Jacob Zuma's second term in office in the midst of wide scale allegations of corruption and fraud. Zuma's ascension to the Presidency, which followed his mobilization of disaffected ANC supporters who were displeased with Mbeki's economic governance, has been discussed in Chapters 2 and 3. However, it must also be noted that at the time of his appointment Zuma was already embroiled in corruption scandals; indeed, Zuma was elected president while facing 783 counts of fraud and corruption.[20] It is also noteworthy that Zuma mobilized the left segments of the ANC after Mbeki had removed him as the deputy president following a court judgement of corruption in connection with sizeable government arms purchases.[21] As noted in Chapter 3, Mbeki's decision generated a deepening of support for Zuma within COSATU and the ANCYL. However, new accusations of corruption soon emerged. Early in his term Zuma was accused of diverting public funds to upgrade his personal home, an allegation that was confirmed to be true by the Public Protector who then ordered the administration to "reimburse a 'reasonable percentage' of the costs of non-security improvements to his property."[22]

The next corruption story altered the course of South African politics. Allegations from members of parliament emerged implicating the Zuma administration in a scandal that involved state penetration by two wealthy private businessmen, the Gupta brothers. The corruption scandal was initially tied to accusations that SOE contracts were repeatedly being allocated to the Gupta family solely due to their political connections, and that Zuma was sharing the responsibility of appointing ministers and company directors with the brothers.[23] The Public Protector launched another investigation into the allegations; however, the investigative findings, although hinting that state capture likely did occur and that the ability of the Gupta family to predict ministerial appointments was troubling, were ultimately inconclusive.[24] Many of the revelations surrounding the phenomenon of state capture were publicized by investigative journalists. Leaked emails from servers belonging to the Gupta family revealed that not only were public resources repeatedly diverted to private companies under manufactured pretences, but that the family network was also involved in systematic attempts to subvert institutionalized accountability mechanisms by influencing the appointment of public officials to strategic positions. The end goal was to replace competent bureaucrats with loyalists who could then engineer corrupt public–private transactions.[25] A number of SOEs were looted in this fashion. For example, Eskom paid half a billion rand to Trillian, an investment fund set up by the Guptas, one day after the firm was approved as a supplier. The money was then funnelled to other consultancy firms and shell corporations controlled by the family.[26] As was discussed in Chapter 2, state capture also generated a prolonged conflict between Zuma and the Treasury after the latter blocked the Russian nuclear power deal that would have enriched a mining company owned by the Gupta family. In the end, the corruption was largely brought to an end through the sheer strength of South African civil society and internal opposition within the ANC, both of which compelled Zuma to resign as President in 2018.

However, a number of questions remain concerning the precise events that might have triggered state capture, as well as the institutional, political, and economic roots of general state corruption in South Africa. One possible explanation is simply that Zuma entered the presidency having already accumulated a string of corruption scandals, and thus the probability of public resource diversion and state capture was already high. While Zuma's personal ambitions and character flaws were most likely a contributing factor to the scandal, this type of explanation attributes far too much significance to one individual. A second explanation might locate state capture within the general history of patrimonial relations in Africa, and thus argue that the absence of a meritocratic bureaucracy in such countries facilitates patronage and public corruption. This argument certainly does capture one component driving state corruption in the South African context; however, as a general explanation it is too simplistic. It was noted earlier in this chapter that neopatrimonialism is not, for example, necessarily incompatible with state-led industrialization or inclusive development. Likewise, there is no reason to assume that a certain degree of neopatrimonialism necessarily leads to the form of state capture and resource diversion that occurred under Zuma. Indeed, as Erdmann and Engel have argued, the literature on neopatrimonialism too often assumes that traditional authority precludes the simultaneous existence of a rational, legal-bureaucratic state structure operating in conjunction with a certain degree of patronage.[27] Yet, as the authors point out, "If we talk about the invasion of informal personal relations into the formal structures of legal-rational relations, we actually presuppose that there is something to invade."[28] Thus, neopatrimonialism is a hybrid of the rational-bureaucratic order and patronage relations, and has its roots in the colonization of Africa.[29]

In the case of South Africa, Lodge highlights three specific factors that contributed to the personalization of power under Zuma. First, the author posits that neo-patrimonial tendencies were present within the ANC throughout the party's history, but were suppressed during its time in exile and through much of the liberation struggle. Second, he points to the party's historical links to underground criminal elements and the post-transition democratic pressures. Third, Lodge argues that neo-patrimonialism under the Zuma administration was partially a reflection of post-apartheid South Africa's broader political economic context.[30] Regarding the first point, Lodge suggests, similar to the general argument put forward by Erdmann and Engel, that neo-patrimonialism has partial roots in South Africa's colonial past. Put briefly, during this period the legal-rational sphere was confined to a privileged administration, and the bureaucratic centre actively sought to strengthen the power of precolonial tribal chiefs as one method of indirect rule. As a result, personalized networks built around family, kinship, and childhood comradery played a crucial role in the formation of the ANC's elite stratum.[31] Additionally, South Africa's colonial legacy and the reality of segregation helped shape the second factor; namely, the ANC's history of colluding with criminal entities and actors during a period when many activities centred around grass-roots mobilization and activism were outlawed by the governing party. Lodge points out, for example, that in 1980 the ANC's intelligence unit, under the directorship of Jacob Zuma, entered into a number of business arrangements with criminal syndicates in Johannesburg in order to secure weapons for the establishment of internal military operations.[32] As Lodge notes, "Criminal networks incorporated into the organization during its insurgent phase would certainly strengthen any patrimonial predispositions within the ANC leadership."[33]

Finally, Lodge links the first two factors to South Africa's post-apartheid political economy. The author draws certain parallels between South Africa and Russia (while noting the many differences as well, such as diversification of ownership and democratic constraints in the former country), such as their dependence on primary commodity exports in the context of an institutionalized setting where the state controls access to monopolistic licensing rights. Moreover, certain aspects of market ortho-doxy, such as external investment flows and privatization, have served to further enhance oligarchic accumulation through the preferential state access that certain private actors enjoy.[34] Additionally, in South Africa neo-patrimonialism has filtered through the country's Black Economic Empowerment (BEE) and Radical Transformation agendas. As Lodge states, "In this setting, politically biased contracting is morally excusable as a strategy to reverse historic racist inequities."[35] This was a crucial component underwriting state capture, one which also highlights the political motivations that drove forward the narrative of "white monopoly capital."

Indeed, in their 2018 book, *Shadow State: The Politics of State Capture*, Chipkin and Swilling argue that a key dynamic driving state capture was the belief, widespread among the Zuma centred elite, that state procure-ment policies promoting investment to the benefit of private business associates could be justified by the principle of radical economic transfor-mation. The authors identify the roots of this phenomenon partially in the BEE agenda as well as the 1994 reform of the state procurement board, which essentially decentralized the state tender process at the urging of the Treasury and other bodies, thereby creating a number of procurement bases across the state apparatus. This policy in turn reduced oversight and eliminated the centralized system of procurement that could have potentially utilized billions of rand in a controlled fashion to embark on a coherent path of economic transformation and nationalism.[36] Thus, it is not surprising that one of Zuma's electoral pledges was the repurposing of state institutions with the aim of recentralizing procurement to pursue the agenda of Black Economic Empowerment—while also enabling rent-seeking and, at times, circumventing the Constitution based on "political conviction."[37]

The SOEs played a central role in this dynamic of state expenditure and neo-patrimonial rent-seeking. At the heart of the scandal was the utility giant Eskom, which featured prominently in the ANC's narrative of a viable developmental state. Under this pretence, the parastatal procurement budget was employed to generate rents, far in excess of market prices, for businesses associated with the Guptas—as well as individuals associated with the Zuma faction. Much of this was justified on the principle that such contracts would stimulate investment in accordance with the principles of radical economic transformation and hence disrupt "white monopoly capitalism."[38] Moreover, the procurement scandal evolved in the context of a general parastatal crisis involving rising company debt and tight capacity. Bowman has noted, for instance, that the ANC's privatization plans for Eskom, which were eventually abandoned, constrained much needed capacity construction. Additionally, commercialized pressures from the capital markets, as well as persistent racial inequality and demands from an energy-intensive industrial core, all helped foster the conditions under which state capture could emerge.[39] As has been noted in previous chapters, this type of rent-seeking eventually placed the Zuma administration in conflict with Treasury officials who, driven by their technocratic socialization and understanding of the global credit rating agencies and capital markets, sought to check what was perceived as reckless spending. Overall, the phenomenon of state capture in South Africa has illustrated that in the absence of a coherent industrial policy, as well as ongoing bureaucratic fragmentation and persistent inequality, rent-seeking is far more likely to emerge through state-predation than in the form of the productive public-private coalitions that have been historically associated with the developmental state.

While the analysis offered in this conclusion has been primarily structural in terms of the focus on incentives, it has also shown that there is room for political agency to shape the country's future economic trajectory. Moreover, the phenomenon of state capture illustrates the manner in which the dynamics of state-predation might unfold when public and private incentives are aligned, or misaligned, in a perverse fashion. In the previous chapter it was argued that the notion of "white monopoly capital" as the primary structural barrier impeding inclusive development in South Africa was based on an inaccurate perception of the post-apartheid economic landscape—as well as a misunderstanding of the historical role of oligopolies in driving industrialization in developing countries. However, the Zuma administration was able to utilize this very concept of "white monopoly capital," in addition to the official Black Economic Empowerment policy, as a rationale for generating unproductive rents for an elite inner circle of public and private officials. Rather than divert funds into the construction of a social investment or truly viable developmental state, the principle of radical economic transformation (in conjunction with Zuma's own history of corruption and the aforementioned neo-patrimonial tendencies within the ANC) compelled the Zuma faction to funnel economic resources into businesses owned by specific families and allies. While it might be tempting to frame this form of predation and "capture" as a general failing of state capacity, this chapter has suggested that the event was in fact an outgrowth of very specific political coalitions and economic conditions. This should not, however, be interpreted as a permanent or fatal characteristic of the post-apartheid state. As has been shown in other chapters, it is perfectly possible for popular struggle to alter official policies and programmes. Indeed, given the strength and priorities of the business community, as well as the interests of international finance and the fragility of the limited social welfare programme in place as laid bare by the disruption caused by COVID-19, the destabilization of the current neoliberal order via civil unrest and worker struggles may offer the only route to a truly effective developmental state in post-apartheid South Africa.

NOTES

1. Shaukat Ansari, "The Neo-liberal Incentive Structure and the Absence of the Developmental State in Post-Apartheid South Africa," *African Affairs* 116, 463 (2017), pp. 206–232; on the issue of incentives and industrial policy see also Lindsay Whitfield and Lars Buur, "The Politics of Industrial Policy: Ruling Elites and Their Alliances," *Third World Quarterly* 35, 1 (2014), pp. 126–144.
2. Laura Routley, "Developmental States in Africa? A Review of Ongoing Debates and Buzzwords," *Development Policy Review* 32, 2 (2014), p. 161.
3. Ibid., pp. 161–162.

4. David C. Kang, *Crony Capitalism: Corruption and Development in South Korea and the Philippines* (Cambridge University Press, Cambridge, 2002), p. 34.
5. See Peter B. Kwon, "Building Bombs, Building a Nation: The State, *Chaebol*, and the Militarized Industrialization of South Korea, 1973–1979," *The Journal of Asian Studies* 79, 1 (2020), pp. 52–53.
6. Ibid., pp. 53–70.
7. Ibid., p. 66. Clearly, this type of "corruption" did not thwart state-led industrial development.
8. Barrington Moore, *Social Origins of Dictatorship and Democracy* (Beacon Press, Boston, MA, 1966). Moore highlights three routes to modernization that were followed by several former agrarian economies in his data sample that transformed into industrialized countries. Britain and the United States are placed in the category of "bourgeois revolutions," while Germany and Japan, it is argued, followed the reactionary route of "revolutions from above." The latter essentially involved a highly cohesive landowning class centralizing power and extracting resources through force for industrialization. Central to Moore's analysis were the type of coalitions forged between the various socioeconomic classes in each case, and how these alliances facilitated industrial development and led to either democracy or autocracy.
9. Nancy L. Clark, *Manufacturing Apartheid: State Corporations in South Africa* (Yale University Press, New Haven, CT, 1994), p. 16.
10. Richard F. Doner, Bryan K. Ritchie, and Dan Slater, "Systemic Vulnerability and the Origins of Developmental States: Northeast and Southeast Asia in Comparative Perspective," *International Organization* 59 (2005), p. 328.
11. Ibid., p. 330.
12. Ibid., p. 329.
13. David C. Kang, *Crony Capitalism,* pp. 16–17.
14. See Robert H. Wade, "The American Paradox: Ideology of Free Markets and the Hidden Practice of Directional Thrust," *Cambridge Journal of Economics* 41 (2017), pp. 859–880.
15. Linda Weiss and Elizabeth Thurbon, "Developmental State or Economic Statecraft? Where, Why, and How the Difference Matters," *New Political Economy* (2020: Published online), pp. 3–4.
16. Thandika Mkandawire, "Thinking about Developmental States in Africa," *Cambridge Journal of Economics* 25 (2001), pp. 289–313.
17. Philippe Burger, "Facing the Conundrum: How Useful is the 'Developmental State' Concept in South Africa?" *South African Journal of Economics* 82, 2 (2014), p. 169.
18. Ibid., pp. 175–177. As Burger also notes, and as has been highlighted throughout this monograph, a developing country which adopts the

model of a "transfer welfare state" to maintain political support will eventually face a number of economic contradictions. The most notable is the strain placed on the fiscal apparatus of the state over the long-run as a result of repeated social welfare transfers in the context of stagnant growth and investment.

19. Jesus Felipe, Aashish Mehta, and Changyong Rhee, "Manufacturing Matters...But It's the Jobs That Count!" *Cambridge Journal of Economics* 43, 1 (2018), pp. 139–168.
20. Rod Alence and Anne Pitcher, "Resisting State Capture in South Africa," *Journal of Democracy* 30, 4 (2019), p. 12.
21. Ibid., p. 9.
22. Ibid., p. 12.
23. Ibid.
24. *A Report of the Public Protector*, "State Capture" (October 14, 2016), pp. 14–16.
25. Rod Alence and Anne Pitcher, "Resisting State Capture in South Africa," p. 13.
26. Khadija Sharife and Mark Anderson, "Down the Guptas Financial Rabbit Hole" (Organized Crime and Corruption Reporting Project, September 18, 2019), Last Accessed August 9, 2020: https://www.occrp.org/en/investigations/down-the-guptas-financial-rabbit-hole.
27. Gero Erdmann and Ulf Engel, "Neopatrimonialism Reconsidered: Critical Review and Elaboration of an Elusive Concept," *Commonwealth & Comparative Politics* 45, 1 (2007), pp. 95–119.
28. Ibid., p. 104.
29. Ibid., p. 106.
30. Tom Lodge, "Neo-patrimonial Politics in the ANC," *African Affairs* 113, 450 (2014), pp. 1–23.
31. Ibid., pp. 5–6.
32. Ibid., p. 10.
33. Ibid., p. 11.
34. Ibid., p. 19.
35. Ibid., p. 18.
36. Ivor Chipkin and Mark Swilling, *Shadow State: The Politics of State Capture* (Wits University Press, Johannesburg, 2018), pp. 105–106.
37. Ibid., pp. 107–108.
38. Ibid., p. 117.
39. Andrew Bowman, "Parastatals and Economic Transformation in South Africa: The Political Economy of the Eskom Crisis," *African Affairs* 119, 476 (2020), p. 398.

Index

A

African National Congress (ANC),
2–8, 13–17, 27, 29–31, 33,
39, 41, 42, 45, 46, 51, 58–63,
66–68, 73–76, 78–82, 84–101,
103–109, 111–114, 116, 118,
120, 121, 123, 126, 142, 146,
151, 166–173, 175

Apartheid, 1, 2, 6–8, 10–13, 15–17,
20, 21, 24, 26, 30, 32, 41, 42,
45, 75, 76, 78, 80, 83, 88, 104,
106–108, 110, 118, 141, 166

Automotive Production Development
Programme (APDP), 143, 144

B

Bonds, 11, 24, 47–53, 55, 57, 60–62,
66, 68, 69
    government, 47, 49, 50, 52, 53,
    55, 57
    ten-year, 48, 50, 52, 57

Boughton, James M., 110, 111, 118,
122

Brazil, 34, 56, 131, 135–137, 139,
140, 144, 153–155, 165

Bureaucracy, 5, 15, 32, 42–45, 63,
66, 76, 104, 117, 120, 129, 130,
132, 133, 139, 162, 169

Bureaucratic expertise, 43, 160, 164,
165, 167

C

Capital controls, 11, 17, 18, 21, 28,
34, 48, 53, 54, 56, 58, 106, 113,
151

Cash-transfers, 5, 6, 51, 61, 63, 65,
138, 140

Chile, 105, 121, 137, 139

China, 140, 153, 155, 167

Coalitions, 4, 6, 7, 13, 31, 54, 58,
59, 65, 74, 78, 80, 81, 92, 93,
95, 108, 136, 159, 163–166,
172–174
    economic, 4, 6, 7, 54, 64, 160,
    166, 173

177

political, 4, 12, 54, 65, 74, 92, 93, 165, 166, 173

Conglomerates, 8, 11, 12, 18, 25, 31, 32, 34, 113, 129

Congress of South African Trade Unions (COSATU), 5, 6, 15, 16, 35, 39, 46, 58, 66, 73–76, 78–91, 93–95, 97–101, 166, 168

Craven, Patrick, 75, 86, 87, 99, 101

D

Democratic Alliance (DA), 74, 92, 95, 123

Department of Economic Planning (DEP), 16, 17, 104

Department of Trade and Industry (DTI), 5, 14, 19, 30, 36, 39, 46, 56–58, 60, 66, 79, 83, 97, 126, 142–145, 150, 151, 157

Developmental state, 7, 37, 44, 45, 63, 66, 67, 114, 121, 125–127, 129, 130, 140–142, 144, 146, 150, 152–154, 159–165, 172–174

E

Economic Freedom Fighters (EFF), 1, 74, 75, 88, 91, 92, 95, 100, 167

Erwin, Alec, 46, 78, 81, 112

Export(s), 3, 12, 18–20, 22–25, 29, 30, 36, 38, 44, 56–58, 60, 62, 128–131, 134–145, 148–150, 152, 163, 171

F

Financialization, 7, 12, 20–23, 25, 27, 32, 36–38, 56–58, 64, 65, 68, 126, 142, 156

Fiscal, 3, 5, 14, 27, 38, 42, 46, 48, 50–53, 55, 59–62, 64, 69, 82, 89, 108, 111, 114–117, 123, 175

expenditure, 3, 59, 64

restraint, 3, 27, 48, 62, 108

G

Gupta family (Guptas), 59, 68, 168, 169, 172, 175

H

Hirsch, Alan, 14, 35, 59, 68, 112, 122

I

Incentives, 7, 22, 25, 32, 37, 41, 46, 50, 53, 65, 73, 120, 128, 130, 143, 144, 151, 159, 160, 162–165, 172, 173

economic, 7, 22, 25, 50, 73, 128, 160, 162–164

political, 7, 50, 120, 160, 162, 172

Inclusive development, 45, 47, 126–128, 132, 137–140, 142, 151, 152, 159, 161, 165–167, 170, 173

India, 7, 107, 118–121, 123, 131–135, 139, 153, 154, 161, 165, 167

Industrial upgrading, 127–129, 131, 138–140, 159, 161–163, 165–167

Inequality, 2–4, 16, 23, 30, 32, 36, 41, 51, 52, 63, 65, 67, 73, 87, 127, 130, 133, 137, 138, 146, 151, 153, 155, 156, 161, 166, 167, 172

Inflation targeting (IT), 3, 21, 55–57, 63, 106, 118, 138, 142

International Monetary Fund (IMF), 50, 54, 96, 103–107, 109–118, 121–123, 153

J

Jim, Irvin, 85, 87, 88, 95, 99, 101, 146

L

Liberalization, 2, 3, 5, 6, 8, 14–19, 21, 24–27, 29, 30, 32, 37, 41, 42, 46, 49, 50, 52, 55, 57, 62, 63, 65, 73, 103, 106, 110, 112, 115, 117, 126, 130, 134, 143, 148, 149, 153, 166
  financial, 3, 5, 6, 27, 29, 41, 46, 52, 57, 62, 166
  trade, 3, 6, 21, 24, 30, 42, 62, 106, 112, 126, 134, 143, 148, 149

M

Macro-economic Research Group (MERG), 16, 17, 42, 45, 103, 126, 142, 151
Mandela, Nelson, 8, 58, 111, 112
Manufacturing, 9, 10, 12, 19–23, 26, 31, 58, 125, 127, 128, 130, 132, 134, 137, 138, 141, 149, 167, 168, 175
Marikana massacre, 83, 91, 98
Military, 83, 127, 129, 131, 134–136, 139, 147, 154, 160, 162–164, 166, 171
Minerals-Energy-Complex (MEC), 10, 12, 13, 18, 20, 30, 31, 34, 35, 60, 95, 141, 149
Mining industry, 8–10, 26, 27, 31, 83, 89, 90, 98, 141, 151
Monopoly capital, 25, 36, 39, 126, 129, 146–149, 156, 157, 171–173
Mosley, Layna, 7, 47, 49, 66
Motor Industry Development Programme (MIDP), 143–145

Multinational corporations, 5, 62, 73, 128, 135, 145

N

National Party (NP), 8, 11–15, 17, 79, 92, 103, 105, 106, 113
National Treasury, 18, 45, 46, 57, 66–68, 79, 88, 104, 106, 118, 142
National Union of Metal Workers (NUMSA), 74, 85–88, 95, 146
Neoliberalism, 6, 7, 29, 32, 34, 63, 64, 82, 95, 105, 108

P

Pepinsky, Thomas, 6, 53–55, 64, 67
Privatization, 15, 35, 45, 66, 79–82, 97, 98, 113, 123, 137, 138, 171
Public debt, 42, 49, 51, 52, 55, 62, 114

R

Radical economic transformation, 171–173
Ramaphosa, Cyril, 60, 87, 95
Reserve Bank, 4, 5, 16, 21, 25, 36, 38, 42, 43, 45, 46, 48–50, 53, 55, 56, 62, 63, 65–69, 73, 88, 103, 108, 111, 113, 115–119, 121, 125, 142

S

Segregation, 1, 2, 8–10, 13, 15, 16, 30, 76, 80, 166, 170
South African Communist Party (SACP), 6, 14, 16, 31, 39, 58, 60, 73–76, 80–82, 86, 93–95, 97, 99

South Korea, 7, 37, 43, 44, 127–130, 132, 133, 135, 137–140, 149, 152, 153, 161–164

Stagnation, 3, 12, 32, 36, 48, 52, 61, 62, 65, 113, 129, 132, 134, 135, 137–139, 147–150, 156, 157

State capacity, 31, 43, 44, 127, 160–162, 164–166, 168, 173

State capture, 3, 7, 33, 59, 60, 95, 160, 168–172, 175

State-Owned-Enterprises (SOEs), 10, 15, 28, 59, 79–81, 115, 136, 137, 141, 151, 169, 172

Streeck, Wolfgang, 6, 42, 64, 69

T

Thailand, 145, 156, 163

W

World Bank, 2, 3, 19, 33, 96, 104, 105, 113, 115, 116, 118, 119, 121, 153

Z

Zuma, Jacob, 4, 7, 58–61, 68, 69, 85, 89, 90, 92–95, 100, 101, 123, 146, 160, 168–173

Printed by Printforce, the Netherlands